This book is dedicated
to the children of America,
their school boards,
teachers, school officials,
and their architects.

is the beginning, and especially when you have to deal with anything young and tender?"—PLATO, *The Republic*

A primer about the building
of the American public school plant
produced in the public service by
the Joint School Research Project:

Aluminum Company of America,
Eggers and Higgins, architects,
and Walter McQuade.

Schoolhouse

EDITED BY

Walter McQuade

CONSULTANTS

Di Stasio & Van Buren
structural engineers

George A. Fuller Co.
construction consultants

Michael J. Kodaras
acoustical consultants

Slocum & Fuller
mechanical and electrical engineers

ADVISERS

William W. Caudill, architect
Bryan, Texas

Dr. Walter D. Cocking, editor
The School Executive

Dr. John H. Fischer, superintendent
Baltimore Public Schools

Charles D. Gibson, chief
Bureau of School Planning
California State Department of Education

Dr. Frances R. Horwich
"Miss Frances"—Ding Dong School, WGN-TV
Chicago, Illinois

Dr. Frances Ilg
Gesell Institute of Child Development

Dr. Francis Keppel, dean
Graduate School of Education
Harvard University

John Lyon Reid, architect
San Francisco, California

Dr. Arthur H. Rice, editor
The Nation's Schools

O. H. Roberts, Jr., past president
National School Boards Association

PUBLISHED BY

Simon and Schuster
New York

Contents

CONTRIBUTORS

Ann Aikman, C. Gates Beckwith (architectural),
R. O. Blechman (cartoons), Louise Cooper,
James M. Fitch, Jr., Abner A. Layne, Harry J. Middleton, Jr.,
Joseph E. Tole (production consultant)

FORMAT AND TYPOGRAPHY

Ray Komai

ART AND EDITORIAL ASSISTANCE

Henry J. Bade, Peter Bradford, James L. Cady,
Mary Grace, Audrie L. Knapp, Mary E. Mueller,
Robert W. Spadafora, Ruth Weinstock

PHOTOGRAPHERS

For listing and individual credits see page 268

PRODUCED BY

Walter McQuade
39½ Washington Square South
New York 12, N. Y.

We wish to thank many groups and individuals who gave us their time and other assistance in researching and preparing this book, among them the many teachers, principals, and superintendents who welcomed us to their schools—especially Mr. Clark Dexter of the Hollow Tree School and Mr. Ralph Perschino of the Tokeneke School, Darien, Connecticut, and Dr. Will French of Syosset High School, Syosset, New York, who granted permission for special photography in their schools.

The extensive information on materials included in this book would have been impossible to obtain and correlate without the painstaking cooperation of hundreds of manufacturers all over the United States. To them, the makers of the parts of which our schools are made, our deep thanks and respect.

We would like also to express appreciation to Time Inc. for granting leave of absence to the editor so he might complete this book—and to the following organizations and individuals:

American Association of School Administrators; American Institute of Architects; Ford Foundation—The Fund for the Advancement of Education; National Citizens Council for Better Schools; National Council on Schoolhouse Construction; National Education Association; National School Boards Association; School Facilities Council; U. S. Department of Health, Education and Welfare, School Housing Section.

Norman J. Aaron, Fulton County Board of Education, Atlanta, Georgia; Dr. Ethel Alpenfels, Department of Social Anthropology, New York University; Cambridge Consultants, Inc., Boston, Massachusetts; Dr. Harold F. Clark, Teachers College, Columbia University; Dr. A. J. Foy Cross, School of Education, New York University; David M. Ellinwood, of Moody's Investors Service, New York City; Engelhardt, Engelhardt, Leggett and Cornell; Paul Grotz, New York City; Miss Margaret Harris, Assistant Director, Nursery and Elementary School, Little Red School House, New York City; Dr. Henry H. Linn, Teachers College, Columbia University; Cushman McGee, of Pressprich and Company, New York City; Albert J. Milloy, of the First Boston Corp., New York City; Dr. Willard Olson, Dean, School of Education, University of Michigan; Mrs. Lili Peller, New York City; Wade Smith, of Dun & Bradstreet, Inc., New York City; Walt Tyler, of Standard and Poor's Corp., New York City.

The editors of Architectural Forum, Time Inc.; Architectural Record, F. W. Dodge Corporation; Progressive Architecture, Reinhold Publishing Company.

Members of the following architectural firms were of specific assistance in sharing their knowledge and experience:

Roger Allen and Associates, Grand Rapids, Michigan; Alfonso Alvarez and Associates, Upper Montclair, New Jersey; The Architects Collaborative, Cambridge, Massachusetts; Warren H. Ashley, West Hartford, Connecticut; Atkins, Barrow and Associates, Urbana, Illinois; The Ballinger Company, Philadelphia, Pennsylvania; Bannon and Antinozzi, Stratford, Connecticut; Bassetti and Morse, Seattle, Washington; Beardsley and Beardsley, Auburn, New York; M. R. Beckstrom, Moline, Illinois; Bennett and Straight, Inc., Dearborn, Michigan;

continued on page 266

Foreword

Every book should have a foreword. The foreword for this one is an urgent statistic: since World War II more than forty-five million children have been born in our country. If they are to be educated properly, it is estimated that the country must provide more than 500,000 new classrooms in the next seven years. At current rates the citizens' bill for this necessity of national life will amount to twenty billion dollars. Meanwhile, more children are being born every day.

As national problems go, this is a good kind to have, of course; there is an old saying: "May all your troubles be little ones." For where there is room for it, a growing population can be a country's major asset—and there is plenty of room, both geographic and economic, in the United States today. Education creates still more room. Knowledge is the frontier, and it is a crucial frontier, pressed most conspicuously in universities and laboratories across the nation. But that is not where the advance begins. It begins in our elementary and secondary schools. Rockets are shot into the sky from the ground.

To some it may seem strange that these words are addressed to you by a representative of an industrial organization. This book is not a selling device for aluminum . . . why has Alcoa sponsored it?

As soon as you become a corporation, you acquire certain responsibilities. Some of them are set by law. Others are not, but are almost as compelling because they are conventional—they are what a community has learned to expect of a modern organization. But beyond these set responsibilities, a corporation soon finds itself acquiring additional ones. In our case, one of these arose thirty-odd years ago when we began selling aluminum in quantity to the building industry. This market has grown until each year we sell many millions of pounds for this purpose; it is not strange that to-day we now concern ourselves with this industry in general, regardless of specific materials—and particularly with school building. A corporation is like a person. It sensibly cares about the future that it shares with the whole country.

Thus this book. Three years ago we started to cast around for a way to present technical wisdom about the building of schoolhouses, a small part of education but sometimes a confusing one to lay-men. We were fortunate in enlisting the enthusiasm of an editor experienced in writing about buildings as well as people. A substantial firm of architects undertook to supervise the research, and several firms of engineers were also asked to stand aside from their busy practices for a time, to help in the project. Their aim: to extract information on their professional specialties that a lay-man, faced with the involved prospect of building, would be able to understand and use.

Then, still working back toward the source, we realized it would be unrealistic if we did not trace that very important tributary, the flow of finance, which every school board must know about when the time comes to pay for schools. So you will find some introductory information on that, too, and on programming and other vital prelimi-nary aspects of school building. Finally, a group of advisers, people prominent in problems of child development and education, have been good enough to make suggestions and to review each chapter critically.

So that is the book you have in your hands, a body of hardheaded professional opinion—which is to be regarded as such, not as dogma. This is not a book on how to design a school (or how to program education). It is not a book of answers. Rather it is a tool, intended to help you find the answers for yourself—especially if you are a

school board member, a parent, or a layman in-volved in school-building decisions. You will find a great deal of evaluation here—more, perhaps, than has ever been presented in one package for any particular kind of building. Because of the regional nature of construction (which resembles education itself in its localization), no nationwide cost comparisons were found to hold true, so those printed on our charts are examples for one local-ity, in one period. Our engineers maintain they are universally typical in one respect, however: in most cases you get what you pay for in building materials. Today's skimping is likely to be tomor-row's expense in upkeep and maintenance. This is essential to point out because cost, of course, is basic to the problem of school building in almost every community; in a way, it is the beginning and the end of the problem.

But only in a way. Use this book with care. Re-member that the most important aspect of spend-ing money for schools is not spending just as little as possible, but getting value for what you can spend. Your own architect and educator (and their staff and consultants) are the final authority on every sentence in this book. If you are a school board member, use these pages as a vocabulary list for talking with them, but then listen to them. For they can give you lasting quality, and in the end quality is the dominantly important thing in school building, and is the reason for this book. Children are more than statistics.

FRANK L. MAGEE, *President*
Aluminum Company of America

13

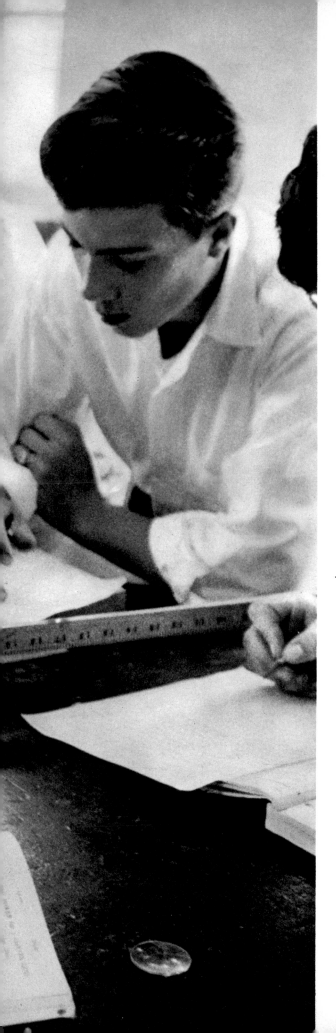

Thinking it over

*"Our arts and tools give to him who can
handle them much the same advantage over the
novice as if you extended his life, ten,
fifty, or a hundred years. And I think it the
part of good sense to provide every fine
soul with such culture that it shall not, at
thirty or forty years, have to say, 'This
which I might do is made hopeless through
my want of weapons.'"*

RALPH WALDO EMERSON, *Culture*

Any building is at heart a collaboration between the architect and the client—but especially a school building. The client in this case is plural, of course, the people of the school district, and in some ways their part of the job is the hardest. They have to *find* the architect. They also have to pay for getting the building up—which in most cases means not only finding someone to borrow from, but also getting the community to agree to repay that loan out of its own pockets. But above all, the people of the community must decide just what they want out of a school building. A good school fits its neighborhood—and in many different ways.

To get a school that fits, the neighborhood has to stand way back, and look hard, and decide some things about itself that are basic, and often very controversial. Perhaps nothing is more controversial today than the question: What kind of education do you want to give your children? It is generally agreed, for example, that one purpose of school in a democracy is to foster initiative, responsibility, and a sense of intelligent participation in its citizens. But how is this to be achieved? By reading Cicero? Or by holding mock political campaigns in the classroom? In most towns, the answer today is probably a combination. There are certainly a lot more mock political campaigns in school than there were thirty years ago. On the other hand, high school students still translate Cicero (or the Theory of Relativity), and will do so in increasing numbers in the years ahead if the recent swing toward more intellectual and scientific subjects keeps up.

A difference, however, remains. America may be headed back to a stricter curriculum, but more liberal methods of teaching it are here to stay. Even in those subjects of severe intellectual discipline, such as the sciences, there is less memorizing today, more discussion, more breaking up into study groups, more laboratory work. The basic scientific attitude is a questioning, exploratory one —a democratic one—and is reflected not only in specific teaching techniques, but in a physical atmosphere which encourages informal and spontaneous exchange. This should make a significant difference in schoolhouse design.

There is also the feeling in America that education should aim at *wholeness*—at developing all of a child's potentialities, not simply preparing him for a profession. This has always been true in a way, but it becomes increasingly important as we slowly, steadily acquire more leisure time—and as people retire younger and live longer. Arthur T. Jersild and R. J. Tasch of Teachers College at Columbia, in a study on children's interests published in 1949, established some facts worth consideration by the school district hesitating between wide and narrow educational goals, between teaching only the three R's, with the minimum in facilities—and offering more than the minimum. Put very simply, what they discovered is that people's interests—which precede skills—are *learned*, and in most cases are learned young or never at all. Even a latent feeling for art, or music, or any of the other enriching aspects of living, does not simply assert itself instinctively if present; it must be found and fed. By adulthood it is usually too late.

These are only a few out of the many educational issues which a community must work out to get the school building it wants, before making this large investment for—and in—its children.

A good school not only fits its community's educational goals; it also fits its tenants—principally children, who are different from adults in many subtle and surprising ways. And it must fit the future too, for educational changes may lie ahead that could wreck your school's true usefulness long before the floor boards begin to sag. These two intangibles—what children like, and the future—deserve some attention even before we get to the lively community activities which normally lead up to the actual construction of a schoolhouse.

Milk time

What do children like
about schools?

"Children would rather make real pies than mud pies."

DR. EDWARD LEE THORNDIKE,
Classroom Lecture, Teachers College,
Columbia University, 1924

This is a difficult question, because the answers are not waiting conveniently in any one place.

Ask a psychologist, and he can tell you a great deal about the general needs of children. But these needs are not easily translated into the kind of specifics which will be helpful to school boards, architects, and builders.

Ask children themselves. They do know two things, the main things: what they like (or sometimes dislike!) about schools is (1) *learning things*, and (2) *the teacher*. And of course they are right: learning and teaching constitute the heart of the school, the building and its equipment are details. But about these physical details, children, particularly the younger children, can't exactly say.

Nor can the teachers themselves—except to point out that the building does matter. In fact if you ask teachers what they personally want in a school building, the answers are quite illuminating, in that what they want just for themselves is usually quite minimal. They need, naturally, a desk or something like it—not as a front-of-the-room badge of authority, or even as a place to sit (a teacher who is truly "teaching" is too busy to sit at her desk; instead she walks around, perhaps stopping to perch on a child's desk for a moment) —but as a place to keep belongings. Teachers want a classroom that is easy to housekeep: dust-repellent surfaces; more cabinets than open shelves; plenty of storage and display space. And most of them want a measure of privacy in that room—the feeling that you can teach in your own way without bothering other classes or being bothered by them. What else? Well, a teacher's room, where you can make a cup of coffee or smoke a cigarette in peace; a parking space for their cars—a covered or shaded one is particularly nice, to keep off the elements. ("You can always tell a teacher's car," one teacher remarked ruefully, "by the way the color's bleached out. And you know we can't afford a new one very often.")

But what teachers *really* want is an environment that children can use and learn from: in other words, what children themselves will like. They want this because they have seen from experience that it facilitates their work, which is education.

What do children like about schools? To get anywhere with this question, it is necessary to ask psychologists, and children, and teachers, and educators, over and over again, and in large numbers. And finally a picture does begin to emerge.

The reason children find it hard to say exactly what they like, or don't like, in their environment is not that the environment doesn't affect them. The reason, as both psychologists and teachers will tell you, is that a child has trouble separating himself from his surroundings; even when he gets into his teens he has not had enough experience to discriminate in the way a grown-up can. It is a little like expecting adults to criticize the solar system. Environment, if anything, affects a child *more*, simply because he does take it for granted as a part of his normal lot in life—absorbing it, soaking it in.

Some of the ways it affects him are quite easy to see. If it is bad, it can impede the teaching process itself, concretely and specifically: if he

can't hear the teacher when a truck goes by outside; if he is too hot or too cold; if he can't see the blackboard for the glare; if his chair is uncomfortable. And if the class is too big—or even if the room is simply overcrowded—you will find the children become more restless and aggressive.

So a bad environment can impede learning. But a good environment is not just neutral. Children react to it. They do this through their senses, particularly eyes, ears, and touch; but also in more complicated ways—ways involving physical motion and muscular coordination; social ways; emotional ways. The influence on a younger child of the space around him, and the objects that fill it, tends to be direct, rather physical, and easy to see; as he gets older, the influence becomes more complex and subtle, more "psychological," but it continues to be very important.

Learning through space

With younger children, one of the things that space can do is actually *teach* them. If you ask a five-year-old what he did in kindergarten that day and he answers "Play" in terribly solemn tones, you can't help smiling. But that sepulchral tone is instructive. Play *is* serious, at five, and work is play, and learning partakes of each. (It is a fine arrangement, and a major problem of education is that it doesn't last. So perhaps it is wiser to swallow that smile.)

At five years old, children are engrossed by space; they are still finding out about the three dimensions—what it is like to be up, as in a tree or a balcony; what it is like to be down low on the floor; what it is like to be far and near, under a table or out in a wide open playfield. They like sitting in a little chair that just fits them, as if it were made just for them; and once in a while they like to be in a big chair for a change, to see what being big must feel like.

The fact that these things are fun for a five-year-old doesn't subtract in any way from the fact that he is *learning*. While his older sister does arithmetic in third grade down the hall, he is "doing," if you like, the properties of space. Pulling a wagon up a ramp is a lesson in gravity, though even his older sister hasn't yet had that word. He is learning, too, the properties of materials, and one of the ways he learns is by touching them. Practically all young children take some kind of furry animal to bed with them. They like to feel—and learn from—all different kinds of textures: a soft, deep piled rug; the cold slickness of glass; the roughness of brick or concrete; the tender pliancy of a growing plant.

By this kind of direct experience, a child learns not only what different things are *like*, but what his relationship to them is. It is a matter of developing his muscles; of learning to coordinate them; of discovering breaking points—both of the things around him and of himself; of learning to plan ahead to avoid mistakes and accidents.

And of course he is learning what it is like to be a member of society, instead of just a family: for the first time he is in a large group. The paradoxical situation of being essentially separate, distinct, and individual, yet part of a group with its own indivisible personality, has been the preoccupation of philosophers for centuries, and a young child is continually studying and testing it. He needs to be part of the whole group at times; at other times break off with one or two other children and go into an alcove (if there is one), or on a couch; at times to be entirely alone and separate, perhaps under a chair. He likes to be on one side of a partition and hand something to a child on the other side, by way of a pass-through, window, or gate. And he is learning the difficult truth that the teacher likes him—but equally; no better than maybe twenty-five other children. At times he needs to be singled out for special affection; to sit with the teacher in *her* chair in a special corner and be comforted in a crisis, perhaps. All these things must be allowed for in a good classroom and its furnishings, which, like the occupants, should be somewhat complex.

Perhaps the point simply is that the smaller children in school, the kindergartners and the first-graders too, have their own way of learning, and it is a great, big physical way. Essentially, that is how they express themselves, not by words so much (though as we all know some of them talk incessantly) but by action. So that where you hand out maps and books and pencils to eighth-graders, the supplies for kindergarten, a great many of them, are on a very different scale: alcoves, balconies, gates, pass-throughs, a small soft rug, a little house. Some very simple devices can be of major importance. In some kindergartens the linoleum on the floor has a large circle imprinted in it, about twelve feet wide. "Well," said a teacher, "that circle just about runs our lives. We're *inside* the circle, we're *outside*, some are in, some are out; sometimes I'm in there all by myself, with the children outside; sometimes the other way. I'm telling you, it's life and death around here." A rug can take on the same magical properties.

Meanwhile, as five and six-year-olds are learning the difference between up and down and between individual and group, so in a more complicated way they are learning about the difference between beautiful and ugly. This is something, of course, that they learn about out of school as well as in it—and beyond the school years into adult life—and it is a difficult and important distinction. It is important not only to intellectuals. Like a

feeling for people, a feeling for beauty, if it is deep and personal, transforms daily life, enriching everything we do—a walk around the block as well as a visit to a museum. Well, how does it come about? Can it be taught? Can the physical surroundings in a school help?

They can, a little. To some extent, of course, a feeling for beauty starts with the simple matter of prestige. If beauty is considered valuable and worth troubling over in the world about him, a child will breathe that in. This does not necessarily mean smothering him with masterpieces. It is partly a matter of detail. Perhaps someone has taken the trouble to plant flowers outside or inside his room—or better, made space where the children themselves can plant them—and maybe there is a pretty vase to put them in when they are cut, instead of an old milk bottle. Details like this accumulate, and make an impression.

But it isn't only a matter of detail. Even quite young children are perfectly capable of responding to a more general beauty, including that of a "pretty" school—not a condescendingly cute one, but one that is genuinely handsome and well designed. Like adults, they are affected emotionally by architecture, and in very concrete ways. "I feel different—prettier," confessed a little girl in a new school building that she liked. "I behave different. I don't make fun of things." Children can appreciate the way space is handled, especially when it is handled surprisingly, so that, for example, when you turn a corner you come upon an unexpected little sunlit court. They certainly can appreciate the beauty of nature, and if the view is nice they will love a glass wall—so long as the glare is killed by overhangs, louvers, or other shading devices. (One third-grader remarked of his new classroom: "I like the no-glare glass except in the A.M. when it glares.")

No one ever learned to swim without water, and you do not develop a feeling for beauty if you never see anything but ugliness. But the parallel goes further than that. In learning to swim, water is not enough; you have to jump in and thrash about. Similarly, adorning a classroom with objects of beauty will not in itself accomplish too much. Action is needed—taking us back again to the teacher. She will ask the children what pictures in a room they like and what ones they don't, and why. She will even find it useful to have something ugly around, so they can clarify the distinction in their minds. She will want a variety of things, changing them about from time to time so the children can form opinions that are their own, not merely conventional. And most important of all in the way of action, of course, are the creative efforts of the children themselves—painting, modeling, building things. The joys and trials of creation are not so very different for the six-year-old with a crayon box and for Mr. Picasso. Both of them must decide what will look nice and mean something, and what will not. It is an important and difficult decision, and a six-year-old who is used to making it will have more understanding for similar decisions made by others.

To handle all these activities, the classroom needs plenty of both display and storage space.

Incidentally, and for what it is worth, children's ideas of what looks good show certain changes as they get older. First-graders usually like modern paintings, but by second grade they are turning more and more toward the traditional; in sixth grade the majority seem to prefer it. As a rule five-and-a-half and six-year olds, and again the elevens and twelves, love bright reds and oranges. In between, research indicates they are apt to prefer pastels. If the teacher wears red shoes the first day of school, she will make a hit with six-

year-olds. Children of that age will go over and touch a red wall. (Unfortunately, the teacher will react differently; in fact she may take up short-hand in secret and quietly disappear to a new career. Perhaps the solution is to save reds for small foreground objects: equipment, play things, shelves, and shoes—and go easy on the large surfaces such as walls, ceilings, and floors.)

The institutional feeling

The overriding problem in education today is just what it always has been—and no doubt always will be—and it can be stated very simply: after the first few enthusiastic years, the average child begins to like school less and less. The process begins in a very small way about halfway through grade school, when it is barely noticeable. But by adolescence it can be really serious. Well, what became of that enthusiasm? What changed?

A number of things did, and some of them are unalterable. In a way, these second thoughts about school are only part of a bigger picture: the birth of skepticism toward institutions in general, including church and home, natural in growing children. And besides, at about nine years of age, a child begins to feel differently about his teacher. Oh, if she is nice, and interesting, and (above all, apparently) *fair*, he will like her certainly, but the warm, dependent intimacy of the earlier years disappears. At six he will wander up to her desk during a quiet classroom moment and confide that he had a marshmallow in his cocoa at breakfast. At nine such an act would not occur to him. He is more independent now—and school correspondingly has lost some of its warmth and savor.

It has lost a lot of its spontaneity too. He has come a long way since kindergarten, when the curriculum consisted of dancing, singing, story-

listening, "playing," and the like. As a child gets older, the process of learning involves less and less the use of his entire self—his five senses, his body—and concentrates down on the mind. A kind of passivity settles over the learning process. Mental work can, of course, be very active in its way—a lively discussion is "active," and so is the solution of an algebra problem—but behind it lies a body of information that has been gained, oftener than not, through the very passive process of reading (or listening) and remembering: it is taking in, receiving, being acted on. And to some extent, nothing can be done about it; no other way is practical.

But beyond these essentially *teaching* problems, isn't there something baleful in the very atmosphere of school—of most schools anyway—a monotony, a kind of unhuman-ness? School is an institution, but does it have to be so institutional?

That children dislike this quality should not be surprising. Adults don't like it either, and some of the biggest adult institutions have learned there are advantages in fighting the feeling of giantism. Look at the help-wanted ads for engineers; they promise good salaries, of course, but the big competition between employers seems almost to be in personal terms of living conditions. Engineers can choose an un-institutional place to live and work. Most children, of course, are not given any choice.

What is the institutional feeling? It is the feeling of large numbers plus sameness. It is the feeling a sardine would have, if he could feel, on his way through the canning factory. It is the feeling a child gets too, in the opinion of many educators, if he sits, day after day, year after year, in a chair just like the chairs, at a desk just like the desks, of a (to him) endless number of other children. He is aware that his room is just like the other classrooms in the school—same size, more or less, same color, same arrangement—and everything, desks, rooms, children, laid out in neat rows like numbers to be added. It is only natural that he gets to feel in a vague way that it isn't just the furniture that's the same, not just the rooms or the layout or the equipment. The children are the same too, or ought to be, and the better part of valor is to sit quietly and do and think like the others. He feels like a statistic.

And sheer numbers have a great deal to do with it. An eleven-year-old girl is delighted to feel "just like" her three friends because they all love horses and hate dolls and boys. It is something else to feel "just like" the 400 children one goes to school with—and worse yet if the number is a thousand.

The institutional feeling, in a word, saps the feeling of self, of personality—which is somewhat shaky in children to start with. They do not have the deep, complex sense of what they are like that a healthy adult does, and, especially at adolescence, they may get pretty concerned about it. Fourteen-year-olds, discussing someone they admire, will say, "She has personality" or "a lot of personality"—not even "a good personality," but giving it a quantitative meaning, as if it were something to acquire and pile up, along with records or bobbysox.

Sameness and size, the sources of the institutional feeling, have their specific antidotes that nothing else can substitute for—neither elaborate auditoriums, nor spacious lawns, ice cream for lunch, or air conditioning.

Sameness

The remedy is of course variety. *Must* classrooms all have the same size, shape, color, fenestration, and furniture? Must a school corridor—which is not just a traffic artery, but is also a very major social center, especially for teenage children—must it *always* run absolutely, relentlessly, inhumanly straight, without turn or indentation, for 300 yards? (Well, it sometimes seems 300 yards.) The answer is that of course it doesn't have to. It is also perfectly possible to vary ceiling heights, between classrooms and halls for instance; and to vary the lighting. Fluorescent lights are certainly very easy to read under, but a child doesn't spend all his day reading; perhaps cafeterias, student lounges, or guidance rooms would be nicer places to visit if they were lit by the shadowy, more human glow of incandescent lamps. Skylights, as in an art room, also provide a pleasant change of lighting pace.

Variety is, after all, stimulating. If a person is subjected to *differences* around him, in a subtle kind of way he naturally becomes more sensitive to differences of all kinds; and isn't the understanding of differences the very heart of education? Socrates felt that it was.

Size

The question of size has been bothering planners, educators, and architects quite a lot lately, what with booming birth rates, and of course a case of sorts can be made on both sides. For instance it is possible for a school to be *too* small: so small that the children feel bored and unchallenged. And a big school, especially for the older grades, has compensations. Its population is usually more varied, bringing students from many different backgrounds up against one another. It can provide certain opportunities much more easily than a small school: a full and varied curriculum with specialist teachers, really first-rate laboratory equipment, a full-sized student orchestra, a good professional dramatic coach. A very big school may actually be better for a certain type of student: the sixteen-year-old boy who is outgoing and able, a good athlete, good scholar, and president of his class—he is happier, and learns more, being president of a class of a thousand than a class of a hundred. If this boy were typical, there would be no problem.

But he isn't. And so there *is* a problem, absent in smaller schools, which an excessively large school must face up to: the feeling, on the part of many children, of being lost.

This feeling takes different forms at different ages. A first-grader can get literally lost, between the school entrance and his room, and wander around corridors for what seems hours before summoning the courage to ask for help. More often, he finds his way by himself all right but continues, all the same, to *feel* lost, in the sense that he isn't oriented; he doesn't really know where he is in relation to his older sister in fifth grade (tucked away somewhere in that vast, complicated building), or in relation to his home (since he

arrived after a—to him—journey of miles and miles by school bus or car). For both physical and psychological reasons, things simply look bigger to a six-year-old than to an adult; and anyone who doubts it should revisit the scenes of his childhood and just see the way they have shrunk. It is for this reason that younger children should have classroom entrances close to school entrances, bathrooms next to classrooms, and playgrounds close at hand—in the lower grades, just outside the room if possible. That way, they know where they are, so to speak. About the age of eight or nine they can go farther—in fact they will want to, because they are beginning to expand in all kinds of ways then, and they feel an urge to cover new territory. Nevertheless, most educators feel a good elementary school shouldn't get much bigger than 500 to 600. "If the principal can't remember the names of all his students, the school is too big" is a commonly stated criterion.

Secondary schools can of course be larger, but where they are too large an adolescent may feel almost as lost as a six-year-old—not physically so much, but socially, personally. He needs at this age to make a personal mark of some kind, he needs this quite desperately at times; and very humble tokens of it can mean quite a bit to him. In a moderate-sized school, when he walks down the hall he knows most of the people he passes, and they will say, "Hey, Jake," to him, and that is very simply an acknowledgment that he exists, as a separate individual with a personality of his own. He will not get the same feeling in a school that is too big. Of course he probably has a circle of friends, but that isn't enough, he needs to make a wider mark than that, and since this is difficult to do just by being himself, he will try to do it in more formal ways. If he is a first-rate athlete, or very "popular" socially, or if he is good enough

to become editor of the school paper, it will make a big difference; excellence in studies, though sometimes looked down upon if it is his sole claim to fame, can also give him satisfaction, some sense of being somebody. But in a very big school the competition is pretty tough. The average adolescent, possessed of no outstanding talents, may react in a variety of ways: by outrageous haircuts, by turning wildly bohemian, by joining cliques or gangs; or, perhaps most frequent, by just drifting along rather meekly and dispiritedly, and not very happily. In an unspectacular way, he is suffering —and so is his schoolwork.

The best remedy for these problems of course is the simple one: don't build too-big schools in the first place. Unfortunately it is an expensive remedy. Everything else being equal, three small schools will always cost more than one big one. A point to remember is that everything else doesn't *have* to be equal. Every school board faces the question of where to spend and where to save. They can save a lot on size—but not always wisely; perhaps it is wiser to take the savings out of a variety of smaller items—auditoriums, for example, which many educators feel are not essential in elementary schools, where children are happier putting on shows within their classrooms.

But where a very big school is the only possible financial answer, all is not necessarily lost. There are ways of being big without seeming so big. The most common of these perhaps is the so-called school within a school—in which sophomores, juniors, and seniors in a high school, say, are segregated into separate wings where they go their own ways except at lunch, gym periods, and assembly hours. This solution creates problems of its own, however: what fifteen-year-old wants to spend practically all his time with other fifteen-year-

olds? He will soon be sixteen, and eventually even seventeen, and he is interested in the people who already are; indeed, he may be quite fascinated by them. This is true at all ages: a five-year-old at the zoo may be so absorbed in the "big boys" (of six or seven) next to him that he doesn't bother with the elephants—or even with a popsicle. Children need frequent contact with children of other ages; it gives them, again, a sense of self—of what they are now, have been in the past, and are going to be next year, and the year after. For these reasons some educators feel it would be better to divide the students not according to age, but simply numerically. A tenth-grade class, housed in the same wing with the eleventh and twelfth grades, would get more chance for varied contacts.

A really good architect can help too. He will give you a floor plan that children can find their way around in easily, spaces that feel human and intimate, and details that take the curse of impersonality away from vast dimensions. For example, he can design a high school social room big enough to hold large numbers, yet with areas hospitable to small groups—an alcove perhaps where five or six can get together and yet be in sight of the crowd.

And as always, most important of all is the atmosphere created by the staff of the school. Where classes are small, where teachers and administrators are skillful, friendly, and concerned with the child as a person, not just as a mathematician or a linguist, the problems of excessive size have a way of dwindling if not disappearing.

The feeling of ownership

To say that the average child lacks a sense of his personality may sound far fetched. Any observer can see that children do possess personality

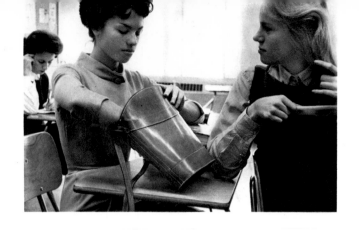

(in fact far too much of it, it sometimes seems). Perhaps the answer is that if they have it, they don't know it, or don't know much of it.

Well, how *do* children think of themselves?

Differently, at different ages. In the early stages, perhaps, it is by a kind of simple definition. Someone who knew almost nothing about it might define Detroit as a city in Michigan; and a child might say, "I am a little girl, here is my mother and father." As knowledge increases, where the Detroit expert might say *this city makes cars and has buildings and streets and people,* the little girl might think: *I play and eat and sleep and I have toys and clothes and a bed.*

The picture of the self gets richer and more complicated with age but some of the basics remain—and what one "has" is one of these basics. Of three men with identical incomes, you may find one drives a black sedan, one drives a two-tone convertible, and the third goes everywhere by taxi. In the end, it isn't convenience, or comfort, or money that decides them; it is the idea they have of what they are like.

The average adult in America has a great many things: a house, a job, a car, a bank account, a voting record. The child has surprisingly little that is truly his, beyond toys, clothes, a "collection" or two. Even his room at home doesn't really belong to him, he isn't allowed to do as he likes with it (and maybe the reason some children hate to clean up their room is not that they are lazy, but that they want *their* rules, *their* clutter—it makes the room seem their own).

Children long for and need personal property, the more personal the better. Proof of this exists in the almost pathetic value a child will put on outwardly valueless possessions: an ordinary stone that brings "luck" to its young owner; a red pencil he found on the street; baseball cards from a pack

of bubble gum; an empty snail's shell. Little boys' pockets are traditionally crammed with such treasures. At some ages, notably seven, this longing for things of one's own is especially acute, but it is generally true throughout school. They want their own desks, their own lockers, a place in science lab to set up an experiment that can go on for several weeks without danger of being disturbed. Older children might like private cubicles to study in, in a library. A chair that fits his own size is not just more comfortable for an eight-year-old, it is more *his*—and it will also save him, if he is bigger or littler than the other kids, from some pretty merciless teasing. He likes schoolroom furniture that moves, enabling him to some extent to pick his place in the room. And at nine and ten, cabinet and display space becomes crucial; these are the "collecting" years.

He also will like things to seem his as a part of a group, he will love the feeling that his surroundings, now that he is seven and in second grade, are distinctive and quite different from what they were when he was only six and in first grade. He will be delighted to have a big platform in the room where he and the other second-graders will spend months building a miniature city; there was nothing like *that* in first grade; and when he gets to third grade he will be glad to see they don't have it there either, for now he is a whole year older, and moving into loftier matters.

This feeling is perhaps strongest between first grade and kindergarten. In some cases, a first-grader may not even speak to his old kindergarten teacher if he passes her in a hallway; he doesn't wish to be reminded that he was ever so babyish as to be in her class. Others may actually seek her out in order to show her how sophisticated they have become. When a school in Illinois first installed movable furniture in the post-kindergarten grades, the six-year-olds on the first day of school were crushed: where, oh, where was that emblem of their growth, their graduation into "real" school, the desk and chair bolted down to the floor? They might as well have stayed five (though they got over it with some tactful help from the teacher).

The possessions and privileges that distinguish children from other children, both older and younger, will naturally vary with age. Where second-graders like a platform to build a city on, the upper grades in elementary school would love a walled-off junkyard, full of cartons, discarded lumber, old truck bodies, worn out engines, and the like, to work on during recess or after school. The city of Copenhagen, Denmark, maintains just such a junkyard for children, and it is wildly popular.

In high school something very different would be appropriate. High school and junior high are a special problem in many ways. It is here, just at the moment when education moves into higher gear, when children are really capable of extensive learning, that school morale drops to its lowest point. In fact, some educators are coming to feel junior high school is a mistake. Twelve- and thirteen-year-olds, they believe, are at a naturally intellectual age, but are thrown off balance in junior high by the complicated social life, which they are not really ready for. Perhaps a separate wing in elementary school would suit them better.

But basic to everything else is that familiar symptom of adolescence: the rebellion against authority. It is worse in some children than in others, but it exists in all of them, it is part of the equipment for growing up. The problem is complicated by another well-worn teenage trait: a bottomless capacity, in fact need, for comforming to other teenagers. So that once an opinion is established—such as that school is a bore—it is very difficult indeed to overthrow it. These mass opinions appear in different forms at different schools. Sometimes education itself, the academic side of school, is held in disdain, but the social side, and athletics and extracurricula, these are "all right," they are desirable, a self-respecting person may indulge in them without losing status, and will in fact gain by them. More rare, though it has been known to happen, is the school where the opposite is true; where a kind of sophisticated pride resides in academic work, but where anything social or partaking of "school spirit" is sneered at. Sometimes *every* aspect of school is beyond the pale. This is pretty much the case in a high school on Long Island—a very large school, significantly, serving five suburban towns. It happens to have one of the best athletic programs in the vicinity, its teams consistently beat the other teams they play, but they have trouble recruiting players; where in 1931 more than a quarter of the boys came out for varsity football, recently only thirty-five were playing by the end of the season from a total of 2,000. In spite of their excellent winning record, the athletes are regarded as fools for trying, for school spirit itself, in any form, is ridiculous. If they are eccentric enough to go out for the team, they still haven't the nerve to wear their varsity sweaters.

This is a drastic case, but similar afflictions plague many junior and senior high schools. Adolescents do feel, in that deadly kind of mass-opinion way, that school is something imposed on them by authority—which to some extent it inevitably is—and they are apt to resent it. And there is no simple cure. Quality is of course the first remedy: a good teaching program, with small and stimulating classes. But it also helps if you can make students feel that the school belongs to them—not to the community, or to the principal, or to the faculty, but to the children themselves. This is one of the major values of the student social room or lounge, and of student councils, of student newspapers and dramatic clubs, of athletic programs, and of those questionnaires that sometimes are submitted to children before the building of a new school, asking them what features they would like to see in it.

And of course this matter of mass opinion, of the prestige of the right things and the disgrace of the wrong, can be worked both ways. Academic prowess will get a better reputation sometimes if the students with top grades are allowed to spend free periods in a student lounge or outdoors, instead of in study hall. In the cafeteria of a high school in Florida there is a raised platform built for the school band to play on, which has to be used for eating since the school has grown so fast. At first no one wanted to eat there; but now that it has been designated the special dining place for the student council, everyone does.

More basically, children will tend to be proud of a handsome, well-equipped new school—and it is worth noting that most teenagers, there is just no doubt about it, like "modern"—they like glass walls (if they aren't glary), horizontal lines, and all the other earmarks of the modern style. Perhaps they simply feel that, being the new generation, what is new suits them; perhaps the modern school seems less school-like and more adult, like an office building or factory; perhaps a nostalgic feeling for period architecture comes only with age; in any case, this preference comes up over and over again.

A kindergartner said to his mother: "It's my room, my teacher, my school, my desk—even the toilet is made just for me!"

That school belongs to *them*—not just as indi-

viduals, or as third- or tenth-graders, but as *children*, distinct from adults: this is something in the whole atmosphere of a good school that kids will respond to over and over. This means, especially in lower grades, that doorknobs should be at a natural height for children to reach; thermometers and clocks should be placed where they can be read; blackboards should be low enough for the smallest child in class to write on with dignity; curtains and shades should be easy to work; display space should be accessible so they can put up and take down things themselves; so should cabinets. Ceilings can be lower than for adults. The whole atmosphere of both classroom and school should be such that a child feels competent in it—feels he can explore, experience, and learn from it—and take care of it—without hurting things or himself. He should be able to make mistakes—because mistakes are educational too—but inexpensive ones, not ones that will make him afraid to try next time. This doesn't mean everything has to be foolproof; there is something to be learned from fragility too. In fact children will be able and happy to take responsibility for one or two fragile things—*if* the general environment is arranged and planned so they can move through it freely and without fear.

One little girl who liked her new kindergarten room was asked why, and after a moment of thought she said, "This room says yes."

That is what all the classrooms should say; because if it isn't said in school, it isn't going to be said anywhere else. At home, in spite of dolls and wagons and pets, the facts remain: curtains are not to be pulled at, rugs aren't for sliding; out in the backyard is a flower garden; on the street, more and faster cars. Even the corner store, where a little boy can go by himself and pick out licorice or bubble gum, is on the decline; more and more he has to wait till his mother is ready to go to the shopping center, and get in the car beside her and drive there—and be careful not to get lost, once he's there. As life in America gets more centralized and departmentalized, there is less and less for children to do in a free, leisurely, spontaneous way. The world, more and more, says no.

Just how you go about making a room or a school say yes is a complicated question; some of the answers are suggested in this chapter, but the total answer of course cannot be given in words; it is given in blueprints, by a skilled and imaginative architect. Architecture at its best transcends the merely efficient.

Children not only like schools that say yes; they take better care of them. This is a point brought up over and over again, often with astonishment, by custodians and principals, though there is no reason for surprise. Adults are just the same. Nobody feels inspired to take pains over something that is ugly, and is made of shoddy materials, and doesn't work right, and doesn't fit right. Children, like other people, have both protective and destructive impulses, and the point is to arouse the protective ones. In a crowded tenement neighborhood in New York City, an experimental school was opened up one recent September with great misgivings. It had gay materials, lots of windows, and a playground full of unusual "creative" play equipment; it stood out in the neighborhood like a healthy thumb. The local policemen said the windows would be broken in no time, and the colors defaced. Nearby in the same neighborhood is an old school. In the course of the school year, children repeatedly got into the old school, set fires, stole tools, and broke windows; but in the new school there wasn't one case of breakage or theft. Instead there was a different kind of problem. Afternoons and Saturdays, two hundred and fifty

children were climbing over the walls to get into the playground. Finally the principal decided to keep the playground open after hours and make it easier for the kids. **1929200**

What do children like about schools? Well, beyond all this, try asking them, as we did. You will get a host of answers, some perceptive, some wildly impractical, but almost all of them stimulating. In some cases it is like asking a child what he wants for dinner and he says, three banana splits and a cup of coffee. Some will say earnestly that what they want most is a school that is cheap. A great many seemingly inexhaustible little dynamos will say, no stairs; they are too tiring. They like weeping willow trees.

Their answers will vary with the kind of neighborhood they come from. At a school in a rundown part of Harlem, a fourth grade class was unanimous, to everyone's surprise, in liking the window: a narrow clerestory strip near the ceiling, with almost no light and no view at all. They liked it, they said, because they didn't have to worry about falling out of it; or about breaking it when it was being opened or closed; or about rocks being thrown through it.

It is just about impossible to compute statistically the likes and dislikes of children. Because they aren't statistics, but human beings, something different keeps popping up, just when you think you have settled the matter. Children in one third grade were asked to pick something they either liked or disliked and write a short essay about it. Here is one of the negative answers. It has nothing to do with schools, but a good deal to do with the variety of human nature:

"I hate bandaid plastic strip advertisements because they say that bandaid plastic strip stick to eggs but they don't. That's why I don't like it."

3

1

4

2

The first day of school frequently
is the hardest. Tearful farewells to
mothers are almost the rule.
Here a boy (left) says goodbye, then
resists the new life, refusing
to join in, to become a part of things,
until, in the end, he loses,
but wins.

5

8

6   7

9

10

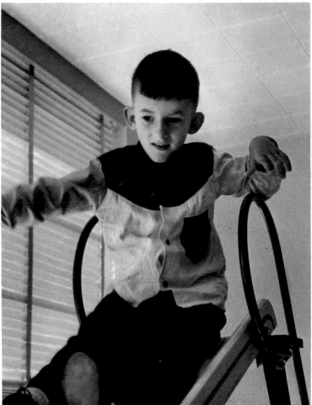

The future

"It is my belief that flight is possible . . ."

—WILBUR WRIGHT
in a letter to his father,
September 3, 1900

About the time World War II ended, and the postwar world sat glistening in the sun, there was an exuberant idea abroad in school building circles that perhaps schools should not even be permanent structures—that they could keep better pace with progress if they were designed to be replaced every generation. But this appealing notion soon faded, despite the tremendous replacement rate that has taken place since the war in other types of buildings. (On Manhattan alone, during the past ten years, old office space has given way to new by 20,000,000 square feet.) What has become clear is that our *public* buildings have not shared in the replacement boom. Some of the "temporary" buildings thrown up in Washington during World War I are just being removed now. The squirrels are going to miss them.

So there is no such thing as a temporary school —and therefore no escape from a long, discerning look into the educational future. Every expert has his own idea of how things are going to change in the next several decades, and some of these ideas can sound quite drastic. But the school board that ignores them is looking for trouble. Today's theories may well predict which schools, new now, will be obsolete before their bonds are paid off.

Some of the changes are quite easy to spot because to some extent they are already with us. The teacher shortage is one of these.

We have plenty of children, of course; usually, somehow, we can get a roof to put them under, happy or miserable. Getting people to teach them is another matter. Not enough new teachers are entering our schools, and each year 8 per cent are leaving. In fact, if the United States is to maintain its present pupil-teacher ratio, it is estimated that the teaching profession will have to draw in more than one-third of the graduates of U. S. colleges in the next seven years. Not just graduates of teachers' colleges—but *all* colleges.

This is not likely to happen, of course. In spite of pressure today to improve the teacher's lot, it will take a major evolutionary shift in salary and status to compete effectively against the lure of other careers. Evolution comes hard. Meanwhile the shortage is already showing itself in changed teaching techniques and—more slowly—in changed schoolhouses.

To be specific, few people really want the size of classes to continue to get larger—least of all today's harassed teachers—but many people are convinced that some stretch is inevitable under the strain of the statistics. To help ease some of the tension of numbers some educators advocate programs of "teachers' aides," larger classes with one fully trained teacher and a couple of less completely qualified assistants to help out. (This can mean different shapes for classrooms.) Some believe that the university teaching system, with rankings of professors, assistant professors, associate professors, etc., must inevitably be extended down at least into high schools, with an interlocking schedule of lecture and lab courses. (This can mean having more and bigger lecture rooms in schools combined with more, and better equipped, laboratory space.) The twelve-month school year (which means summer air conditioning in many areas) is a suggestion too.

There are others who maintain that the answer is television—and most educators will grant that

TV is a uniquely good way for teaching children certain things. For example, today's cigarette commercials, as one of our advisers, Dr. Frances Ilg, has remarked, actually are a wonderful way to learn spelling—especially such words as *throat, filter,* and *satisfaction.* Children have a basic, hypnotic fascination with the TV screen, perhaps connected with the pigmy image it projects of adults. Children aren't scientists, and TV to them is a form of magic—whatever appears on that little screen has the kind of force that only magic can have. Another of our advisers, Dr. Frances Horwich—Miss Frances of the famed "Ding-Dong School"—finds that the children she meets in the real, everyday world are apt to back off the first time with a look of awed astonishment. "How did you get out of the box?" they want to know, and she is still looking for a good answer.

But there is vigorous disagreement whether TV, much as it might assist in teaching, can replace an appreciable number of teachers. A few observers even think that TV teaching requires not fewer teachers in classrooms, but more. Someone has to understand children and answer questions, and the machine can't. Before deciding further about TV teaching, much of the educational world is watching several extensive experimental projects in TV teaching backed by grants from the Ford Foundation's Fund for the Advancement of Education. They are watching with an interest scarcely less than children's fascination with the TV screen itself.

Until the answers to many questions of curriculum and teaching technique, including the teacher shortage, are clearer, there is one shrewd hedge available in school design: flexibility. Almost everyone agrees that it is worth going to some trouble and expense to avoid building a schoolhouse that will lock the teachers into present curricula and class systems, that might prevent experimentation in class sizes, or preclude the ability to go along with whatever teaching patterns do evolve. For instance, more individual teaching can be made possible if large spaces can be subdivided to create rooms for three, five, or ten pupils in a special field, such as calculus in a small high school. If at the same time two "standard" rooms can be combined, it is possible to free a teacher to work with one of those small groups.

Architecturally this means erecting long spans with few supporting columns, so that partitions can be knocked down and classrooms rearranged, re-sized, without knocking down the basic school structure. It means building movable partitions, if your budget can stand it. It means including conduit or runways for TV and other transmission lines even if you don't intend to use them right away. *More* than enough electrical outlets should be scattered around the classroom to allow for new ways of using existing teaching aids—movies, phonographs, operating models.

The future is not just a problem of power outlets of course. For example, in the matter of larger classrooms, psychologists point out that it may become important to offset the press of large "audience" teaching with compensating facilities which give children real privacy at some period during the day—the intimacy of two or three young children working in a small space, or—when they are older—a system of booths or cubicles in libraries. With this in mind, some re-

search programs are even developing machines to teach children certain subjects, addition, for example. (Recording machines are already widely in use to teach languages.) This would mean that the child would be entirely alone during a period of each day or each week in school. These devices have some of the fascination of pinball machines. They also have the great advantage, when the child masters something, of advancing him immediately to the next learning task. Holding the interest of a classroom full of children who have different learning speeds can tax any teacher even if she isn't massively outnumbered.

And besides children in schoolhouses there is the matter of adults in schoolhouses. During one year recently, forty-eight million adults attended some kind of organized adult class, ranging from evening courses in metalworking to amateur theatricals in the school auditorium, and this has a direct meaning for school builders today: put up your buildings so that parts of them, the shops, some classrooms, the gymnasium, the theater, can be unlocked, heated, and lighted separately, for future economy. And plan these community areas for eventual air conditioning; they will be used in summer too.

The list of community uses of schools is very possibly an endless one. It is common, of course, to find Chambers of Commerce and other civic organizations holding their meetings in school lunchrooms, with refreshments served afterward. (The superintendent of schools in Los Angeles pointed out some time ago that his schools had the largest string of eating places in the city.) The schoolhouse traditionally also is the election polling place in many areas throughout the country. Citizen committees and parent-teacher associations hold their meetings at the school; so do American

Legion posts, and women's clubs. Special public hearings on political issues frequently are held at the schoolhouse, where a crowd can be accommodated (and where their cars can be parked). Social and folk dancing is another popular community activity in many towns in the school gymnasium or lunchroom; rural communities frequently stage Halloween or Christmas parties in the schoolhouse. Health clinics, for both children and adults, use school buildings, to dispense polio shots and other types of vaccinations. Adult acting groups rely on the school facilities for practicing their plays and presenting the finished productions. Community "sings" and county fairs convene, and in some areas church services are conducted at the school. In New England and the Middle Atlantic States the traditional town meetings meet in the schoolhouses. In southern states, citizens use their school facilities for family canning of fruits, vegetables, and meats. Slaughterhouses, poultry houses, laundries, deep freeze lockers, and repair shops for farm equipment are also found within the rural school plant. The Red Cross, in times of local disaster, almost always uses the school as a headquarters for emergency service, feeding, and housing.

There are strong reasons to believe that adults are going to use schoolhouses more, not less. An increase in leisure time is one of these. In the past fifty years the average industrial work week has shrunk from fifty-one hours to forty hours, and the rate of shrinkage has been accelerating as the age of automation clicks in. In the next forty years, with developments in solar and atomic powering, many sober statisticians actually expect to see this work week halved. Also, as advances in food, drugs, and medical technique extend active life, the great American off-duty group—the children—is being joined now by a new mass, the

elderly. Except for churches, there aren't really too many other places but schoolhouses to center their activities in most communities, and as our continent becomes more populous, pressure will increase. Educators also are hoping to lure many of these active elders into helping teach—or correcting test papers, at least.

Population estimating is chancy at best, but present predictions see 220 million people in this country in 1975, when today's new schools will still be only teenaged. Even at that, the U. S. will hardly be crowded—there will still be a little over eight and a half acres per person. (In England today there is less than one acre per person.) But there is also a thickening pattern of compression of population, of urbanization; city planners already are thinking of the Atlantic Coast from Boston to Norfolk as a single, continuous metropolitan area, and this is true also of groups of cities on the Pacific Coast and in the Midwest.

To the school board today this may signal that the smartest thing they can do is to look for a hundred-acre farm near town and buy it. This may sound impractical, but it is actually being done in some of today's hardest pressed, most bond-battered metropolitan suburbs. In another thirty years the squeeze on accessible open space in our towns may be tough enough to make such a tract invaluable; it might well be possible to invite a town park, the library, public health offices, and public employment agencies to consolidate with the school system in its real estate planning, to the great advantage of the entire district. For one thing, adults who *use* schools or school grounds don't generally vote down school bond issues.

Most experts expect that such consolidation would require physical changes in the massing of schools, with a growing shift to the "campus" plan so that a number of separate buildings connected by walks could be used separately as well as together. The gymnasium, for instance, would be more like today's university field house; the school might well get a swimming pool as a community dividend. (This has already happened in a number of U. S. communities.) Also, a smaller auditorium, designed as a theater, is recommended in schools today by many educators and architects. Besides being cheaper to build than barn-like "assemblies," it is really more useful. The performers, children or adult, are usually at least as important as the audience; it is frequently to their benefit to run a show several nights, not just once. Mass congregations like graduation ceremonies can use the field house.

Togetherness may be the slogan, even the fetish, of our decade, but there is some reason to think that occasional *aloneness* will acquire more and more value in the crowded future. If school districts think in terms of big sites, they can also plan for secluded nature walks and other meditative places as well as plenty of open playground and baseball fields, to be used by adults after that wonderful short work day.

Inside schoolhouses, beyond designing for long span flexibility and plenty of power outlets, it may be wise to consider mobility. This means more than movable walls and partitions (though on this point we still, today, can't approach the ingenuity of thirteenth century Japan). Another kind of mobility involves transporting things—from hot

Haircut. Sometimes children grow suddenly.
An example of this swift change:
three pigtailed sisters make a visit
to a hairdresser's, and emerge what seems
a few years later.

lunches to book racks—in and out of the classroom on wheels. This is a way to save cafeteria space, and take advantage of remote storage space. (Few classrooms have enough storage, especially really flexible classrooms). Conveyors, lifts, and wagons are not architecture, but they can affect a school design immensely. And it has been established that a schoolboy considers pushing one of these vehicles to be quite an honor.

Besides generally wanting to teach all pupils more, educators hope for two special break-throughs in the coming decades. These are in the education of handicapped children and, conversely, in the development of specially gifted children. What these problems may mean in the future of today's school plants is difficult to define, but the feeling is that the first specialty calls for a certain amount of seclusion—but not remoteness—from the rest of the school. Handicapped children often need some privacy for protection until they learn to get along with other people, but it is an error to remove them entirely from the usual. A campus-type school or one with long wings might be the

most prophetic architecturally, better than a single block, unless the block is broken by courtyards. Architecturally, gifted children are a lesser problem than retarded or handicapped children; but gifted children, to learn as much as they can, need variety and opportunity, which can mean special teaching rooms in addition to regular classrooms. The tasks of educating gifted and handicapped children are not small; together these make up about a tenth of our school population.

There also are several break-throughs in materials which architects and manufacturers have been looking for. New methods for divorcing glare from lighting, both artificial lighting and daylighting, are one quest which is advancing well; another is the continued development of materials that need little or no maintenance. The third search is acoustical—some method for blocking sound by other means than bulk. The solution for this final need still seems remote. Some people even deny it ever will happen—but in 1900, although plenty of people thought it would be nice if they could fly, Wilbur Wright was not widely regarded as a prophet.

Getting going

School building is a process that calls for enthusiasm, but a measure of doubt is not a bad ingredient either—doubt that the past is perfect, for one thing, that, for example, the traditional size of elementary classrooms is necessarily the most efficient size.

But perhaps the first question to ask is: Why do you need a new school? Over-crowding in the present school? Double shifts? An antique, uncomfortable, unpleasant building? Is the old school too far from where new neighborhoods are springing up? Is it a fire trap? Is it barely adequate this year when you know a new surge of children will hit it next? In other words, what is your problem?

But even defining the problem is only a starting point; the real questions—the tough ones—lie beyond: *How* inadequate are the accommodations, how obsolete the facilities? Most new school buildings begin in questions such as these. And they begin, as often as not, in the mind of the superintendent of your school system. Part of his task is to spot the problems early, before they become acute, so there will be ample time to anticipate trouble and plan durable solutions.

Superintendents of schools in the United States have jobs that would at times confound a Leonardo da Vinci. Directly responsible to a board of education, each one is, as often as not, actually running the single biggest business in his town, with more employees than anyone else, the

largest (but tightest) budget, and the biggest plant (25 per cent of the population of the U. S. is going to school, after all—a higher proportion than is engaged in any other one occupation).

Sheer administrative size is only the beginning of the superintendent's difficulties. His raw material is children; his product—their mental and social growth—is more subtle than smoke, and considerably more controversial. At a city administrative conference, a superintendent may well look across the room at the Commissioner of Parks and sigh enviously—*he* just has to worry about trees staying alive, not how many of them are being admitted to colleges of their choice. And there are not only the children to think about; there are also the parents, the teachers, the bus drivers, the janitors, and sometimes the political pressure groups. Fortunately, most U. S. superintendents are not only dedicated men (for fair evidence, compare your superintendent's income with that of a local utility president); they are

also professionals trained in the technical complexities of their field, the key executives in the building of new schools.

The board of directors in this process is the board of education, a group of citizens elected (in most school districts) by popular vote. As a group they have a deep regard for their communities and a willingness to work to make them better; they will also in the end be held legally responsible for the building that is put up. In some districts they are also a well-scarred group. Selfless service is no shield against hard knocks.

The next group usually involved is harder to define, but no less vital to successful school building. We are back to the people themselves, and fortunately they are not totally disorganized.

Service associations, fraternal groups, clubs, and social offshoots of church and veterans' organization abound in the U. S. and get things done. The Masons, for example, have over 4 million members in the United States. The PTA has

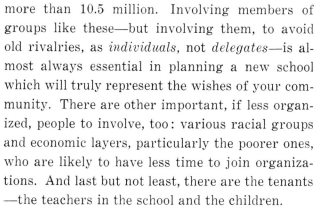

more than 10.5 million. Involving members of groups like these—but involving them, to avoid old rivalries, as *individuals,* not *delegates*—is almost always essential in planning a new school which will truly represent the wishes of your community. There are other important, if less organized, people to involve, too: various racial groups and economic layers, particularly the poorer ones, who are likely to have less time to join organizations. And last but not least, there are the tenants —the teachers in the school and the children.

School planning, in other words, requires a complicated blend of local professionals and amateurs. The sharpest characteristic of today's school planning, in fact, is wide democratic involvement. Experts calculate that in a town of ten thousand people as many as 1 per cent of the population should devote personal time and labor to the survey and programming for a new schoolhouse. In smaller towns the effective group may be as large as 2 per cent; in larger ones it shrinks

to ½ per cent (but involves both city-wide and neighborhood groups). This participation is not just a clever process to sweep the populace into voting *yes* when the bond issue comes up, it is to get them to say *yes, no,* or *maybe* intelligently when discussions are under way about what kind of school to build. You may also want to bring in an educational consultant—a professor at your state university or an independent practitioner. He is a specialist, with the added advantage that he is removed from town politics and can be impartial in such matters as real estate wrangles— where the school should best be placed, which land must be condemned. In fact his organization may offer to move in and do everything (usually for a small percentage of the final cost of the

Nap time

school). But few school boards favor this. It seems wiser to insert the consultant at certain balance points, but let the local people do as much of the planning as they can.

In most cases, the community itself begins to enter the school-building picture in numbers when the school board invites a few prominent citizens to help out. Opinions differ, sometimes sharply, as to the degree of independence this group should have. It should not be used as a rubber stamp, but some boards and superintendents, fearful of just that accusation, are much too cautious. Actually, some definite kind of liaison is essential if the citizens' committee is going to get the necessary data, consultants, research assistants, and clerical help. Probably the truth is that advisory groups, in the end, always define themselves. They all operate a little differently. Almost all are bound, however, to report to the board, although less formally they report to the community as well. What they create is a general lay definition of need —of what a school should teach and the kind of

spaces it needs to teach in. In the process they also predict what additional schools may have to be added or replaced in the district in years to come. The committee may even recommend consolidating with one or more other nearby districts.

But their biggest and most serious responsibility is less tangible; just how should the community's children be educated? A citizens' study group which gets lost in the details of counting heads (or washbasins) to the exclusion of interviewing new *ideas* in education, is neglecting its job. Perhaps the new ideas should have most to do with shaping the program.

Here are some of the subcommittees a citizens' group is likely to form:

Inspection and evaluation—These are the people who look over the existing schools to judge their condition and list what they lack. This, again, calls for some technical help from the superintendent or consultant: *how much off for a cracked foundation wall?* To make it easier, there are several standard check-lists, something like report cards, which give point ratings not only on

may shape not just one but many schools.

The immediate fruit of the committees' labors, however, should be a general statement of the needs that the school district faces, and the goals to which it aspires. This statement is presented to the professionals—the superintendent and his staff—who in turn work out a statement of their own, a set of educational specifications that is concise, complete, but architecturally speaking still fairly general. Educational specifications, it is generally agreed, should describe as carefully as possible the amount of space that is needed, and the uses it will be put to, including the equipment it has to house—but they should not attempt to shape that space. That would be like telling a doctor not only what ails you but what color pill you want. Few architects are educational experts; most will appreciate the opportunity to ask "dumb" questions about education, but they will cherish a school superintendent and a board who answer these questions not with exact descriptions of rooms but with ideas for rooms.

A survey undertaken conscientiously by a citizens' group always uncovers many opportunities, in addition to duties, in school building. If your town hasn't built a school in twenty years, participating in the survey may be like walking barefoot into a fully stocked department store, to see what you now *can* include, if you want to. This raises problems of choice, of course. Sometimes communities choose not to choose; they back out the door and go home and build a replica of the old school from a cavernous cellar right up to the decorative cupola riding the roof, from semi-Greek columns out in front to semi-dark corridors in the core. They may get a traditional-looking school out of this decision, but there is a legitimate doubt that they have made their decision in the traditional American pattern.

How to choose an architect

Choosing an architect is not nearly so difficult as choosing a wife—but it sometimes seems so. This may be because while people need architects, they *want* wives.

A competent school board, however, does "want" an architect; it has learned from experience to want one. Its members know that only an architect can domesticate their ideas of what they want in a schoolhouse—the home for their children during nearly half their waking hours. They also know that the earlier you get an architect (even before you buy the site is best), the more he can do for you. And they know how vital it is to get the right one; a spouse, if things get bad enough, is usually divorceable, legally, but not a million dollar building. There it sits, full of taxpayers' money and dreams. It has got to be used. So it had better be good. Beyond all this, an architect who is a real master of space planning may also actually save you his fee, when ultimate construction costs are figured out. He will certainly do his best to. Professionally, it can only help him. Legally, he is your agent, bound by law to look after your best building interests, forbidden to make any money from anyone else involved in the design and construction operations.

One of man's earliest instincts is to find a pleasant shelter—not just dry enough and warm enough, but *pleasant*. This extra and essential element, though it can be neither computed nor defined (our affection for certain places is fully

as complex as our affection for certain people), is what really keeps the architect going as a professional. He does not have pain to send him clients, as doctors do, or anger, as lawyers do. And the architect's world is full of rivals: contractors, developers, builders eager to deliver any kind of building as a complete package "with no charge for the design." Still, the architect has been around since the time of the pharaohs (who possibly were offered "package deals" for pyramids too), and today architecture is a confident, vigorous profession. The most obvious symptom: the simple fact that we are no longer copying the past for our buildings. The national nostalgia of the past half century for Roman fire houses, Gothic water tanks, and Baroque movie theaters has pretty well blown over. Today even the wildest and funniest of our buildings usually has some tie to reality—even if it is a roadside duck shop in the shape of a gigantic concrete duck.

This change did not come solely from boredom with the past; it grew through a healthy interest in the possibilities of new materials and new ideas of how a building can serve its occupants. Modern building techniques and materials have given the architect a freedom which his colleagues of a century or so back never dreamed possible. He doesn't first have to ask: How many columns, and how thick, does this building require? He asks: Who is going to use this building? What will they use it for? He is free to fit the building, like a footprint, to the activities it is intended to shelter, and he has thrived on this new freedom. The result is that it is no longer possible to separate its delight from its usefulness as organized space. You no longer say to yourself, in looking at a good school: "This corridor is useful; this cornice is decorative." Not all modern architecture is good, or suitable, or original, of course. There are modern clichés; there is modern pretentiousness. But in modern schoolhouses, architects have been able to embrace industrial progress without raising the shibboleth of coldness in environment.

It is probably true, as one school architect put it, that "while the children do not always get the school they deserve, the school board does." If you are on a board, or are one of the thousands of other citizens involved in school building, a wise preliminary might be for you to devote special attention to cultivating your response to buildings. The way to do this is to walk through many schools and try to drink in their total effect, the atmospheres they create. At this point, do not focus on details. If you will, take a look without your glasses.

When looking over the field of architects, you'll want to keep them on, of course.

But even then how shall you choose? Dazzled by color slides and glossy photos, buried in a mound of charts and unit cost comparisons, bewildered by cryptic references to *elevation* and *section, stud,*

joist, and *clerestory*—how shall you know which of the rather frighteningly well-equipped men who appear before your building meetings will prove to have the frontal lobes of a cost accountant and the heart of a poet? Which of these clear-eyed men will really see into your building problems and have the concern and sensitivity and time and other resources to give you a building that even the holder of your county's biggest tax assessment will find irresistible?

On the notion that architects might themselves have some useful things to say, we interviewed or otherwise queried a substantial sampling of first rate architectural firms on how *they* think an architect should be viewed from the other side of the desk. Almost all of them replied at some length and with a natural and deep interest in the subject. According to their reports, there are almost as many ways of picking architects as there are school boards and school building committees. The method of choice ranges from outright political tie-ins in a few areas to a conscientious examination, in others, of every firm within a 500-mile radius of the building site. Both methods leave something to be desired, and while there was considerable difference of opinion among the architects about just how architectural competence can be spotted, there was a rather striking unanimity on just how you should *not* go about choosing an architect to design your school.

Avoid the horse show or mass stock judging method. One and all, the architects agreed that a ten-minute pitch is inadequate for presenting a firm's qualifications, and that the kind of evening when as many as twenty or thirty architects are invited to appear is likely to be unrewarding for all concerned. Almost all the architects reported dismal memories of waiting interminably, in the uneasy company of other architects, only to face a bored board, whose attention must somehow be caught above the roar of band practice in an adjoining room or the distraction of chocolate cake served by the home ec teacher. One distinguished school architect, who has a speech difficulty, recalled such an evening, when every architect within traveling distance had been invited for a ten-minute interview: "My ppppartner said, ddddamn it, *we* should get ttttwenty minutes—my ttteam stutters."

On the whole, you will be better off if you can resist the urge to interview each and every firm registered in your state. Try to allow each firm an hour, including a ten minute break to punctuate interviews, and, beforehand, send them an agenda to follow in the presentation.

Try to decide immediately whether you intend to employ the best architect or the best salesman. In any of the assaults of business life, it is difficult to distinguish salesmanship from professional competence, and where one product is very much like another product, perhaps it doesn't matter. But one building is not just as good as another building. It is up to you to decide whether the suave fellow who seems sure of himself before the listening audience will have an equally sure hand at the drafting board.

This point is a difficult one. There is no rule that the good architect cannot also be a good salesman, and it is not necessary to seek architectural

On the next four pages, young people with things they have made.

genius solely among bashful, introspective types: if anything, professional competence is more likely than not to manifest itself in an air of confidence. It is also true that you and your superintendent and his staff will have to work together with the architect you choose for a long time. So it is a good idea, other things being equal, to vote for an architect who does not get in your hair. It is, however, in the investigation and summing up of all the *other things,* beyond the man himself — white teeth and well chosen words—that the real burden of choice lies.

Refrain from trying to select your architect by shopping for the lowest fee and the maximum in fringe benefits. A promise to "fix" a bond issue, or even to pick up the checks for monthly school board dinners should be regarded as a clear danger signal. "Fee-shopping" is just as hazardous as hiring the cheapest doctor to treat a serious illness. If this seems exaggerated, reflect for a moment on the size of the building expenditure for which your architect will be responsible. Only his personal integrity, reflected in his professional ethics, can safeguard your building investment.

At least one architect recalled a school board meeting where some twenty-five colleagues and himself were asked for competitive bids on their prospective fee. The board was convinced that the matter worked just like competitive contractors' bids, and it took some lengthy explanation to persuade them of the professional character of architectural services for the design of buildings.

More than half the licensed architects of the U. S. belong to a national professional association, the American Institute of Architects, and are bound by the Institute's code of ethics. Part of the code is an agreement not to compete with other architects by fee-cutting. This is very much in the client's interest, because where fees are cut, architectural service is cut in ratio. The A.I.A. has recommended a scale of percentage fees based on building type and total cost, which may be obtained from the A.I.A. chapter in your city.

Lean back quickly if you find yourself veering toward the man who says he can get your school built cheaper than anybody else. Building costs have been rising steadily for twenty years now, and so an architect who sells himself by promising

miraculous reductions raises serious doubts about either his integrity or his wisdom. You will, of course, want to pick someone who is realistic about costs, and who will consider the limits of a tight building budget a challenge to his ability. But there also are times when your architect should argue with you.

Don't automatically plug for the architect with the most schools to his credit. Experience in school architecture will, of course, be a weighty factor, but sheer quantity of experience is less telling than the quality of the work produced. A firm with many schools to its credit may have much to offer you; on the other hand a growing firm working hard to achieve a top-bracket reputation may bring as much or more interest to your job. Repeat assignments from former clients always mean more than the absolute number of previous school contracts. If all of one architect's schools look entirely alike, incidentally, don't take this as evidence that he must have discovered *the* answer. Perhaps, instead, he has just stopped trying. It is basic that schools, like sites and people, *should* vary from one town to another.

There are no rules of preference for the large vs. the small firm, either. As one architect said, "Some school boards are of the opinion that an architect with a hundred draftsmen can design a school in one-tenth the time required by an architect with only ten draftsmen. They really believe it. Actually this is about as sensible as concluding that a woman with nine husbands should be able to produce a baby every month."

Whatever the size of the firm you choose, it is always wise to have a clear understanding that the school project will be supervised throughout by principals of the firm. You should decide also whether you want to employ a full time construction inspector—*a clerk of the works.*

The possibility of pairing a well-known, national firm of school architects with a local firm may come up; some of the country's most famous schools have been the result of such collaboration. The local firm is a real necessity. Don't leave them out unless the outside firm can demonstrate really intimate knowledge of your town's building conditions. Such collaborations, incidentally, should not raise the total fee appreciably.

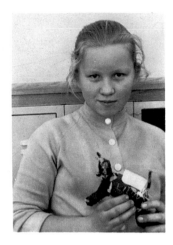

Resist a tendency to overload the preliminary questionnaire you will probably use as a means of sifting firms. A competent architect is likely to share all your own aversion to filling out forms of needlessly encyclopedic proportions. So for his sake and yours, keep your questions concise and relevant. The National Council on Schoolhouse Construction has collaborated with the A.I.A. in preparing a standard questionnaire for collecting the facts that matter. Copies can be obtained from most architects.

Do not expect the architect to design your school program as well as your school building. Not even the most gifted of architects is likely to be a master at curriculum planning, or to know the maximum number of students who can be happily taught by a single teacher, the number of subjects one teacher can handle, or any of the other essential arithmetic that must be worked out before a new school building is designed. Nor is it reasonable to expect him to divine, say, to what extent TV instruction may help compensate for the teacher shortage—although it is quite reasonable to expect him to give you some flexibility of space and

equipment that will help you hedge against future change. It is the job of your superintendent and his professional staff to provide a clear picture of your school needs, and how they may change in the future. The clearer the problem you give your architect, the more likely you will be to get a first-rate architectural solution for it. Don't expect him to provide the services of an educational consultant within his architectural fee.

Don't ask for rough sketches. This is something like asking a doctor for a diagnosis after you have spent five minutes leafing through a magazine in his waiting room. Contrary to some impressions, an architect is not valued for his ability to produce pretty pictures. The real work of architecture lies in the painstaking analysis of building needs: of the many activities that must be provided for in the new building, of safe traffic patterns that permit large numbers of children to move efficiently from one activity to another, of a space plan that will get the maximum of use out of a minimum of building cubage, of construction materials that will save labor and prove durable in use. All these factors must be analyzed—and then synthesized—

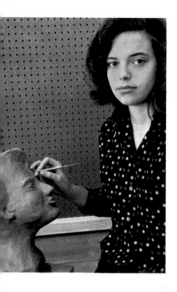  

before even the roughest sketch can be made of the building that is to meet your needs.

An architect who is willing to bring a rough sketch of your building to his first interview puts himself under suspicion as a charlatan. At the least, he is in violation of his professional code of ethics, which says that sketches, plans, or cost estimates must not be offered without compensation. This protects architects from exploitation, but also protects clients; a rough sketch usually contains less than meets the eye.

Remember that a good architect can design more than one kind of school. Don't mentally try on pictures of the schools an architect has already done like a woman at a milliner's trying on hats. An architect's professional education has prepared him not to turn out stock plans, but to provide a highly custom-tailored product that won't suit anybody but its owner. A prize school for Winnetka, Illinois, in 1958 may be no good at all for Pocatello, Idaho, in 1959.

If you are determined, then, to avoid these pitfalls in picking the architect for your new school,

it will be necessary to find some objective starting point in selecting from among the registered architects in the United States. There are approximately 22,500 of them, and approximately 10,500 architectural firms. How, then, shall you begin?

Getting up a good preliminary list of architects worth serious consideration is a crucial part of your task. The superintendent and his staff should be asked first. Your state department of education perhaps will also recommend names, and so can superintendents in other school districts, as well as deans of the architectural schools of your state's leading universities. Other good sources are the three national architectural magazines, *Architectural Forum, Architectural Record, Progressive Architecture*, and the national school magazines, *American School Board Journal, The Nation's Schools, The School Executive*, and *School Management*. The architectural magazines get out a special school issue every year or so, well worth a trip to the stacks of your public library to scan. The professional magazines will also give you a feeling for some of the school building problems being solved, and may even show you work by

firms in your area that you will be interested in following up. Preliminary list in hand, you will next want to think about the many different kinds of service—creative, scientific, technical, and business—that you will be asking from your school architect. The check list on page 63 will help tell you just about what you should expect from him at each main stage of planning and building, and, in general, how he should be paid.

One way to determine how effective an architect is likely to be is to ask for evaluations from his former clients and from contractors who have worked with him. Many school boards have used questionnaires for securing such evaluations, but, again, questionnaires carefully designed to elicit an accurate response. Were the architect's cost estimates realistic? Were there change orders after approval of plans for which the architect (and not the client) was responsible? Was the architect competent in dealing with building code and other regulatory requirements? Were plans, specifications, and other documents completed on time? Were the working drawings clear-cut and complete? How much personal attention did the architect give to supervision of construction? Has the building been satisfactory to children and teachers in use?

Specific questions of this sort, which will also be on the agenda of your interview, should collect a good deal of information about the architectural firms in which you are interested. In all fairness, however, you should try to question as many former clients as possible, and to be on watch for the one who tries to shift responsibility for his own changes or mistakes to the architect. It is sometimes hard for a client to recognize that the architect is not, after all, a magician in stretching building dollars. Funds available for a school

Major steps	What the architect should provide	What the client should provide
(1) Selection of architect	Facts about his firm Lists of previous buildings References (previous clients and contractors) Photographs and cost data of previous work Inspection of previous school designs in use	An open mind
(2) Site selection	Evaluation covering: Site suitability for building, play space, access Utility connections and drainage Character of land, natural growth, and surroundings Subsoil conditions (usually an engineer is retained by school board to make a detailed subsoil analysis)	All possible data bearing on future school needs Unless school district has already contracted with the architect to design school on site under consideration, district should pay lump sum or consultation fee, plus expenses for this service
(3) Signing of the contract for architectural services	Advice as to terms of contract, and suggestion of contract form	Contract specifying: Basis of architect's fee and fees to engineers and other specialists Basis of billing of fees (monthly or at specified stages of planning and construction) Compensation for extras (travel, extra blueprints, work done due to owner's changes after approval of plans) Inspection of construction by architect Ownership of design (drawings and specifications remain professional property of architect) Method of arbitrating disputes between architect and client Method of terminating contract, if it should be necessary, and basis of payment for services already rendered Guarantee that there will be no transfer of interest by contract parties
(4) Preparation of preliminary plans	Rough sketches, diagrams, drawings (these represent various stages of the architect's analysis of the functions to be provided by the building)	Complete data on school needs, educational program, number of students and teachers to be provided for, community uses of building, future needs Approximate cost limits

Major steps	What the architect should provide	What the client should provide

(5) Presentation of preliminary plans, specifications, cost estimates	Site plan
	Plans for all floors
	Perspective sketches of exterior and of principal interiors
	Specification of materials and method of construction
	Specification of heating, ventilating, lighting, acoustic equipment (usually prepared by associated engineers)
	Preliminary cost estimates
		Careful study and review of preliminary plans and specifications
		Evaluation of construction, materials, and equipment specified on basis of
		  (a) economy of maintenance as well as initial cost
		  (b) standards of child health and welfare
		Approval of preliminary plans and specifications, after any necessary changes, with recognition that changes cannot be made in final plans without additional cost
		At least 25 per cent of total architectural fee

(6) Submission of final plans, specifications, and cost estimates	Complete working drawings covering site plan, floor plans, elevation sections, all design details Working drawings of structural, lighting, heating, and ventilating systems Clear-cut and detailed specification of all materials, equipment, and method of construction, to serve as basis for competitive bids Final cost estimates from contractors based on detailed specifications	Approval of final plans and specifications At least 50 per cent of total architectural fee, computed as a percentage of estimated building cost
(7) Review of final plans by city, county, or state agencies regulating building standards	Plans that will conform to code and safety standards of community Applications for all necessary building permits	
(8) Acceptance of competitive bids and award of general contract and subcontracts	Supervision of bidding Advice to client on evaluation of bids and award of contract	Contracts with general contractor and subcontractors
(9) Construction	General inspection of building process, to ensure delivery of construction and materials as specified and proper coordination of work of all subcontractors General administration of all business aspects of the operation	Confidence in the ability and integrity of the architect; support of his translation of the board's ideas into a structure
(10) Furnishing of building	Supervision (upon request) and installation of all furniture and movable equipment	Consultation, and a fee in addition to usual architectural fee
(11) Completion		Acceptance of the building Remainder of architectural fee

building are almost always fixed, and the client who permits his requirements to balloon from day to day, without realistic regard for cost, is likely to end the job feeling disgruntled.

While you will have to deposit a great amount of faith in the architect you choose, it is also true, again, that you have one major resource in the difficult task of selection that is not available in the case of any other sort of professional service. You can look at visible, incontrovertible evidence of the architect's competence. You can open the door and walk into it. Whatever means you use in judging an architect, visiting the buildings he has already designed is an essential step which should never be neglected on grounds of time, trouble or expense. Even if you are considering an architect with no previous experience in putting up schools an inspection of his other work will be rewarding. It is surprising how many school clients sit and talk and interview and ignore this opportunity. Perhaps they think one school house, after all, is about as good as another.

If you are visiting a school building, be sure to see it in use. Talk to the superintendent, the teachers, the janitors or maintenance men, and, perhaps, even the children. The people who use a school can tell you a great deal about the competence of the architect who designed it and about its satisfaction, efficiency, and durability in use.

But trust your judgments as you move through the building. Take plenty of time to get a real feeling about how *you* would enjoy spending a large part of your life in the classrooms, in the play space, the library, the auditorium. These feelings and judgments are a priceless index of architectural competence. If, as one architect said, you "decide for the buildings that move you to enthusiasm," you will not be likely to go wrong in picking the architect.

Convincing the community

*"... the genius of the United States is not best
or most in its executives or legislatures, nor in its
ambassadors or authors or colleges or churches
or parlors, nor even in its newspapers or inventions . . .
but always most in the common people."*

WALT WHITMAN, Leaves of Grass

Standing at the broad plate glass front of the Albright Investment and Loan Company, James H. Albright looked out at South Ninth Street, whose intersection with Main Street fifty yards away marks the business center of Winfield, Kansas. He had spoken volubly to a reporter for an hour about the school bond election which just a few weeks before had split his community, leaving deposits of bitterness which would be evident for a long time to come. Albright acknowledged freely his part in organizing and leading the opposition to the bond issue. He said thoughtfully, "Maybe service of this kind is the price you have to pay if you love your town and want to see it progress."

The sincere bedrock upon which Albright built his opposition—with an uncomfortable near-half of Winfield's voters in concurrence—was, in brief, a powerful fear of more and bigger taxes.

It is a fear to be reckoned with. In most towns, new schools mean new taxes, and a vote is necessary to accept them. The *No* votes have been on the increase. Perhaps the record of what happened in Winfield will provide information useful to other communities confronting the problem.

Like most Kansas towns, Winfield is bisected by a broad sun-baked highway (U. S. 77) which for three-quarters of a mile forms Main Street and houses most of the community's commercial life . . . the clothing stores, the restaurants, drugstores, five-and-ten's and supply outlets which service a community of 10,000. On either side of U. S. 77, a

mile to the banks of the Walnut River on the west (where a crossing at Kichapoo Corral formed part of the old Santa Fe Trail), a mile and a half to the east, the men who make up this commercial center live with their families in shaded neighborhoods of well-built homes. And beyond the city limits, on the flat prairie land, are the prosperous wheat farms which underpin the economy of Winfield and every other town in Kansas.

Like the farms themselves, Winfield is reasonably prosperous. The deposits in its two banks total more than $16 million. It is as proud of its reputation for conservatism as some other towns in the state are of their adventurous frontier backgrounds. Its residents tell the visitor about the city's two colleges (both denominational) and twenty-two churches, and its refusal to accept government help in the construction of public works even during the darkest years of the depression. Since 1948, when the state was released from a bone-dry liquor law and the matter was left to local option, Winfield has kept itself pure; residents have to travel to Arkansas City on the Oklahoma border thirteen miles away ("a transient town," Winfield citizens call it) to buy their refreshment.

The last two decades have brought a certain amount of light industry to Winfield; today thirteen small manufacturing firms carry a payroll of 495 employees. But postwar growth has been modest—the population increased from 9,000 in 1945 to 10,500 a dozen years later.

The two most striking evidences of this growth are the new houses clustered around the rim of the town and a new elementary school that sits in one of the new neighborhoods. This school—the Whittier School—was built several years ago to take care of 375 new children brought by the population increase. The bond issue to pay for it carried easily when it was presented to the voters in 1955. Later, there was some grumbling about the school's design, which was dictated more by consideration of the needs of school children than by Winfield's tradition of conservatism. Stone and glass, it has outside doors to each classroom, skylighted rooms, flexible interiors, and imaginative use of color. But criticism was minimal, and it looked—particularly after enthusiastic reports began to come in from the teachers and pupils who used it—as if the Whittier School was becoming one of the chief marks of Winfield's civic pride.

The construction of the Whittier School was only the first step in solving Winfield's school problems, and the school board recognized it.

Of the town's six elementary public schools, three were problems. Deep, multi-storied buildings, all more than sixty years old, with cramped, fixed classrooms and inadequate lighting, they were deficient by modern educational standards and too small to take care of enrollments.

Superintendent Herbert Hawk and the school board—two doctors, a businessman, an optometrist, and two housewives—decided to approach the problem in the broadest possible community spirit. First Hawk wrote a letter to the townspeople, for publication in Winfield's only newspaper, the *Daily Courier*, describing the situation. The board wrote similar letters to all PTA groups and to every civic organization, inviting them to participate in a citizens' advisory committee which would explore the problem.

The advisory committee—with thirty-five members—first met with the school board in the spring of 1956. Sentiment ran high in favor of action. But that first meeting demonstrated that such a committee was too large and unwieldy for efficiency. So the school board selected a steering committee from the members of the advisory committee, which in turn appointed other subcommittees.

In the summer of 1956, the members of the subcommittee on the need for new schools met and studied a disquieting report from a structural engineer who had been called in to assess the condition of the schools: one—the sixty-three-year-old Lowell School—was dangerously weak; the second school—Irving—had structural defects which, although not so serious as Lowell's, were nonetheless important.

A concerned group (four businessmen, a farmer, a teacher, and a housewife) made its own inspection of the Lowell School. Climbing dilapidated stairs, poking through furnace rooms and basement recesses, dodging attic rafters, they soon realized the engineer had not exaggerated. Then the original thirty-five-member committee voted its recommendations to the school board: the Lowell School should be replaced with a new building as soon as possible; the Irving School should be replaced in four or five years; decision on the third school—Bryant—should be postponed indefinitely. One or two members voted for renovation rather than replacement, and some concern was voiced over mounting bonded indebtedness. But there was no serious opposition, and, with its recommendations made, the committee disbanded.

The superintendent and board then drew up a list of "educational specifications" for the immediate task of replacing the Lowell School and gave them to the architect—William N. Caton—who had designed the 1955 Whittier School. His preliminary plans satisfied the board completely. The new school would have three more classrooms than the old, which would not only take care of swelling enrollments in the Lowell district but would even help relieve congestion in other districts.

The architect's cost estimate, with a margin of safety, was $255,000.

The board then consulted an investment banking firm specializing in municipal bonds, and a maturity schedule was set up which would integrate the new bonds with the present tax levy and allow the combined levy to remain even and consistent over a fifteen-year period.

Now there remained the matter of deciding when to put the issue to the public for a vote. In Kansas, second class cities have elections every second April, which would mean the forthcoming April for Winfield. Or a special school bond election could be called earlier. Some board members felt it was urgent to get the matter settled immediately. But the Midwest was in the grip of drought that fall, and the cautious majority feeling was that it would be wise to wait until the spring rains came to talk about money. So in January the board announced that in the April city

election it would ask the citizens of Winfield to vote a $255,000 appropriation for a new building to replace the Lowell School.

The school board planned a campaign to get information to the voters through several channels: (1) a speakers' bureau (composed of board members), to appear before every civic group in the city; (2) the publication of an inexpensive, clearly written school building fact booklet to be distributed to every home in the city; (3) a series of articles, each taking up a different phase of the problem, to appear daily in the *Courier* during the last days of the campaign. (Wallace Keith, the *Courier* editor, agreed to handle the articles in his news columns.) The PTA groups in the city started their own tub-thumping as soon as the board announced its plans. The issue was talked up in PTA meetings, in PTA publications, and over neighborly morning coffee sessions initiated by PTA members. "Convince at least one person," became the PTA slogan.

Then a few weeks before election, the city commission announced that in that same election it would ask the voters to authorize $430,000 for the replacement of the sewer system. The citizens of Winfield, it now developed, were to be confronted with issues totalling three-quarters of a million dollars. Shortly after this announcement, a long letter entitled "The Road Ahead" appeared in the *Courier*. It was signed by James H. Albright.

The letter presented a disquieting array of figures. The city's total bonded debt, it pointed out, was $871,000. The cost of the new school and the new sewer system would bring that up to $1,556,000 and the Winfield taxpayer's 1957 tax would be about 75 mills. Nor, Albright persisted, would this be the end. A school board encouraged by a favorable vote on this issue would in short order bring two more school proposals to the pub-

lic; and there were yet other community needs to be satisfied. "It is not difficult to see that our bonded debt could very easily go above three and one half million dollars which . . . would mean your taxes would be $100 or more per $1,000 of your assessed value," Albright wrote. "Such a tax load would be confiscatory and ruinous."

Albright saw no way out of providing the new sewage system. But the line had to be held somewhere. He urged all his fellow citizens to vote "No" on the school bonds.

His letter also urged the alternative of remodeling the Lowell School (at a cost of about $90,000). This would leave Lowell without the three extra classrooms and the multi-purpose room the board wanted, but he submitted that they were not really necessary. He offered a wide range of other justifications for opposition: (1) $255,000 was too much money; if Winfield *had* to build a school, it could do it more cheaply. (2) Perhaps a permanent structure was not even necessary; some communities were putting up inexpensive frame buildings designed to be used for a period of fifteen to twenty years. (3) The Whittier School, which the proposed school would resemble, was, with its modern design, its color, its glass, its radiant heating, too fancy and full of frills. (4) School board members had not thought the matter over enough before making their proposal.

Albright, a former mayor and member of the city commission, is an influential man in Winfield, and his letter hit the town with stunning impact. "It really set the grass afire," he reflected.

Herbert Hawk was disheartened by Albright's letter. Hawk is called by many in Winfield—supporters and critics alike—a "teachers' superintendent." His interests focus precisely on the city's public schools, and he brings a dedication of some thirty years (he is ex-principal of the high school) to the cause of continuing school improvement. A retiring man, he is more comfortable inside the school system than on Main Street ("I'm not much of a joiner") and he prefers to find and meet his challenges *inside* the structure of the system—with the introduction of new teaching methods and materials, for instance, or the strengthening of curricula. But when a threat rises from the outside he is not hesitant to meet it. He penned a fast reply, rebutting several of Albright's points.

The school board drafted a long reply of its own, also answering Albright's objections and adding a caustic observation on Albright's vision of the future: "The city total mill levy for all purposes might possibly be in the neighborhood of 100 mills at some future time. We wish to point out however that children are created from year to year. We feel that we must provide them with suitable educational facilities in order to insure their future, and that the total tax levy is more or less secondary."

The articles prepared by individual members of the board, each explaining a specific issue connected with the bond proposal, began to appear in the paper that same day. These articles told in detail the reasons why Lowell had been found to be dangerous and inadequate, and how the financing would be arranged—specifically, how it would be worked in with the existing bond schedule so that only for a few years would it mean an increase over what the taxpayer was now paying.

But the tent Albright had staked down was broad, and into it flocked dissenters of all persuasions—the honestly worried and the irrationally worried; those who were critical of the building's design; those with a grudge against the school board or any of its members. "We had been waiting for something like it and we didn't know where to look for it," according to one elderly resident.

"We are wondering how long we can exist," wrote an ex-postal employee who was living on his retirement allotment. Albright himself told a reporter: "You've got children to think of and you've got the teachers to think of, sure, but you've also got the little man with a fixed income to think of. When you let the tax load get too big you're making it so he can't own a home and he'll have to spend the rest of his days in one of these rest homes."

Albright's most surprising—and influential—support came from Wallace Keith, editor of the *Courier*, who had served on the citizens' committee which had begun the review of school needs and had participated in the recommendations made to the school board. Keith's opposition centered on the contention that there was no need for the extra classrooms in the new school. Conceivably more significant was a distrust he had of the school administration itself. Its members made no effort, he said, to circulate among, to exchange ideas with, to win the confidence of the merchants and the bankers who "are the backbone of this town." Although he honored his agreement to run the board members' stories in his news columns, Keith began using his editorial page to fight the issue.

The opposition stimulated by Albright and supported by Keith erupted a scant two weeks before the voting day.

One week before the election, large advertisements began to appear daily in the *Courier*. Each contained a sketch of a school built or in the process of being built elsewhere in Kansas, purporting to show that each was being constructed less expensively and more efficiently than the proposed Lowell School. Each ad called upon the community to "Vote No" and "ask the Board of Education to submit a more practical plan." The ads carried a grand signature: "Committee For Progress."

The "committee" and its advertisements attracted interest and attention quickly. "The Committee For Progress seems to be an intelligent, interested, and informed group," said one man, voicing the sentiments of many of his neighbors.

Others, however, were disturbed and angry. "Who are they? How were they chosen and whom do they represent?" demanded a housewife. An advertising salesman at the *Courier,* a supporter of the bond issue, ran an elaborate ad of his own, which quoted John Ruskin to answer the committee: "There is hardly anything in this world that some man cannot make (or build) a little worse and sell a little cheaper, and the people who consider price only are this man's lawful prey." "It seems to me," the ad continued, "this definitely applies to the present bond election. This ad is run by one who Does Not believe in using a High Sounding but Name-Hiding Misleading signature. W. T. (Bill) Tressider."

The committee's anonymity bothered many citizens. Later, Albright acknowledged to a reporter that his "leadership" had been instrumental in forming the committee. It had included, as well as himself and Keith, a "number of businessmen along Main Street." He defended its anonymity: "These men are in business. They couldn't let their names be known without a lot of hysterical women taking reprisals against them." (Keith, however, had second thoughts about the matter. He announced in an editorial after election day that the policy of the *Courier* in the future would be to accept no advertising from groups whose membership lists were secret.)

Some citizens were irritated not only by the committee's anonymity but also by its appropriation of the word "progress." Mrs. Louise Wilcox, a vociferous supporter of the school board, swept indignantly into the newspaper office and asked how one might apply for membership in the committee. "They say they're for progress," she announced heatedly. "Well, I'm for progress, too. So I'd like to join." Her application for membership was not accepted.

Passions rose sharply in the final days before election. The biggest and most closely followed battles were fought in the pages of the *Courier.* The letters column—now an entire page—was filled daily with impassioned declarations on both sides of the issue.

Jim Albright wrote another letter. In this one he charged the school board with "loose procedure." The letter pointed up what everyone in town now recognized: debate was no longer simply whether the need for a new school justified an increase in the tax burden; the issue now embraced a direct attack on the school board.

The two physicians on the board made it clear that they recognized this as the issue. Dr. Warren Bernstorf ran an advertisement which put the matter bluntly: "The present Board of Education of the city of Winfield has had a total of approximately fifty-six years experience in school management. Mr. James Albright had a very brief two years as a member of the city commission. Who do you think is the better qualified to direct the future of the children of the Winfield schools?"

Dr. Wendell Grosjean wrote that because of the nature of the opposition, "the result of the coming election will, in fact, reflect either a vote of confidence or a vote of no confidence in the Board."

Support for the board—and the bond issue—began to rally. The PTA groups got together information, which they published, charging that the buildings praised in the committee's ads were of inferior construction. Not only the PTA units, but the City Teachers Association, the American Association of University Women, the Chamber of Commerce, and the Junior Chamber of Commerce all made their backing publicly known. The teachers at Lowell offered to forgo their salary increase for the forthcoming year as a gesture of support.

The principal of the Lowell School reminded his readers that it was unlikely that Superintendent Hawk, after thirty years of service to Winfield

schools, would "deceive anyone with regard to expensive and extravagant construction." "We voted for and elected the school board members," wrote a mother. "By so doing, we placed in their hands the responsibility for the educational welfare of our children." "It would seem the better part of judgment," wrote Mrs. Wilcox, "to trust the members of the board to do the job to which they have been elected." There were many others. The Ministerial Alliance backed the board, two of the city's ministers speaking in favor of the bond issue from their pulpits.

Yet in spite of this heartening support, the issue seemed in grave doubt as the campaign entered its last days. The inroads cut by the opposition ran deep . . . in the shops and stores along Main Street, where consciousness of an obligation to preserve fiscal soundness provided almost a fra-

ternal bond . . . in the small quiet homes where the retired, the widows, the pensioners lived.

And then, in the last few days, in a spontaneous demonstration of that amorphous force called "community spirit," little candles lighted in support burst into flames of activity in neighborhoods all over town. At no time had a personal, door-to-door campaign of persuasion been proposed or considered. Now, however, a group of mothers from the Lowell PTA hurriedly got together and devised just such a course of action. "We realized," said one of the women, "that we couldn't get that school just by wishing. Things were serious." They organized a block-by-block plan of contacting all the registered voters in their district.

The other PTA districts, stimulated by the Lowell group, followed suit and the town became a frenzy of female activity. "Some people thought we were crazy," said a dedicated worker, "but we changed some votes. We know that." In each of the districts, voters' names were put into three lists—those who were known to be supporters, those who were known to be against, and those who were known or assumed to be undecided or whose opinions were not known at all. The workers concentrated on this third group first. ("They're the important ones; they can make the election go either way.") Then they tackled the certain opponents. They made their contacts both by visit and by telephone, presenting facts, answering questions, urging. "Some of the fence-sitters had to be persuaded through figures," a worker admitted, "but some had to be intimidated. I made at least a dozen people think that if a fire broke out in the old school it would be their fault."

Another group of mothers used intimidation of another sort. They bought a full page ad to be run in the *Courier* the Saturday evening before Tuesday's election. The ad professed faith in the school

board, and urged an affirmative vote on the bond issue. They went up and down Main Street soliciting signatures for the ad. Getting the endorsements of those merchants known to favor the issue was no problem. But they frankly hoped to worry secret opponents (the anonymous members of the "Committee For Progress") into adding their signatures. They succeeded. Although no one ever knew for sure precisely how many of the ad signers had contributed to the earlier attacks there were enough to "disgust" Editor Keith.

Another group of women had 3,000 handbills printed. On the night before the election, they were distributed to every home in Winfield. The handbill's message was simple: "You have had much to read and think about, but when you go to the polls, remember this: the only effective measure of our 'progress' as a community is our children. They are our obligation and our hope. Vote Yes for their new school."

On voting day, the PTA groups provided baby-sitting and transportation services.

Winfield voters approved the school bond issue, 1,490 to 1,172. The sewer bonds were defeated by almost the same majority.

In a wounds-binding spirit, the *Courier* ran an editorial headed, "Let's Build That School." And both Keith and Albright acknowledged afterward that they were not totally disappointed that the issue had carried. Albright told a reporter: "If they [the board] had been defeated they might have come back with a plan too far the other way and we might have got a school put up that nobody would like. I wouldn't want people to be able to say, 'Jim Albright is responsible for *that*.' ")

Superintendent Hawk and many of the others who had worked hard for the school personally regretted the defeat of the sewer bond issue. What Hawk primarily regretted, however, was that the two issues had been included in the same election: "I would say that it is a mistake to include a school bond issue in any general election. I'd never want to do it again. Wherever possible, the school issue should stand on its own merit."

There is validity in this observation, very possibly for other communities as well as for Winfield. There is validity in all the lessons posed for Winfield in its experience—if they can be recognized.

"What would you say was the most important thing we learned?" Superintendent Hawk asked the assembled board members several weeks following the election, after a reporter had put the question to him.

There was unanimous agreement that the most important thing to do in putting a school bond issue across is "to get the information before the public"—all the information, at every stage of the operation, using every medium possible. But perhaps Dr. Bernstorf posed the issue more succinctly—and accurately. "Don't," he advised, remembering the valiant work undertaken by the PTA members, "forget the mamas." For the issue is not simply getting the information before the public; it is getting it before the public in such a way that the public votes favorably. Our system of public education is built on the assumption that an aware citizenry acts wisely; but we also know that people informed and uninformed alike (although perhaps not to the same degree) can be influenced.

The chief question, then, is: How do you influence them, what techniques are available and appropriate to use?

The mass media technique implicit in the Winfield school board's broad advice to "get the information before the people" is a sound enough beginning. Specifically:

(1) *Speakers*, bringing the case for a *yes* vote before local groups, can form an important part of the publicity campaign. School board members often are the most useful because their views are recognized as knowledgeable and authoritative. Where dissension throws a school board into too harsh a spotlight, it may, however, be more effective to recruit *other* leading citizens—informed and interested ones—for the tougher speaking assignments.

(2) *Newspaper publicity*, particularly in small communities, often is the most effective single communication channel available. Because a school bond issue is news, the editor, whether he is a supporter or not, will devote a substantial amount of space to the subject. A continuous supply of well-written news releases, each developing a new and timely facet of the story, will almost always be used, frequently in toto. Prominent citizens quoted in favor of the issue, particularly if their reasons are different, are always news.

In Winfield, *Letters to the Editor* was easily the most widely read page during the two weeks prior to the election. In that instance, the letters were written spontaneously; there is nothing, however, to keep an organization from stimulating correspondence. Pictures, too, are valuable. One clear photograph showing fifty children crowded into a shabby classroom may attract the support of people apathetic to written and spoken appeals.

(3) *Radio and television* appearances in larger communities can usually be arranged through the station managers as a public service. Either prominent citizens or teachers and students from the overcrowded school itself may be helpful in arousing attention and support.

(4) *Local advertising* should not be under-

estimated: display ads enjoy high readership. If expense is a problem, as it usually is, regular advertisers in favor of the issue often are willing to include a short message in their own ads urging their customers to support the bond issue. This costs the school bond campaigners nothing.

(5) *Electioneering devices* (sometimes described as hoopla or razzmataz) are easily the most colorful of all the aids. Many an urban calm has been disrupted (and enlivened) by torch-light rallies, snake dances, parades, and sky writing. Many a street has vibrated to the blare of a loudspeaker and the thundering troupe of doorbell-ringing children. And where dramatization has not been used, repetition has. With mountains of brochures, handbills, posters, automobile stickers, and milk-bottle tags, citizens have been urged to make known their faith. (Such devices can be employed by the opposition as well. The voters of one town awakened on the morning of their bond election day to find their milk bottles decked with the ironic message. *"Let's Go—Vote No!"*)

Are these devices effective? Many an after-

action report gives them credit for the success of a bond issue. And Tarrytown, New York, once blamed its failure to put a new school across on the maximum of dignity—and minimum of electioneering—with which it presented its case. Probably the only valid rule is that it depends on the community itself—in conservative towns, voters' resentment may easily be aroused by the suggestion of frivolity or extravagance.

Of course, in *no* community is the exploitation of any one—or perhaps even any combination—of these techniques likely to bring victory by itself. They are assists, of proved value. They should not be ignored. But neither should these techniques, in themselves, be overestimated.

School bond campaigners to be successful must be aware of certain more basic truths about persuasion:

—it is rarely *facts*, more often *feelings*, which insinuate themselves into a voter's consciousness. (This might do violence to our comfortable belief that an aware citizenry acts wisely, but there it is.)

—facts, for that matter, which disturb the voter's preconceptions do not easily get through to him, no matter how forcefully they are presented.

—people more readily accept information on matters they are already interested in. (The lesson here is clear enough: a bond issue embraces many areas of interest; exploit them all, and you find a wider audience.)

—man still takes his influence most directly from personal contact with his fellow man. This includes, importantly, the persuasive door-to-door, shop-to-shop work done by the PTA groups in Winfield; it includes the neighbor-to-neighbor telephone conversation; it includes the carpool chat. All of these reach an incalculable number of voters in a most—probably *the* most—effective way.

—there are, in any community, certain indi-

viduals who are more important than others, in that they exert influence on those around them . . . even, in certain instances, on those who are most resistant to influence.

These individuals are a town's opinion-makers. They are not always the wealthiest, the most active, the most distinguished in a civic sense. They do not always occupy important positions. (A newspaper editor, for instance, *may* be an opinion-maker; but often he follows rather than makes opinion.) They might be found anywhere, in drug-stores as well as law offices; they may be house-wives as well as ministers. But, whether because of personality traits or a reputation for knowledge-ability, they exert a remarkable influence over their fellows—indeed, their opinions are often sought; and the wise planner of a bond issue campaign will find out who they are and enlist their aid in any way he can. Sometimes, of course, the assistance of these "influentials" cannot be obtained; they are to be found instead at the head of the opposition. In that case the only thing to do—and it is important—is to anticipate and

counter their objections before they have a chance to take grave effect against the issue.

In every part of the nation, new schools and improved facilities stand as monuments to citizen action. Sometimes civic participation is a spontaneous thing, rising out of the urgency of a particular problem, retaining its formality long enough to see the problem solved, then retiring once again to the arsenal of weapons with which democracy's best battles are fought. Sometimes it is a continuing force, always active, always in motion. Sometimes it is purely local in character, fitted to needs so unique that it has hardly anything in common with civic effort in other communities. Sometimes it is part of a nationwide movement formalized in the National Citizens Council for Better Schools, an organization whose purpose is to promote local citizen activity for improved education.

What kind of community support is best? Which should a board of education encourage?

The answer is not simple or easy. There is no doubt that Winfield was lucky. There the community support which literally put the bond issue across could just as easily have remained passive, frustrated into inactivity because it had no plan of action to follow. Had a formal, continuing citizens committee existed, it would have provided such a plan of action. And taking over, in an organized way, some of the tasks of publicity and voter-education, it might have accomplished other valuable ends as well. It might from the beginning have identified the issue as a broad one and prevented it from becoming the unpleasant contest it did between the school board and the opposition to the board, and bond issue.

The existence of a permanent committee might also, however, have brought new problems to Win-

field. Citizens committees are, by their very nature, open to all citizens—often a good, even desirable, condition, but not always. In Winfield's case, a continuing citizens committee would undoubtedly have included the most active of the new school's opponents—some of whom, like Jim Albright, were among Winfield's influential group. The result could be compromise in the quality and/or design of a school.

An effective committee can never be simply a servant of the school board; its hold on the public's confidence would be short-lived. But neither—except in the rare case of a genuinely inadequate board—should a committee set itself up in competition with the board. And if the board relinquishes any of its authority, the community and the entire cause of public education very likely will suffer.

In general, it would seem that larger cities, where the number of citizens responsive to school needs is higher, offer the best chance of continuous committees working successfully with boards of education. In smaller communities (six out of ten U. S. school systems have fewer than 300 pupils) the individual school boards should weigh the matter well, for in the end the right answer will be dictated by the temper and character of the community itself, as well as the exact nature of the local school problem.

In the matter of convincing the community, rules are hard to come by. But there is encouragement for those who are determined—and dedicated—enough to take it: interest in public education in America is itself a force *potentially* more powerful than the fears which can gather to shape opposition to schools. And it is a force which can be exploited. Dr. Bernstorf's advice is applicable, wherever the fight is being fought: "Don't forget the mamas."

To win

$$$

"Nothing in the world is too good for our kids."

—ANONYMOUS

"What are we building anyway, a palace?"

—ANONYMOUS

Since the earliest days of public education, these two cries have been as inevitable a sound in the school building process as the sock of hammer on nail. They represent extremes of attitude more than they do finished buildings, of course. In the U. S. today you will find fewer educational palaces than princely communities; on the other hand, there are almost no neighborhoods, wealth aside, who don't recognize that some things are "too good" for their kids—that a seven-year-old mathematician, for instance, needs paper and pencils more than an adding machine.

But in school building today money is an especially anguished subject, shrouded in wear, worry —and confusion. Few entire school plants, fully equipped, cost as much as a mile of super-highway, for example, yet it is the schools that are under the sterner cost pressure. In some cases this pressure is squeezing much of the juice out of schoolhouses, leaving them stripped, temporary, and in fact uneconomical—that is, unable to meet complicated long-range challenges, thus defeating the intent of both the proponents and opponents of bond issues. This miasma of alarm and misunderstanding surrounding the subject of money in school building is our reason for including this chapter of financial observations in a book which already wears the dollar mark prominently. The results of our research will not turn the house lights on, but they may serve here and there as an ushering flashlight beam.

Economy in education begins long before the actual building does, before the foundations are dug or the footings are even blueprinted; it begins with a motive. In school *building*, the motive toward or away from money-saving is the educational program, which defines the rooms and other facilities needed. The architect is the professional who must fill this prescription with a building.

The prescription for public schools has changed twice, broadly, in the last two hundred years. The first change was the move from one-room schoolhouses into multi-room buildings, which began many years ago. As of 1955, there still were 39,061 one-room schoolhouses in the country, but almost no new ones are being built. A second historical change, however, is just now getting into high gear, and it represents an enlargement of the task of education in the U. S. It is the adding of "program space" to the classroom space. Program space includes all the letters that have been added to the three R's in two centuries of public education: domestic and mechanical skills, music, leisure time activities; special treatment for children with speech or reading difficulties and other physical or emotional handicaps (as well as for gifted children); special science facilities; health services; vocational guidance, and also vocational education in skills varying from typewriting to aeronautical engineering. Many schools today also are helping out with pre-school care for the children of working mothers; others are being asked by nervous communities to teach high school students to drive cars safely. As pointed out in Chapter III, parents—and grandparents—are using schoolhouses more and more too, for purposes ranging from music and craft shops to libraries. This all means "program space."

Some people assume these new school functions are something foisted on the public by over-zealous

want, frivolous or not. It was the search for fur coats that opened the American Northwest. Maybe our economy demands a new word, *want/need*, to define the democratic hunger that propels us forward in the material world—and, incidentally, creates much of the wealth that school taxes draw upon. In any case, many school features which would have been luxuries a generation ago, now may need to be reclassified. Some schools need more playgrounds today because there are fewer open fields left for children to play in. And many need more rooms for extra-curricular activities— "club room space"—because out-of-school extra-curricular activities are not what they used to be. For confirmation, consult your local police statistics on juvenile delinquency.

educators. Perhaps they are, sometimes, but in two years of looking we have found few examples of this. Instead, it seems, the public requests them —and then can't quite believe it when the bill comes in. So blame is directed, all too often, at the architect and the school board, rather than at the needs and wants of the community. This is human, but it isn't always realistic.

Just as human and unrealistic is the irritated defense of some harried school campaigners. "So America spent $2.5 billion for school building a year ago," they retort. "All right: so we also spent $10.5 billion for alcohol, $1.7 billion for toilet articles, $5.7 billion for tobacco, $2.4 billion for radio, TV, and records." But perhaps they aren't completely practical either, for in a sense the U. S. needs all these things, too, just as it needs schools and super-highways (and safe drivers). The commercial power of a democracy may well lie in the effectiveness with which people get the things they

Although the educational programming does govern the over-all economic strategy, this does not mean that there is not a great deal of economizing still to be done in the trenches, and on the drafting boards. Construction is costly, costlier than it used to be. However, the usual opinion about this too is somewhat garbled, we found.

The mid-twenties, like the mid-fifties, were a time of high costs, zooming birth rates, and accelerated school building. Using published records of the building industry, it is not difficult to see that one of today's typical modern schools would have cost about a third as much in dollars to build then as it does now, figured item by item—*if* it could have been built then. But today's schools do *not* cost three times as much to build as the schools that actually were constructed in the 1920's . . . perhaps they should, but they don't, generally. Somewhere along the line, someone must have learned to bring their comparative cost down, to design and build them better, to build more value per inflated dollar. In school building we are get-

Alcohol Expenditures: $10.5 billion
School Building Expenditures: $ 2.5 billion

ting *more*, comparatively, for our tax dollars than we did twenty-five and thirty years ago.

At this point, if you are finding scant comfort in this smaller relative cost increase, it may be revealing to stand back and take a look at what has happened to the dollar itself in the last three decades of depression, war, and prosperity.

In 1925, a pound of coffee cost 50 cents in the same store where it cost $1.02 in late 1957. The usual obstetrical fee in 1925 was about $50; today it is about $200. A new Ford car cost $580 in 1925; today, $1,879. Even more significantly, a brick-layer who earned $1.50 an hour in Kansas City in 1925 was worth $3.70 an hour last year. A carpenter's hourly rate was $1.12; at publication date it is nearer $3. Only marriage licenses and birth

certificates seem to have held the price line.

Also, to pursue the subject, any such comparison of cost between products also involves differences in the products—what you're getting for your money now as compared with what you got then, even for less money. This applies to school-houses as well as to homes and cars. In the 1920's the usual washing machine you got when you bought a house was a tub in the cellar. Last year an estimated 160,000 automatic washers (and many fewer cellars) were available as parts of new one-family houses. Although a Ford does sell for more than three times what the 1925 model went for, in 1925 this same car would probably have been worth more than a 1925 Rolls-Royce. Indian maharajahs probably would have bartered fleets of elephants for one. Do you remember the cars of the twenties, the beloved Model T, for example? Do you remember starting one? There was no left-hand door by the driver's seat, so you had to climb in from the other side to set the spark and throttle levers in place so that the car could be cranked to a start. The cranking itself required considerable muscular effort and was a little dangerous as well, because if the handle spun backward it could seriously injure the cranker. As soon as the engine began to roar, the driver rushed to the trembling footboard to re-set the spark and throttle levers. On a cold morning this process had to be repeated several times.

Perhaps we could get along without starters, hydraulic brakes, and directional signals today, as we did in the twenties. But we don't get along without them. We *want/need* these products of progress. And the last thirty years have brought improvements to school building no less tangible than improvements in our ways of traveling. Here are a few of them, some costlier, some cheaper than the old ways, but almost all under attack from time to time by people who confound economy with tradition:

—the old schools were designed for a "sit and learn" educational program. For this rote and lecture system we bought fixed, regimented rows of desks and chairs. Today we buy movable furniture and equipment—even to the very walls of the classroom sometimes—to do basic teaching better.

—the old schools were usually monuments designed to impress the adults. They were imposing municipal edifices with towers, arches, columns, cupolas, echoing lobbies, waste space attics and basements. (Not infrequently they had the proportions of palaces, if rather gloomy ones.) Today we invest in schools that are planned for the children, scaled closer to their size (eight-foot ceilings

as compared to twelve-foot ceilings in those days), built without the waste spaces formerly required for conspicuous consumption on the part of the community, in its pride.

—the old schoolrooms got daylight from one side only, from high windows covered by dark shades, with large blank wall spaces in between. Today we can have large, continuous sections of glass, sometimes on the roof as well as the walls, with better natural illumination. This is not extravagant.

—the old schools had dowdy, dim lighting fixtures. The new schools have integrated fixtures that produce many times more illumination, and make classrooms more efficient and comfortable.

—the old schools were heated by steam-fed

radiators which projected into the classrooms, were hard to keep clean, and were sometimes dangerous to active children. The new schools have integrated, built-in heating systems.

—the old schools, lacking cross-ventilation, frequently were stale and uncomfortable during the hot months; the best new schools are so designed that each classroom has two-way ventilation.

—the old schools had several stories with expensive stairs, fire escapes, and heavy construction. In many cases these old stairways constituted fire hazards. Most of the new schools are efficient one-story buildings with light, inexpensive frames (although necessarily these new schools do occupy more land).

—the old schools had floors of oiled wood—squeaky, and hard to keep clean. New school floors are covered with attractive, easier-to-keep-clean compositions.

—the old schools had black chalkboards that absorbed light, collected dust, and were fixed in their places. The new schools have colored, glare-resistant chalkboards that often can be moved around the room in accordance with the needs of a particular teaching situation.

—the old schools frequently had institutional trough-like washing facilities and surprisingly dismal and unsanitary toilets. Many of today's schools have sinks with hot and cold running water within the elementary classrooms, and toilets that are nearby, not banked centrally.

—the old schools were often located on such small sites that the building itself took up most of the area, leaving little space for outdoor play. The best new schools are built on sites of many acres with outdoor playing fields, tennis courts, and landscaped areas.

Children, young ones at any rate, know very little about progress, and if they are short-changed on design improvements of the last few decades, they probably will not complain. They wouldn't complain of a vitamin deficiency either, but we do our best to feed them properly.

A more precise example of this shift in standards and values:

Henry L. Wright is a California architect who has served as chairman of the A.I.A. national committee on school building. In 1928 his firm built a two-story school at Pomona—Roosevelt School—at a cost of $7.50 per square foot of floor area. It was a successful school for its day.

But Wright points out that today, although local building costs in California have about *tripled* in thirty years, the same number of children could have a better schoolhouse at a cost of only $12 to $14 per square foot—less than *double* the 1928 rate. This new environment, as envisioned by Architects Kistner, Wright and Wright, would include improvements like these: in 1928 the classrooms were oblong, and about 750 square feet in area; today they would be a more versatile shape, square, and larger, about 960 square feet. The electric lighting then totaled about 300 watts, with two light bulbs per classroom; today it would be 3,000 watts, and there would also be 200 per cent more glass in the walls. Inadequate heating was included then (gas-steam radiators with no vents); there would be adequate, uniformly distributed heating today, and good natural or mechanical ventilation. There would be acoustical treatment, where there was none in 1928. There would be colored walls where there was unpainted plaster. The central corridors of 1928 would be replaced by windowed corridors. Where construction was merely fire-resistant in 1928, it would be earthquake-resistant today. The Italian Renaissance masonry construction of Roosevelt in 1928 could today be brick, poured concrete, or frame and stucco in contemporary style. The large central washrooms would be replaced by units more accessible to classrooms and located to serve different age groups. The new school would not be two-story, but single story with play space related to the classrooms.

And the new school would actually be a third *cheaper* to build than the old one would be to duplicate precisely from the original plans!

In your community, if it is not too far from the norm, the over-all cost of building a schoolhouse probably runs about 20 per cent of the yearly total educational budget. This also sounds expensive, but most families' own housing budgets run considerably higher, and if you cut a full 10 per cent off your community's budget for its new school, what really will you save? A 10 per cent cut in a school drops only about 2 per cent in yearly educational costs in your district—2 per cent which may come back magnified into a two-headed monster to haunt you in upkeep costs and in efficient educational space. In a comprehensive school-building study for the state of Ohio in 1958, Architect David A. Pierce compared the eventual cost in his building area of two flooring materials for schools over a period of thirty years. The more expensive flooring, terrazzo, would cost $1.15 per square foot to install; the less expensive one, asphalt tile, 33 cents per square foot. But extend costs over thirty years, and the situation reverses. The reasons: the

cheaper flooring requires periodic replacement and eight times as much custodial time for maintenance. Pierce points out that over thirty years, the total custodial services for a schoolhouse may vary from as little as 40 per cent to as much as 65 per cent of the building's initial cost, depending on its materials and design. In the end, in his area, the more expensive flooring costs less money.

You can compare floorings, but can you compare total schools? People certainly try. In Winfield, Kansas, the "Committee For Progress" dug up cost figures for schools all over the state to try to prove that Winfield's own design was extravagant. But the comparisons were unfair, and they usually are unfair.

Why? Because in comparing two things, they must be equal things, and schools are very rarely equal. They vary in size, in design, in quality of construction, in site factors, in interior finishes, in the timing of their bond lettings, and—perhaps most important of all—in the quality of their educational programs. No perfect system has yet been evolved to compare, simply, the cost of two school buildings for what they offer in educational facilities, even if they stand only a quarter mile apart. When comparisons are brought up, however, there rarely is time to scrutinize them closely, and so they blossom into slogans, frequently misleading ones—and very effective bond-killers.

Some people compare school costs by putting a

price tag on each classroom ($40,000 is a frequent figure today). But classrooms are dissimilar. This can be like comparing orange juice with milk. Besides the *per classroom* standard, there are several other common methods of comparison. They are used honestly, if indignantly, so let's look at them.

The square foot method: this involves calculating floor area and dividing it into total cost. For example, a school 40 feet wide and 200 feet long will have 8,000 square feet of floor. If it cost a total of $120,000 to build, the cost of each square foot would be $15.

One trouble is that the initial calculation of square footage usually varies somewhat—even two draftsmen will rarely agree—so that strict rules have to be observed for this game. Will outdoor corridors, sheltered by canopies, be included? Will storage space in the basement count? Unheated garage space? Does the figure per square foot include the book shelves in the library, the cost of blinds as well as windows? . . . all fees or just the contractor's bid?

Also, a simple square foot comparison, like most other comparisons, leaves out the essential factor of upkeep and maintenance. Indeed, it is a method loaded with opportunities to leave things out, in a way that only a great deal of laborious and expensive checking can uncover.

The cubic foot method: this projects the square foot system into three dimensions. The significance of the height of our 40 by 200 foot school is considered. If it is 11 feet high, the cubic content is 40 times 200 times 11, or 88,000 cubic feet. Divided into the cost (assumed $120,000) it is $1.36 per cubic foot.

It is easy to see that this method is susceptible to the same ailments which can kill the meaning of a square foot comparison—and others too. What about attic space in a school with a pitched roof?

A big attic can bring the per cubic foot figure way down, but how much is the attic space actually worth in terms of use?

The cost per pupil method: if you've heard of a school that cost $200,000 and has an enrollment of 150 children, it obviously cost $1,333 per child. But is the school elementary or high school? What facilities has it? How many sit in each classroom? Is it on double sessions? How are the classrooms lighted? Is it used by adults as well as children? How much of this space is actually used for teaching and learning, not boiler rooms or spectator space in the gym?

The best way to compare school costs is by a combination of methods. In 1951 the California

State Legislature, alarmed at the influx of new residents and the resultant expense in building schools, began to look into the problem, and it was then that the state A.I.A. committee went to work. These men undertook a survey in which more than 100 architects reported the construction of their schools in detail—in *similar* detail, the difficult part of the procedure. They developed workable forms to make it easy for contractors to report costs in a truly informative way (if left to himself, the usual contractor will lump all concrete work together, for example, even though some of it is for driveways or sidewalks, not the building itself). In the beginning they also tried to assign a "quality" rating to schools reported, but the reporting architects naturally tended to upgrade their schools so this was abandoned.

Ultimately, what the survey demonstrated was that where ten qualified California architects were given the same problem, there was not more than a 5 per cent cost variation, at most. A school building might cost as little as $5 per square foot, or as much as $22, but the difference resulted directly from the building value received by the client, appraised very dispassionately.

When that indignant man stands up beside you at the bond issue meeting and complains, as he almost certainly will, about "educational frills," or a "solid gold schoolhouse," there are no sure-fire arguments to hurl back, of course, but an angry challenge is many times blunted by a searching question. Here are five, which may help a school board out of a common and dangerous position: that of being forced to compare their proposed school building on an equal basis with a building for which they have no respect and which would not fit their community. These questions are a set and should be asked as such:

(1) Was the school built cheaply with high maintenance requirements and little teaching equipment; or well, with moderate maintenance expense and up-to-date equipment? What fire rating has it?

(2) What is the total cost *per pupil* at present, including everything but land cost? What will be its cost *per pupil* at maximum enrollment?

(3) How many square feet of *classroom* area does each student have? To add to this, how many square feet per student exist in *program space*—gymnasiums, social areas, shops, theaters, and other important non-classroom areas?

(4) What ground rules were used to arrive at the square footages?

(5) Will it be used by the community as well as by the children?

When that man does stand up at the bond meeting and makes his accusation of extravagance, perhaps the worst mistake the school board can make is to assume he is just a crank. He may be a cost analyst. Whatever he is, if he lives in the school district he has a right to an answer, and the answer will exist if the school board has gone deeply into the real possibilities of economy for the kind of school they need. Architect Alonzo Harriman, who practices in Maine, has pointed out: "There is no royal road to truly economical school design, no gimmick or trick construction that will magically halve building cost. Savings come as the result of hard work, guarding always against expense in all items, paying intense attention to details and keeping continually in mind the money behind every line the architect draws."

By now the list of economies is long and well known to professionals. But the thread, remember, is the program. After that, there is no single, great, sweeping saving to be made in building ex-

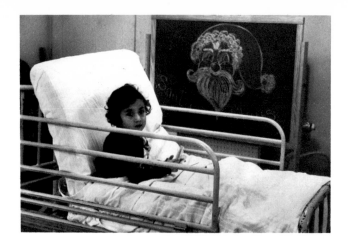

cept in the avoidance of disastrous mistakes. An example of one to avoid: a year or two ago, an East Coast town had to go back to the voters for an extra $300,000 when their site turned out, to their surprise, to be almost solid rock. Know your site; ignorance can bankrupt you. Basing everything on last year's cost estimates can be just about as embarrassing.

It has become almost a convention in economy schools to combine rooms: gymnasium with assembly hall; cafeteria with assembly or study hall; corridors (widened) with cafeteria-study. Mistakes can be made here, easily. For instance, combining the cafeteria with the gym is an alluring idea, but a grease spot on the floor can break a leg. Another reality to remember: a multi-use room may be very costly in school-staff time (and salaries) throughout the life of the building because the room has to be set up anew for each different use.

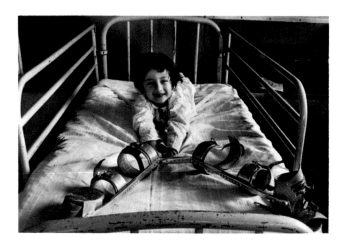

But suppose this man says, "You have too many corners in the building. It isn't a simple enough shape—that's expensive." Your critic may well be right. A straight exterior wall is easier to build, thus usually cheaper, than one which zigs and zags. Later, the chapter on structure will have some things to point out on economy in building: repetitive framing, modular design, use of modern industrial techniques, and so forth. In addition to these points, the school board and architect should watch their developing design, hawklike, for any evidence of unessential complexity—not only in walls, but in roofs and in decorations—for wasted cubage and for square feet of floor area that do not have definite, labeled, necessary uses.

There will be jogs in your plan and there will be reasons for them; just be sure to have those reasons on tap when the community critique begins, when that man stands up and clears his throat.

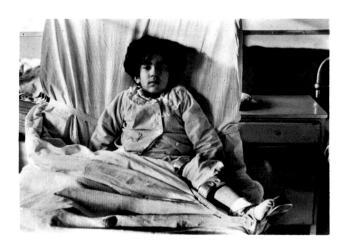

Many children have to try very hard. Here are some patients at the Blythedale Children's Hospital and Rehabilitation Center at Valhalla, New York, being helped and trying to help themselves.

Shopping the bond market

The principal source for financing new schools in the U.S.A. is a vast, submerged pool of investors' money with springs which rise to the surface in New York, Chicago, San Francisco, Los Angeles, and the banks in your nearest big town. The keepers of the springs are usually friendly enough when school boards approach, cup in hand. They want to buy bonds; it's their business.

And it is a big business. The total of municipal and state bonds now out is a little brother of the national debt, nearly fifty billion dollars. Of this staggering sum, when last counted, about twenty billion dollars worth were held by individuals and personal trusts, about thirteen billion by commercial banks, about seven billion by insurance companies, a little over five billion by state and local governments, about one billion by corporations, and the rest by savings and loan associations, foundations, pension trust funds, mutual savings banks, and the U. S. Government's own investment accounts. In recent years an average of 72 cents of every dollar spent for capital outlay (building, buses, equipment) in our schools has been raised this way, through bond issues.

Most school bonds are general obligation bonds, which pledge the full taxing power of the school district; but there is also another type, limited obligation bonds, which are payable from specially earmarked revenues such as sales taxes, motor vehicle licensing, and gasoline or business taxes. General obligation bonds are the kind buyers prefer. The reason: specific revenues always can dip, but only a few cities or school districts have ever been forced into general bankruptcy. By far the most alluring thing about school bonds and other municipal bonds to investors is the fact that their yield is free from the federal income tax.

What is the cost of borrowing?

Interest rates on most school bonds recently have ranged from 3 per cent to 4 per cent. For instance, a community which needs a school costing $500,000 may have to pay 4 per cent for that money over the course of a twenty-five-year bond issue; the total interest would amount to $260,000, in addition to the $500,000 repayment. There is nothing really surprising about this; compared with the individual school board member who buys a new car with no cash down and three years to pay, the school district is not doing badly. And the individual who buys school bonds instead of a new car surely is entitled to the 3 to 4 per cent interest he earns on his investment.

But it is the difference between paying 3 per cent interest and 4 per cent interest that can be delusive, that sometimes can be disastrous.

On a typical twenty-five-year bond issue, that 1 per cent difference, over the years, can add another 13 per cent to the total cost of the school. A school district which hopes to pay 3 per cent for a $500,000 school might easily have to settle for a $435,000 school, in effect, if it has to go up to 4 per cent interest to get financing. The difference can represent almost two classrooms in the finished school. That is a big 1 per cent.

The difference between being able to finance at 3 and 4 per cent, or even higher, depends principally on *who* and *where* you are. If you are a wealthy school district, with lots of stores and factories on your real estate (and a good tax system), your credit is probably good. If you have nothing much on your land but scrub pine, your credit likely is less good. But also important in getting bond money are the condition of the market when you go shopping, the kind of bond you propose to sell, and how long it will run.

Timing

All the money that a good architect can save, plus a substantial fraction of the revenue a sound tax program will raise, can easily be lost if a school board has to go shopping at the wrong time: for example, when the market is flooded with other new bond issues. The bond market is actually no different from any other market place; there is rivalry in selling. The sure way to sell bonds is to lower their price and pay higher rates of interest.

In 1948 the town of Whitefish Bay, Wisconsin, went to the market with a $987,000 issue whose average maturity was ten and three-quarters years. Their net interest cost was 2.08 per cent. In 1957 the same town went back with an issue of $750,000 averaging fifteen years maturity, and had to pay 3.94 per cent. It happens to big towns too: in 1948

Timing on the Bond Market

Los Angeles raised eight million dollars in bonds averaging eleven and a quarter years maturity. They paid 2.35 per cent interest. Less than ten years later, for a bond issue of ten million dollars running thirteen years, they had to pay 3.96 per cent interest. Whenever the demand for money is greater than the supply, interest rates are forced up. When the reverse is true, they go down.

Faced with a buyer's market in bonds, and an immediate and drastic need for new schools at home, communities can occasionally find another way out. A minority are still able to pay as they build, without borrowing. For example, Portland, Oregon, has spent almost $40 million on school building since 1945, all out of current revenue. Substantial aid in school construction is also avail-

able from about a quarter of the state governments, and in very special situations the federal government helps too.

Once in a while, if rarely, a different kind of break comes along. Eight years ago a wind-tanned man of about sixty with a farmer's furrowed eyes and hard hands approached a number of New York investment houses to place a bond issue for several hundred thousand dollars. He was on the school board of a small southwestern town and happened to be traveling. When, in answer to his questions, the brokers quoted him the going percentage, he bobbed his head and said he might have to look around and see what he could do elsewhere.

He came back a few days later to ask again; the going interest had drifted a decimal fraction lower in that time, but he still thought it seemed high so he left his telephone number and went back to his farm in the Southwest. A month later the call came through. The bond market had eased again, permitting a lower bid—but too late as it turned out. The farmer had got tired of waiting and had taken the issue himself. The water table on his farm was very close to the surface indeed, and as it happened it wasn't water; it was oil.

A bond is like a bank account in reverse; *you* pay the interest. And with bonds, this slow repayment of debt and interest eventually comes, year by year, from those local property taxes that pay for almost all of public education—teachers' salaries, chalk, and report cards, as well as walls and roofs. This kind of tax is very blunt, not a bit subtle. Unlike other taxes he pays, the taxpayer usually has the opportunity to approve or disapprove it directly. For this reason it sometimes seems more painful than most.

The Puritans laid the pattern in Massachusetts in the early 1600's, taxing all "householders," after donations collected during the church service had proved inadequate to run their schools.

Later, after the Revolution, as the colonists expanded west, schools were supported by federal land and money grants. The Northwest Ordinance of 1787 required that the sixteenth section of every township in the frontier lands be reserved for the maintenance of schools. (The frontier was then the Appalachians, but the idea continued as the West moved west.) This gift of real estate was a great boon to education, but it was managed, or mismanaged, unevenly.

As the nineteenth century moved on, the states began establishing free school systems, and asked school districts to pay their share by levying local property taxes. Land ownership was a good measure of wealth in the agrarian economy of the day, and this was the index generally adopted. Borrowing to build schools, by means of school bonds, first came into use about 1820.

After the Civil War, as the re-assembled United States shifted from an agricultural economy to an industrial one, and wealth became concentrated in manufacturing areas, great inequalities began to appear in schools, and the states had to step in more and more with rules—and money—to keep standards up. By then, also, the percentage of school revenues from sources other than property taxes had begun to taper off. For example, by 1890, the old land grants were bringing in only about 5 per cent of the total U. S. school budget. Something else was happening, too, and is still happening. An industrial society was demonstrating that ownership of real property is less and less significant as a true index of wealth. Income means more.

The states and the federal government recognized this swiftly and shrewdly and began dipping into newer sources. The states tapped sales taxes, business taxes, income taxes; the federal government, income and special excise taxes. By 1900, only about half the citizens' total tax bill was collected on property, and today the proportion is down to 10 per cent. The larger cities shifted their approach too, applying licensing and sales taxes to help pay their bills, including school bills; few school districts, however, have administrative units big enough to cope with the collecting process, and so the simpler property taxes have more and more become theirs.

In one recent year our total school expenditures came from these sources in these amounts: $6,217,818,552 from local districts; $4,524,075,864 from state capitols; $401,149,584 from Washington, D. C. This is not the budget for school *building,* however, but for everything, from pencils to electricity and teachers' salaries; except for state help and some P.W.A. help during the depression, this task of providing walls, roofs, and warmth never really has been lifted from local communities' shoulders to any significant degree.

In America's fastest-growing communities, according to several investment bankers whom we interviewed, property taxes are today so high that they have reached a "psychological saturation point." But even more of the financial experts pointed to the inefficient state of these taxes as they are used today; over-all their yield represents only about 1 per cent of the market value of property, a very unbusinesslike percentage indeed. Even some small counties and towns are being drawn into using other supplementary taxing methods to collect essential revenue. Why?

The main trouble seems to be assessments. There is an almost bewildering diversity of local systems for appraising the worth of property. In some places—Oklahoma, for one—property owners actually report their own assessments, a situation full of temptation. In most places a local assessor does the estimating, supposedly on the basis of real market value or income-producing worth, but then slices this, in establishing the tax base. It is possible for townships located right beside each other to base taxes on 10 per cent to 100 per cent of value. If the valuation is low, obviously the tax rate should be high, but the intricate local political situations which develop around such variables can hamstring a school outlay program.

The localities with the best borrowing power are those which have made that stern adjustment to reality called for in most state codes: assessments near market value. Thus they broaden their tax base. Sometimes, unfortunately, they also penalize themselves in the amount of state educational aid they will get. A good deal of realistic reform is due in state equalization methods, many experts think. Another obstacle to money-raising comes when the state puts a ceiling on the amount of total debt (bonds issued) that its school districts can legally incur. Some of these limitations are as out-of-date as a 1935 dollar.

A school district must decide not only when to borrow, but when to pay off. How long should bonds run?

Your actual costs may exceed your hopes by a wide margin if you choose a thirty-year bond issue when you could have squeezed current revenue to pay for the school in twenty. Like a man who puts some cash down when he buys a car, the short term borrower eventually spends less. He pays interest on a smaller sum for a shorter time. This is not to say that long term borrowing (more than ten years) is, in itself, a poor idea for a school district. More often than not, it is essential. It depends on what kind of district you are.

The rocketing district

The district with the toughest (and commonest) problem is one that is growing fast—so fast that it needs a great many new school rooms all at once, but at the same time is also looking for money to pay for other municipal improvements. Further, most districts in this dilemma are primarily residential, with little industrial or commercial property to tax. These are the bedroom suburbs, where the only taxpayers besides home owners are the shopping centers.

Such a community has very little cash on hand; besides, its current revenues are pretty well committed for a variety of services, from new sewers to police cars, so there's nothing left to use as down payment on new classrooms. And since the district is already increasing its tax rate rapidly to pay for its sudden growth, it simply is not desirable to issue short term bonds that will boost the immediate tax bill even higher.

Long term bonds seem the only answer left. But today's budget is not necessarily tomorrow's. The chances are that things won't always be so tight in the district. New retailing and industrial property revenues will come in after a few years, and some costs (such as new fire engines) will be paid off fairly quickly.

So the district should not commit itself to a permanent long term bond issue. It should try to float a long term issue but retain the right to "call" (pay off) a specified portion of the bonds as soon as it can, before they reach their scheduled maturity. In this way the district, when it begins getting more revenue, will be able to reduce its carrying charges as it goes along. What starts out as a thirty-year bond issue may end up running only twenty or twenty-five years. The district will be reducing the total cost of the school by cutting

down the length of time that it must pay interest on the full amount.

This callable feature on a serial bond will cost an extra fraction of a percentage in the interest rate, but generally it is worth it, if the community foresees any chance at all of reducing its indebtedness in a shorter period of time.

This booming kind of residential town, one that is being carved newly out of the mild suburban wilderness, really needs expert assistance, and is wise to engage a financial specialist to help set up a long range plan. He can recommend bond types today (serials vs. serial annuities, for example); if you give him a good long range educational survey to work from, he can also make it easier for you to build the schools and sewers you will be

needing twenty years from now. And his presence at your elbow when you enter the bond arena will also be reassuring to the bond buyers, the kind of reassurance worth money to you.

The stable, well established district

Some districts know they will need only a certain number of new classrooms every few years; they can predict fairly closely what their population growth will be, and frequently they can count on a sizable amount of steady income in commercial and industrial tax revenue. They're lucky.

In this comparatively comfortable situation, a textbook economist might expect the community to pay for its new schools out of current revenues and savings. But in practice, even a rich community's pocket money is quickly spent; many other expenses besides schools drain off most of the cash. However, by combining current tax revenues and capital reserve funds (savings) with shorter term bonds, such a district can keep its interest payments at a low level.

This plan for cutting interest payments is, in fact, what all school boards should be working toward—even in the hard-pressed, swiftly growing districts. But they won't be able to do it if they get themselves locked into long term bonds that can't be paid off early.

Any district which develops this sort of planning-ahead program will obviously be getting more schools for less money, since it will be spending less for debt service, paying less money for the proposed bond issue. But there is another benefit not quite so obvious: the district which has carefully planned its financial future and keeps cutting down on long term debt is steadily improving its credit. And the better a district's credit, the lower interest it will have to pay next time.

The men who make their living by rating bonds for investors use standards that range from strict mathematical formulae for comparing a community's income with its real worth, to a general appraisal of the kind of mayors a town habitually elects. They also have very long memories. What the bond raters really like is a community with a budget split like this: 75 per cent for current expenses (including interest on debt) and 25 per cent for capital expenditures (street lights, school buses, fire engines, office furniture, etc). There is a safety valve in this kind of community budget; in an economic pinch the 25 per cent item can be trimmed temporarily without unsettling the basic program. This is the kind of budget Dickens' Mr. Micawber admired sadly.

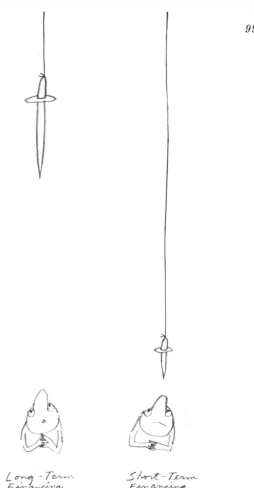

Long-Term
Financing   Short-Term
Financing

The fading municipality

America's moving habits, currently dramatized by the dash to the suburbs, make school trouble for the cities too. Even when new people move in, they generally are poorer than the ones who left for the suburbs. Pockets of slums develop, which mean imbalance—crowded classrooms in some districts, empty ones in others. Some types of business run down and tax delinquency increases. New bridges, tunnels, and roads seem even more urgent than schools, and the city also is trying to protect itself by means of taxes which won't drive still more business away.

Some cities up to now have had a very easy time with public schools. In Boston, for instance, parochial schools absorb so many pupils that until quite recently the city was easily able to finance new schools out of current income without borrowing on bonds. But in general, although the cities are not so immediately desperate as the suburbs, their long range trouble can be solved only—it seems—by using all available methods to redevelop themselves both industrially and residentially. Meanwhile, city school districts that are fiscally independent of the rest of the city budget are in the strongest position. They run their own store.

Rural communities

Out in the clover, still unreached by the swirling orbit of suburbs, the country district seldom has to build a school, but when it does, the expense seems immense. This kind of district almost always goes in for long term bonds, twenty-five or thirty years —or longer, if state laws permit it. The expense of building is unlikely to recur soon and such longer run debts require less increase in yearly taxes. If the district tries to pay for its school *too* fast, in fact, the bond issue probably is in deep danger of being voted down by an alarmed electorate.

The consolidated school district

If the picture up to this point seems gloomy, here is a happier note. In many parts of the country, school districts have been grouping together, assembling their assets to command greater recognition in the bond market and more efficiency in centralized administration. In Corning, New York, several years ago, sixty-one districts consolidated into one; in the U. S. as a whole, the number of separate school districts has been more than cut in half over the past fifteen years. This is not just the old rural custom whereby several thinly populated communities get together to build one school and buy lots of buses; the new kind of consolida-

tion sometimes takes in urban, suburban, and rural. If a large enough area is included, great stability is achieved. Population moves are less disruptive within one large district, than from one small district to another. And in emergencies, children can be transported to school in another neighborhood until the new building is ready in their own. A public clamor for higher education may make consolidation even more advantageous in the future: the need, a near one now, to build public junior colleges on a wide scale. The public is demanding them; only states, big cities, or large consolidated school districts will have the resources to supply this new educational demand.

Some of the conditions which make a school district a poor or good investment risk have been described. But how do you know? It's easy; go to *Moody's, Standard and Poor's*, or *Fitch's*, and see what your credit rating is. *Moody's*, for instance, rates *Aaa, Aa, A, Baa, Ba, B, Caa, Ca, C*. The difference between an *Aaa* rating and an *Aa* for a twenty-year bond on the recent market would be about $\frac{1}{4}$ per cent in the interest rate you have to pay; the difference between *Ca* and *C* might be as much as $\frac{1}{2}$ per cent.

School bonds in general rate well; *Moody's* places 98 per cent of them in its first four categories—very high marks indeed. It is *Moody's* practice to rate all districts that have a total debt outstanding above $600,000; *Fitch's* and *Standard and Poor's* rate issues of $1 million or more.

The state you vote in will make a difference. Some states, refusing to let their school districts default, move in and bolster them in time of trouble. New York, Massachusetts, and Connecticut are in this category. Others, however, have always remained aloof, and investors know it. Some states, California for one, actually market their school districts' bonds for them as general obligations of the state, usually at cheaper rates. But sometimes a sizable city can do even better than its state. For example, Tucson or Phoenix can borrow on better terms than the state of Arizona. Baton Rouge, Shreveport, and New Orleans have better standings than Louisiana. In Tennessee, Nashville and Memphis can borrow on at least as favorable terms, for most of the state's wealth is concentrated in these two cities. In Massachusetts, Springfield, Newton, Wellesley, Winchester, and Salem can beat the state.

Some states limit by law the amount of interest their school districts can pay on bonds, yet do little to help the districts market them. This is tough; it hampers local capacity to raise money. Most states, however, help rather than hinder. County support can help sell bonds too, as it does in New York State.

But what investors are most interested in is the community itself: its record of payment, its industrial base, its attitude toward schools, its administration, its long-term plan, and its debt structure. The last is an inescapable index. If the over-all local debt already exceeds 10 per cent of the actual (not *assessed*) value of the taxable real estate behind it, you will have to pay high for your school building money.

Investors are very leary of boom towns. A case in point was Cisco, Texas. In the early twenties it was a small trading center, then . . . oil! Suddenly the town grew to more than 20,000 and there was a desperate need for facilities of all kinds. When the facilities were half built, more oil was discovered in East Texas, where it was much cheaper to develop. Eighteen thousand of the population moved east, leaving those two thousand who remained in Cisco with an enormous debt.

The worst trouble of all, according to the experts, comes when a town expands its facilities in expectation of *future* population growth. During the late twenties, real estate developers in Florida, in the Cleveland and Detroit areas, and in other parts of the U. S. built whole towns in anticipation of a population which never quite arrived. What did arrive was the crash, in 1929, and these new towns were left with too many facilities and too huge a debt for their few citizens to carry. As a result there was a great wave of defaults in municipals in these areas. Investors were burned, and still remember the sensation.

A community can help itself in the bond market by good public relations and by procedural propriety in marketing its bonds. It helps to think ahead; even in the years when no bonds are being floated, some smart districts send financial statements to a mailing list of their potential money sources. This is not a major undertaking . . . there are only 250 to 300 sizable bond houses in the country.

When bonding time comes, issues should be advertised both locally and in financial publications like *The Bond Buyer* and *The Wall Street Journal*. Most big New York bond houses are interested primarily in issues of a million dollars, but they sometimes bid on offerings as low as $50,000.

Again, even if your state law does not require one, it is generally smart to engage a bond counsel to help you in this intricate business (your local district attorney can probably recommend a qualified man). Bonds not approved by a recognized bond attorney cannot be sold on the national market, although local banks might take them. The reason: investors are afraid of loopholes which could permit a disgruntled taxpayer to challenge the bond's authenticity and prevent payment. Most states still do not have laws governing the *notice of sale*—in the absence of such guidance, many bond men recommend following the New York

In retrospect childhood can seem a very simple time,
uncomplicated, uncrowded. But even before a ball
game, there are many things to get out of the way.
For example: the paper route, practice, and—
in this case—the building of a snug dugout so
the little kids won't interfere with the game (maybe).
And then, finally, for a while, there's ball.

form, to provide the basic information needed by potential bond-buyers.

Here are some things that make bond buyers really morose:

—school districts that obviously try to out-guess the market by stalling with very short term issues and over-doing the issuance of bond anticipation notes. (Since World War II the proportionate supply of short term money has been shrinking anyway, and its rates have gone up sharply.)

—districts that compete inside their own borders with other local bond issues, failing to coordinate school needs with other needs of the community.

—districts that are late in presenting annual financial reports, or do it incompletely.

—districts that don't pay off the bond coupons on time when they come due.

—districts that take too much expensive property off the school tax roles.

—districts that hold the bidding day at an inconvenient time, float issues in odd lots, pay their interest annually instead of semi-annually, go to the local job printer to get bonds printed.

—districts that send *too* much descriptive material to investors (bond men wear conservative neckties and don't like to be promoted).

—districts that try to market their bonds before their voters have approved them (this happens!).

—but most of all, districts that have defaulted.

The money market is one of supply and demand. When business is active there is great demand for money and the interest rate goes up. Bond underwriters are wholesalers; they will buy what they think they can retail to their customers. There are, of course, various ways the federal government can stimulate or subdue the market, ranging from changes in basic federal reserve policy, to such devices as extending the tax exempt feature of municipals through mutual investment funds. But these measures are undertaken only as a part of over-all national fiscal policy.

One thing that would help the future of school finance would be a greater involvement of the public. The interest rates are not as good as corporate bonds, but the income tax exemption is interesting (the states also offer exemptions to their own residents). Yet few of the smaller investors, who by repute are the backbone of the stock market, know much about the municipal bond market today. It might pay some to find out.

The site and its climate

". . . there is much less weather than when I was a boy . . ."

—F. SCOTT FITZGERALD,
The Crack-up

Within the continental limits of the U.S.A., you can find most of the world's climates: subtropic, desert, temperate, steppe, alpine. Florida has the climate of Hongkong; Arizona, that of the Middle East; Oregon, that of Japan or England. The plains of Kansas are like the Russian steppes; Maine is like Sweden; western Colorado like Switzerland. Mississippi's climate resembles that of northern Italy, Tennessee's that of central France. With this multitude of geography in one country, the surprising thing about U. S. school buildings, like U. S. accents of speech, is not how much they differ, but how much they're alike.

Climates of this sort are all what the weather men call *macro*-climates—i.e., large-scale climates applying to whole regions. But you will also find tremendous variations within a given macro-climate. Sometimes these variations are natural, as in the San Francisco area where a short drive takes you to the moors of Scotland, the rain forests of New Zealand, or the apricot groves of Israel. Sometimes the variations are man-made, as in the temperature differentials between the heart of a city and its surrounding countryside (the city is *always* hotter, winter and summer). You will even find quite different climates on different slopes of the same hill, as any farmer or orchardist can tell you. These small scale variations the climatologists call *micro*-climates.

You would think that American school buildings would reflect these vast variations. Oddly enough, they seldom do. Yet, when you select a site, not only the comfort and well-being of your children is involved but also the amount you will spend on heating or cooling, snowplowing or irrigation, grass or asphalt. This is the reason that your architect should know his climate, macro and micro. No climate is perfect but there are always ways to exploit its good points and correct or minimize its deficiences.

It goes without saying that the school board must consider many factors besides climate in the selection of a site: size and location; soil conditions and topography; surroundings and accessibility; as well as availability of services (electricity, water, sewage lines, and fire engines). In many towns schools are combined with parks; in new suburban developments school sites are always community cores, and this should be recognized early in land planning. Always look a gift site in the mouth; more than once a generous benefactor has presented a school district with a piece of land that cost twice their site budget before it was made habitable for a building. Get an architect in on this early, on a flat fee basis, if necessary, even before you decide on the firm you want to design your school building.

But once you have narrowed the selection of sites down to several which are equally acceptable for the educational program, for access, for cost (eventual, developed cost, that is) and other criteria, analyze their micro-climates.

A school board in Helena, Montana, for example, has to accept the Montana climate, but the micro-climates of Helena offer a wide range of choice. By placing the school on the *south* slope of a hill instead of the north, you get it exposed to the winter sun and protected from the winter winds. The north slope may be only 1,000 feet away: yet for all practical comfort purposes you may have moved

the school as much as 1,000 miles to the south! Spring will come earlier, winter later, and all the school days will be warmer. (You can easily prove this by checking the date of snow melt, flower bloom, etc., on each of the slopes of this same hill, even before you build.) In Arizona, on the other hand, where all the days are hot and all the nights cold (a typical desert phenomenon), a school located on a north or northeast slope will be as much cooler than a southwest slope as if it were hundreds of miles to the north, in Wyoming.

Of course, there may very well be no hills at all in your town. If not, you should try to employ architectural and landscaping devices to accomplish the same thing. (More about these later.) Even if other considerations force you into a climatically difficult site, professional imagination can usually overcome the worst deficiencies, for every piece of land has some inherent potentials which can be exploited by an ingenious designer or overlooked and lost by a poor one. In the last analysis, your site is merely the raw material for a fine plan, not its guarantee. If your climate dictates shade and trees are missing (as in Oklahoma, Texas, or Kansas), you must decide whether to plant trees or erect shading devices. The mainstay of the science of climatology is the difference in the sun's path from winter to summer, of course: in winter the sun travels low in the sky, and can peer under the overhangs designed to block it in summer, when it rides higher and hotter. If the

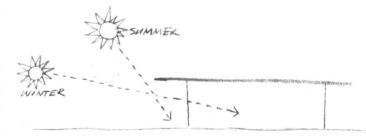

up the classrooms. In hot, wet climates (Biloxi, Jacksonville) a "cool" roof might well be flat with a curb around the edge, to hold a shallow pool of rain water—water also is a good heat insulator and excellent protection for asphalt roofing. If your winters are long and cold, you'll want a "hot" roof—dark in color to absorb heat, snugly closed.

Your climate may also determine the character of the walls and windows, within reasonable limits. Their insulating characteristics should be adapted to local climatic conditions. In the Southwest, with its hot days and cold nights, heavy masonry (more than eight inches thick) is good because it is very slow to heat up and takes all night to cool off. (The Indians, of course, have made use of this principle for centuries with their *terra pise* and adobe walls.) But in most climates you'll need insulation of the conventional sort—mineral wools and aluminum foils or combinations of these materials.

site is exposed to cold winter winds, tree belts, walls, and fences can be placed to break their force. Or the bulky elements of a building (gymnasium, cafeteria, auditorium) might be so disposed as to protect classrooms and play areas from prevailing winds. If, contrariwise, your winters are warm, making shade and cross-ventilation more important, then your trees should be so placed as to stop the sun without stopping the breeze. Decisions like these require your finding the direction of prevailing winds during the school months (your local Weather Bureau will be glad to help you) and orienting your building accordingly.

Climate and the structure

Your local climate may also determine a number of other architectural features—roofs, for instance. If you are building in areas of heavy snowfall (northern New England, the Dakotas, the Rockies) your roofs should be designed for it. Either steeply pitched, to shed the snow; or flat and very strong, to hold it: snow is an excellent insulator. On the other hand, if you are building in Miami, New Orleans, or Galveston, your roofs will have a lot of rain water to shed. Roofs can also be "cool" or "hot," depending upon their very design. If your climate is hot and dry (San Antonio, San Diego, Tucson), you'll want a "cool" roof—white in color to reflect solar heat, with well-ventilated attics to carry off hot air before it heats

In general, classroom walls are best oriented to have southerly exposure, provided they have horizontal overhang to block direct sunlight. (Their optimum orientation, because of the cooler forenoon temperatures, shifts from south toward east in different U. S. climate zones.) If classrooms are placed on both sides of a corridor, then the second-best orientation should be utilized for these rooms, which is, generally speaking, near north. The exceptions are in the cool, and possibly in the temperate zones, where longer cold periods make sun heat welcome, so east-west orientation of the classroom windows is preferable. In the hotter climates it is especially important that classrooms should have cross-ventilation, and the orientation will depend not only on the sun, but on the prevailing direction of the winds.

Climate and the landscape

In all decisions of orientation the finished landscape in which your school is to be placed can also be made to work for you or against you. Configuration of the land, planting, paving, walls, and fences are your natural allies. Properly used, they can make your buildings cheaper to build and operate; more comfortable for students and staff; and better looking for all concerned. Properly used, they can reduce the amount you spend on heating, cooling, and ventilating; the quantity of acoustical and thermal insulation required; the number of lights, blinds, shades, etc. you have to buy and maintain. Improperly used, they can make excessive heating or cooling situations worse.

School programs vary across the country: site developments to implement them will too, depending largely upon local weather. Take, for instance, the problem of playfields. Tennis, basket- and volley-ball courts can be used throughout the school year south of the Charleston-San Francisco line. In the North and in the Rockies, long winters, heavy snowfall, and extreme cold may reduce this to a few weeks in fall and spring. Undifferentiated play areas for younger children are mandatory everywhere, of course. Where winters are long and cold, they should be oriented for maximum exposure to sun and maximum protection from wind: generally speaking, this means open to east and south, protected from west and north. In warmer climates, orientation is obviously less crucial. But wherever you're building, parts of such play areas should be surfaced to minimize the mud problem. In the North, the paving might be black-top, since it absorbs sun heat and melts snow much faster than concrete. In the South, your problem would be rain: here masonry paving would be cooler (though probably more expensive) than black-top. In the Southwest, dust is sometimes more of a problem than mud: if the play areas are properly graded and tamped, dust can be held down by periodic spraying with one of several dust-laying chemicals. Anywhere south of the Savannah-Shreveport-Tucson line, play areas ought to have shade. In the Southwest, you can rely on trees, since your problem is mainly intense sunshine, but along the Gulf and Florida coasts, shading should be rainproof as well as sunproof. In these mild climates, also, corridors can often be of the open gallery type and—if made wide enough—they can easily double as protected play areas in periods of wet weather.

In sizing up a site for drainage of storm water, keep the flash storm in mind. If the terrain can absorb a fall of two inches in a half hour, for example, it will have little trouble soaking up longer but slower rainfalls, nor will the runoff from thaws create a real problem. Where the site is

relatively (but not absolutely) flat with good moisture absorption capacity and not too much paved area, site drainage presents no problem. On the other hand, if the ground is uneven with rocks or stone near the surface, the site runoff will have to be dumped into catch basins, manholes, and runs of piping to some low spot on the grounds where it might be allowed to pond temporarily until it can percolate down into the soil. If this is impractical on your site, then dry wells must be used. Sandy soil is very good at soaking up water; clay is very bad.

Another thing to keep in mind when site-shopping is the probable character of the school to be built on the land, and this also has a generalized link to your area's climate.

In general, in the colder regions of the U. S. architects favor more compact building forms, with enclosed corridors and reduced exterior wall surfaces. As you move south and the weather becomes more temperate, buildings become more elongated, and there is freer use of forms. Then,

in the hot-arid region, buildings go back to the block shapes, with cluster plans and shaded open walks. In the hot-humid regions, you will find, for good reason, many "finger" plans with open walks and emphasis on through-ventilation and shading devices such as overhangs and louvers.

Trees

Of all the elements in the landscape, trees are the most important. Even if your climate is hot and sunshiny, properly placed trees will stop the sun's rays before they overheat the classrooms. But an improperly placed tree in a cold climate could force the teacher to turn up the heat and turn on the lights when, actually, both heat and light are available free, outside. Where you place your trees, in other words, *depends entirely upon where you live.* Baltimore, Maryland, and Sacramento, California, are in the same latitude. A hundred square feet of wall in either place will, on an average December day, receive 40,000 B.T.U. of heat from the sun. But in Baltimore the outside temperature may be 30 degrees, while in Sacramento it's 80 degrees.

Or another example: the cooling effect of wind is directly proportional to its velocity—that is, zero degree *still* air is no colder than 18 degree air in an 8 mph wind; still air at the freezing point (32 degrees F.) is no colder in effect than 50 degree air in an 8 mph wind. In North Dakota, protecting your school from the wind can therefore be the equivalent of raising the temperature 18 degrees, or moving the school hundreds of miles to the south. And trees, planted in thick "belts," make excellent windbreaks, diminishing velocities as much as 80 per cent in their immediate lee. If you're building in a hot climate you may be able to plant your trees so they'll actually help to funnel

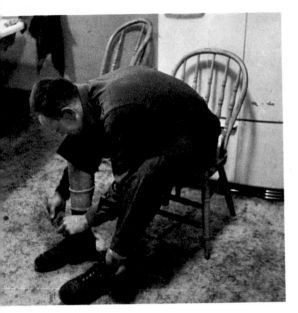

There are things to be attended to in the morning before a high school boy
on a Wisconsin dairy farm is free to climb into his Chevvie and head for school.

the breeze into the buildings.

If your site already has good trees on it, make sure that every possible one is saved. If your site is treeless, make sure there's a budget allowance for planting them. And plant the biggest trees you can afford. Small saplings are easy to transplant but have a hard time getting established except in climates with mild winters and heavy rainfall in summer, especially with young children climbing, swinging, and carving on them. With today's tree-moving techniques, almost any tree can be successfully, if expensively, transplanted and the big companies guarantee to replace the ones which die.

What *kind* of tree you plant depends upon *when* you want shade, and that, in turn, depends upon your climate. If the school is in the deep South, you have a magnificent choice of indigenous trees: for hot-weather shade such deciduous ones as sycamore, sweet gum, tulip poplar; for year-round shade, such evergreens as the live oak, magnolia grandiflora, swamp bay, and pine. With irrigation, most deciduous trees will grow in the Southwest, though the native willows and poplars (cottonwoods) are the hardiest and fastest growing. If you live in the Midwest or Plains states, the tree problem is more difficult, with bitterly hot summers *and* bitterly cold winters. Deciduous shade is probably preferable: the maples, oaks, sycamores, and thornless Moraine locusts, with willows and cottonwoods again for the drier areas. In New England, the Rockies, and along the West

Coast from San Francisco up to Seattle, the full range of native conifers is available; but care should be taken not to place them where they'll cut winter sun from classrooms or play areas. On the other hand, of course, the conifers are ideal for windbreaks and snow barriers.

Lawns

Lawns are the second major feature of any landscape design. Everybody admires their appearance and complains about their cost. And they are costly, both to install and to maintain. Yet the sad fact is that, for most parts of the country, there is no other practicable way to keep large areas under what the landscape architect calls "control." Paving is expensive, usually ugly, always hot, and sometimes dangerous. The so-called ground covers (pachysandra, ivy, myrtle, honeysuckle) are more expensive than grass and cannot survive school-age traffic. So, no matter where you live, you'll probably end up with a large portion of your school grounds in grass. In the Southwest, you'll have to irrigate. In the Southeast, if you want an evergreen lawn, you'll have to sow twice a year (and sod slopes) since the evergreen perennials such as Kentucky Blue or the creeping bents can't survive the summer heat. Only southern Florida, in this area, with its coarse St. Augustine grass, has a true evergreen perennial lawn. In the North (Lincoln-Chicago-Pittsburgh-Boston), evergreen perennial lawns are possible—though of course they're under snow for several months in winter. Actually, the only ideal lawn country in the U. S. A. is the cool and rainy Northwest (Portland-Seattle-Vancouver).

Lawns, like all vegetation, make excellent air conditioners: in hot weather temperatures immediately above them will run 20 degrees cooler than over a paved area immediately adjacent. They make excellent air filters, catching and holding air-borne dust on thousands of blades. They are the world's best glare reducers. Like carpets indoors, they even make good acoustical absorbents. Thus, they are good investments for the entire community. Try not to skimp on their costs. Build them well, plant the grasses recommended locally, fertilize them properly—and you'll save money over the course of coming years.

Shrubs and vines

The most common error in school ground landscaping is that shrubbery is handled on a residential scale. For example, shrubs are often used as "foundation planting" around the base of the buildings proper. There could scarcely be a worse way to use them. This practice, borrowed from residential work (even there it seldom really makes sense), raises all sorts of problems. Because of roof overhangs, they seldom get enough water, especially in winter. They take a beating from the kids and—if they survive that—soon grow so big as to interfere with window washing, painting, and caulking. There are, of course, plenty of good uses for massed shrubs. A thick planting of mixed shrubs along a busy highway will not only keep children from dashing across the traffic at unpoliced points: it will also, to an astonishing degree, reduce the noise, dust, and fumes of that traffic. Massed shrubs can screen unsightly buildings, serve as snow fences and as pedestrian traffic barriers. But shrubs should be selected for hardiness (use local ones wherever possible), long life, and easy maintenance—avoid hedges which need continual clipping, for instance.

The same general considerations apply to vines. They make fine sun shades on arbors and trellises but few of them are hardy enough to survive the children. Clinging vines—ivy, ampelopsis, hydrangea, etc.—are handsome but, unless you have solid masonry walls which will never need painting, don't get them started on your buildings. Some of them will try to come through the walls.

Avoid annual or perennial flower beds. They're too small in scale to amount to anything, too fragile to survive the children, and very troublesome to keep up: you can maintain a couple of acres of lawn on fewer man-hours than a bed of annuals. The only exception to this rule would be the garden plots of the children themselves in some schools, or that rare community whose PTA will keep flower gardens in apple-pie order.

Layout of walks and paths

The "keep off the grass" signs which dot most public spaces, the pathetic little barricades at path intersections, the trodden-down shrubs at sharp corners are the marks not so much of perversity in children as of obtuseness in the people who designed them. For all pedestrian traffic, like water, automatically takes the line of least resistance. On a flat area it will take a diagonal short cut instead of a right angle turn every time. On a steep slope it will usually work out a zigzag ascent or descent. School grounds would be a lot handsomer if designers recognized this fundamental truth. In fact, in new layouts there is an increasing tendency not to install permanent paved walkways until after the children have had a few months to tramp out their own paths. These are then paved, with the result that "traffic violations" are reduced and "keep off" signs are not necessary.

School plants are constantly increasing in size. Thus they are coming to play an increasingly im-

portant role in the appearance of the community as a whole. For this reason they should be landscaped to be as good to look at as they are for the school population to live in; and they should maintain their good looks around the year. This means twelve full months of maintenance, not just eight or nine. Moreover, a twenty-acre school plant reaches the dimensions of many a city park. You can't expect an old-fashioned janitor to handle this kind of job in his "spare" time. For this reason, all landscape materials should be selected for durability, long life, and low maintenance.

Landscaping today is expensive, and many school boards, thinking of it merely as an ornamental luxury, are likely to economize on it. That is why trees have been emphasized here as shade-giving, windbreaking devices; lawns as air conditioners; shrubs as acoustical insulators; the entire landscape plan as a "climate-conditioner" to produce more economic and more comfortable school plants. All this is literally true but, of course, there is a wonderful extra reward in this kind of science. A well-planted school yard is also beautiful, a stabilizing influence to its neighborhood and the community it serves. In congested neighborhoods, it may even be the only open area for many blocks; it deserves special attention.

Structure

"The exact cost of my house, paying the usual price for such materials as I used, but not counting the work all of which was done by myself, was as follows:

BOARDS	$ 8.03½,	*mostly shanty boards.*
REFUSE SHINGLES	4.00	
LATHS	1.25	
TWO SECOND-HAND WINDOWS	2.43	
ONE THOUSAND OLD BRICK	4.00	
TWO CASKS OF LIME	2.40,	*That was high.*
HAIR	.31,	*More than I needed.*
MANTLE-TREE IRON	.15	
NAILS	3.90	
HINGES AND SCREWS	.14	
LATCH	.10	
CHALK	.01	
TRANSPORTATION	1.40,	*(I carried a good part on my back.)*
IN ALL	$28.12½"	

—HENRY DAVID THOREAU, Walden, 1854

MADISON, WISCONSIN, *"The state historical society completed a replica of a log cabin yesterday and figured its cost at $2,193. Back in Wisconsin's pioneer days, a settler could throw up a de luxe cabin for less than $5, historians said."*

—UNITED PRESS dispatch, November 27, 1957

The structure of a school is no more the school itself than the clothes you are wearing are you, of course—the school is the child and his teacher. Yet a community cannot change its school's structural clothing very often, so the fabric of the school and the way it is stitched together is of enduring importance. And this "clothing" must also hold itself up with its own strength—a function expected of few garments apart from old suits of armour and new corsets.

A school building has to stand through many years of hard knocks. It has to resist the push of wind, the penetration of cold and rain, the massive weight of snowdrifts, the attacks of termites (and children), earthquakes, erosion, rhythmic dancing, and eventual remodeling. Remodeling is of special point; the manager of an office building in New York recently pointed out that in fifteen years, every partition except the walls of the president's office had been torn down and rebuilt. Because teaching techniques seem to be entering a period of change, partition walls should not be rooted any deeper in the floors of new schools than in office buildings; if they are, transplanting will be difficult.

Schools, structurally speaking, are not a class unto themselves. From the days of log cabins they have always reflected the methods by which small commercial buildings like banks and warehouses have been put up. Cost pressure, as school boards well know, has been heavier on schools than on any

other building type, but the quality of structural design sometimes thrives on a lean diet.

For example, it used to be that most schools were put up with what is called bearing walls, walls that supported the roof. Not only were the outside walls weight-supporters, but so were partition walls. These walls generally were made of masonry, thick and strong, or a system of closely spaced wood studs.

But today most schools, like people, are built around skeletons. Isolated columns and posts support a framework of beams, girders, and trusses, which in turn carry the roof. Between these structural bones are the membranes and skin of the walls and roof that keep out the weather. Backing up this skin (except for glass areas) is a layer of building flesh, the necessary insulation. This skeletal system has become general structural practice not only for schools but for banks, ware-

houses, and office buildings, and the reason is this: in an age of specialization it separates the load-bearing job from other jobs walls do, and allows them to be slimmed down. The skeleton frame (whether made of metal, reinforced concrete, or timber) is the strength; the skin merely has to serve as a shield against the weather and fire. This kind of framework structure also permits a great deal of freedom in inserting windows, doors, ventilators, and future extensions; and inside, most of the partitions can be shifted at will because they don't hold anything up.

The simplest kind of skeleton construction is called post and beam. This is the kind of building with blocks that young children do, standing two blocks on end and resting a crosstick on them. A refinement, rigid construction, comes later with a new toy, the erector set, when beams and columns are fastened together with screws. The reasons:

they can't be knocked over as easily; each part of the framework can borrow strength from the others. The shape is important too; for instance, you can resist much more force with two arms clasped together, braced against pressure, than one arm held straight. A simple beam is like one arm; a *truss* is made of several arms clasped together. This grouping is taken even further by what is called a rigid frame, which makes the whole skeleton of the building a kind of openwork truss, or braced box.

The disadvantages of skeleton construction lie in the fact that the skeleton frame is solely structural. Other qualities, such as fireproofing, acoustical and thermal insulation, must be added. But by the same token, this can be an advantage, because today in building, manufactured specialties are frequently more dependable than craft specialties. The big advantage of skeleton frame construction is its speed. Time—labor time—is money.

Bearing walls, on the other hand, retain some advantages, which include their weight, which is generally useful for retaining heat (and, in summer, coolness) and excluding noise, and their stability, which makes elaborate bracing less necessary. The disadvantages are the other side of these advantages: stability by weight is often expensive, both in handling and in the foundations it requires; also, a few windows or a door in a heavy wall may negate its acoustical advantage; also, it is not so easy to change the temperature rapidly to meet sudden weather changes in a heavy, heat-absorbent building as in a light one.

There is another way of building, a fairly new way for the United States. It takes advantage of the strength which thin planes gain when they are bent into certain shapes and held in them. For example, a piece of paper can't even support itself when you hold it up by one corner. It slumps. But

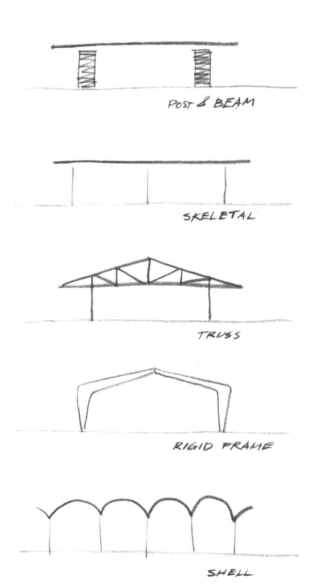

POST & BEAM

SKELETAL

TRUSS

RIGID FRAME

SHELL

curve it and it can hold up a box of matches. The other standard example of the strength in "shell construction," as it is called, is the ordinary sea shell. It doesn't have a skeleton—its strength comes from the fact that when you push one part, all the other parts contribute strength to resist your push. Today roofs of reinforced concrete are being built in the United States which actually are thinner in proportion to their spans than hen eggs or the thinnest sea shells. They span large areas and permit the insertion of long, lightly framed walls and windows. Even thinner than the concrete shells are folded and curved roofs of light metal; some of these graceful structures are almost like tents without tent poles.

Few of these roofs are yet used over schools, however, because few people know how to build them, and because many building codes are reluctant to accept them. But some banks and warehouses are being roofed with these thin "umbrellas," which probably means that schools will not be far behind in putting them to use.

Somewhat surprisingly, whatever structural system—wall bearing, skeletal, or shell—they do select, architects and engineers begin to design from the top down, not from the bottom up. Although this is not the way a great oak grows, it has its own undeniable logic: all weight travels downward with gravity. The designer begins his calculations not with the foundations but by assuming an anticipated top load on the roof in pounds per square foot (defined everywhere by local building codes). In the snowy north this may be forty pounds; in Texas it is twenty pounds. To support this load and the weight of the structure and the roof itself, whether it is marble chips on asphalt, or shingles, he has to pick a roof frame, and here he runs into the problem of span, which usually determines his choice of framing. Also involved, of course, is the shape of the roof, which is determined partly by pure structural logic, partly by the lighting scheme, the site relationship, and other factors. The big decision, however, is span —how much clear space should there be in the building between columns? How long should the beams or trusses be?

In a theoretical sense the designer probably begins with the idea of creating large spaces without *any* columns at all inside the building, with the entire weight held up by columns in the exterior walls. He puts a roof deck under the finish roofing to pick up its weight and the snowload, runs crossbeams under the roof deck to gather that weight and carry it to the main beams, and then he stretches the beams (or trusses) from wall to wall where columns or the walls themselves hold them up. But like wall-to-wall carpeting, wall-to-wall spans can get expensive. Long beams become very deep, very heavy, very costly, not only because they contain a lot of material, but because they usually are difficult to handle and ship. As their span widens, their own dimensions and weight have to increase rapidly. To illustrate this, engineers swap stories about such structures as the framework supporting the flat roof of a big U. S. aircraft factory: if its crossbeams were one foot longer, they would have to be twice as heavy—and you pay for steel beams, like steak, by the pound.

Other choices for spanning besides steel beams and trusses may be: laminated wood members— "manufactured" timbers—made up of numerous layers of wood glued together under pressure for a considerable increase in strength; lighter-weight metal beams, which some building codes are beginning to recognize; and—very important in either wall-bearing or skeleton construction—precast or cast-in-place reinforced concrete slabs,

There are easily as many ways of putting a schoolhouse together as there as bridge hands. On the chart which begins below, and on charts placed through the next 63 pages of this book, are indicated a few typical cards in the hand of the schoolbuilder—some of the more commonly used, familiar assemblies of walls, partitions, floors, lighting, etc. with comments on their qualities drawn from the professional experience of our building consultants, and with comparative cost indications noted in one locality in one period by the technicians of the George A. Fuller Company.

Not all these comments apply precisely nationwide, of course, nor do all the bar chart cost comparisons; labor and materials vary considerably from one town to the next. But the comparative costs indicated in these charts, both first cost and twenty year cost (including maintenance, insurance, and, when necessary, replacement) can be checked out locally by your architect and builder, who will also have comments on special advantages and disadvantages of these techniques for your own use. Throughout the comparisons, our classroom is sized at 28 feet by 32 feet, with a ten foot ceiling, and the job size assumed is the construction of an eight-classroom wing. Costs are comparative within each chart.

STRUCTURAL FRAMING

FRAMING SYSTEM	NECESSARY DECKSPAN WIDTH	FIRE RESISTANCE	BUILDING SPEED	REMARKS	COST COMPARISON
Vertical support: lally (steel pipe) columns, 4 inches in diameter, set at corners; Roof framing: rolled steel beams (size, 21 WF 68) spanning 32 feet; cross members of rolled steel beams (size, 12 WF 27) spanning 28 feet, spaced 8 feet apart	8 feet	Incombustible, but fire-rated under one hour without applied fire-proofing	Fast; can be riveted, bolted or welded	Long spans, few footings; no walls bear weight (they can easily be rearranged without affecting the structure)	installation cost / maintenance and insurance cost for 20 years
Vertical support: 3½ inch lally columns set at corners and midway in longer wall; Roof framing: rolled steel beams (size, 16 WF 36) spanning 28 feet; cross members of 10 inch bar joists (light, open web steel beams) spaced 2 feet apart; steel beams (8 WF 17) over columns	2 feet	Incombustible, but fire-rated under one hour	Fast; bar joists can be handled without elaborate hoists	Column-free and flexible; if framing is left exposed, dust is sometimes a problem, and the ceiling cannot be used well for indirect lighting	
Vertical support: 3½ inch lally columns set at corners and midway in longer wall; Roof framing: rolled steel beams (size, 16 WF 36) spanning 28 feet, spaced 16 feet apart; steel beams (8 WF 17) over columns	16 feet	Incombustible, but fire-rated under one hour	Very fast; one step is omitted when roof deck takes over the structural task	Has advantages of relatively few columns and no weight-bearing walls; also has clear ceiling with only one cross beam (but cost of wide span decking must be taken into account)	

STRUCTURAL FRAMING continued

FRAMING SYSTEM	NECESSARY DECKSPAN WIDTH	FIRE RESISTANCE	BUILDING SPEED	REMARKS	COST COMPARISON
Vertical support: 3½ inch lally columns set 8 feet apart on long side; Roof framing: 18 inch bar joists, spanning 28 feet, spaced 8 feet apart; light steel beams (8 by 13) over columns	8 feet	Incombustible, but fire-rated under one hour	Fast	Fairly clear ceiling; there are numerous vertical columns, yet they don't impose any serious limitations in flexibility; the end walls can still be removed structurally	installation cost maintenance and insurance cost for 20 years
Vertical support: 3½ inch lally columns set 8 feet apart on long side; Roof framing: steel angles (size, 4 by 6 inches) over columns, with cross members of laminated wood beams (size, 5¼ by 18 inches) spanning 28 feet	8 feet	Combustible; many codes frown on timber construction, but it does retain strength even when charred	In theory fast, but in practice usually only fair; two separate building trades are involved	Fairly clear ceiling; many people like appearance of exposed laminated wood beams, especially if stained and waxed instead of painted	
Vertical support: 4 by 7 inch wood columns set 8 feet apart on long side; Roof framing: 4 by 6 inch steel angles over columns, with cross members of laminated wood beams (size, 5¼ by 18 inches) spanning 28 feet	8 feet	Combustible, but see above	Fair	Same advantages as above, but wood columns take up somewhat more space	
Vertical support: 4 inch nailable steel studs (slim steel columns) spaced 4 feet apart on long side; Roof framing: 18 inch bar joists, spanning 28 feet, spaced 4 feet apart; 3 by 4 inch steel angles over columns	4 feet	Incombustible, but fire-rated under one hour	Fast	Light, easy construction, allows cost-saving in roof decking, but tight spacing of the studs in the walls limits flexibility	
Vertical support: 3 by 10 inch wood columns set at corners and midway in longer wall; Roof framing: wood trusses, 36 inches high at one end, sloping up to 48 inches at other, spanning 28 feet; cross members of 4 by 12 inch wood, spaced 4 feet apart	4 feet	Combustible	Fair	A simple structure with few columns, allowing substantial flexibility; usually, however, a suspended ceiling must be added below the trusses	
Vertical support: 3½ inch lally columns set at corners and midway in longer wall; Roof framing: steel trusses, 36 inches high at one end, sloping up to 48 inches at other, spanning 28 feet; cross members of 4 by 12 inch wood, spaced 4 feet apart	4 feet	Combustible	Fair	Remarks above apply here also	
Vertical and roof framing are combined: the rigid steel members (size, 18 WF column and girder) span 28 feet, spaced 16 feet apart; cross members are steel beams (size, 10 WF 21) spanning 16 feet, spaced 7 feet apart	7 feet	Incombustible, but fire-rated under one hour	Very fast, with proper hoisting equipment	A spare, trim way to build with few elements	

FRAMING SYSTEM	NECESSARY DECKSPAN WIDTH	FIRE RESISTANCE	BUILDING SPEED	REMARKS	COST COMPARISON
Vertical and roof framing are combined: the laminated wood members (size varies from 5⅛ by 5 inches to 5⅛ by 40 inches) span 28 feet, spaced 8 feet apart; roof slopes up 3 inches per foot toward peak at center of span	8 feet	Combustible	Very fast	Numerous columns, but placed on exterior walls where they will not interfere with the rearranging of interior partitions	installation cost maintenance and insurance cost for 20 years
Vertical support: weight-bearing walls of solid concrete (which become the partition walls between the classrooms); Roof framing: laminated wood beams (7¼ by 18 inches) spanning 32 feet, spaced 7 feet apart	7 feet	Combustible	Walls slow, roof fast	A simple, solid way to build, but with no flexibility whatsoever (the partition walls are permanent); Also, running the beams the long way throws shadows on the ceiling, reducing its effectiveness as a reflector of daylight from the windows	
Vertical support: solid 8 inch concrete weight-bearing walls (the partition walls between the classrooms); Roof framing: long span steel or concrete roof deck	None needed	Depends on deck selected (the walls have a 4 hour fire-rating)	Walls slow, roof fast	The simplest way to build and apparently the cheapest; cost includes partition walls, but the cost of long span roof decking will probably eat up the money saved using this framing method; inflexible	
Vertical support: 8 inch lally columns; Roof framing: reinforced concrete slab, spanning 31 feet by 27 feet, poured on floor slab and jacked up columns into place	32 feet	Incombustible, with 4 hour fire-rating	With proper scheduling, fair	A very flexible way to build, with few columns and a clear, clean ceiling for reflecting light; heavy, it sometimes calls for expensive foundations; cost figure, however, includes roof decking	
Vertical support: 4 foot wide, weight-bearing, prefabricated aluminum panels (cross bracing provided by partition walls); Roof framing: steel beams (size, 12 WF 25) spanning 28 feet, spaced 4 feet apart	4 feet	Incombustible, but fire-rated under one hour	Very fast	Very flexible	
Vertical support: 14 by 20 inch reinforced concrete columns, poured in place, set at corners and midway in longer wall; Roof framing: 14 by 20 inch reinforced concrete beams, poured in place under a 6½ inch reinforced concrete slab	None	Incombustible, with a 4 hour fire-rating	Slow, needs framework and setting time	Heavy construction but few columns; fairly flexible for rearranging partitions; maintenance low; cost includes usual roof deck	
Vertical and roof framing are combined: the prefabricated, prestressed concrete frames span 28 feet, spaced 8 feet apart; columns are 10 by 12 inches, beams 5 by 18 inches	8 feet	Incombustible, with a 4 hour fire-rating	Fast, if heavy equipment is used	Heavy construction but still quite flexible, columns do not interfere with the moving of interior partitions	

FLOOR FINISHES

DRAWING AND DESCRIPTION	WEAR RESISTANCE	SOIL RESISTANCE, CLEANING AND MAINTENANCE	RESILIENCY	REMARKS	COST COMPARISON
⅛ inch hardened cement finish on concrete slab	Good	Poor; frequent cleaning needed; must be refinished every ten years	Very hard	Cement base costs little, is too hard a floor to be comfortable; infrequently used in classrooms, sometimes used in corridors, shops and inexpensive toilet rooms	installation cost / maintenance and insurance cost for 20 years
¾ inch terrazzo finish, with ¾ inch cement underbed on a concrete slab	Very good	Very good; needs cleaning once a week with detergent and water	Very hard	Terrazzo base is easy to clean and sanitary, but not resilient and sometimes noisy; seldom used in classrooms, often used in corridors, vestibules, toilets and shower rooms	
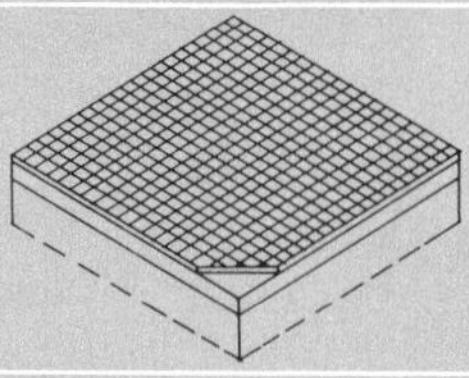 Ceramic mosaic tile, ¾ inch setting bed on concrete slab	Very good	Very good	Very hard	Used in toilet rooms, showers, food service areas, but seldom used in classrooms	
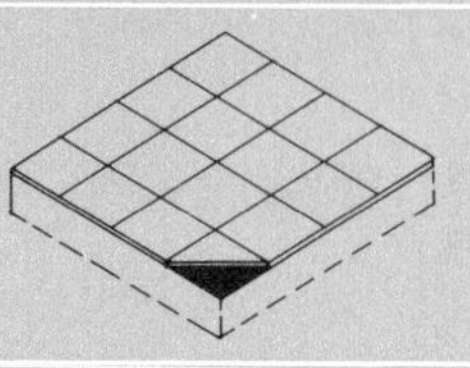 ⅛ inch asphalt tile finish installed in mastic on concrete slab	Poor, usually needs replacing every ten years	Fair; must be cleaned and waxed once a week	Fair	Low first cost; finish requires careful maintenance	
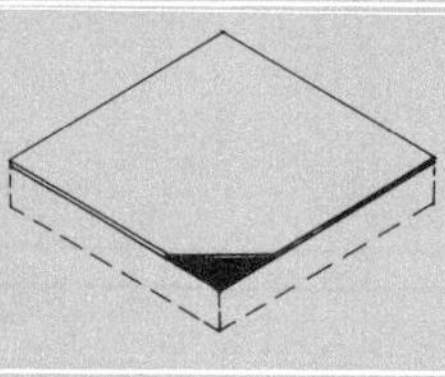 ⅛ inch linoleum finish installed in mastic on concrete slab	Good	Fair; must be cleaned and waxed once a week	Fair	Serviceable; a sanitary floor for classrooms, corridors, assembly and administration rooms	
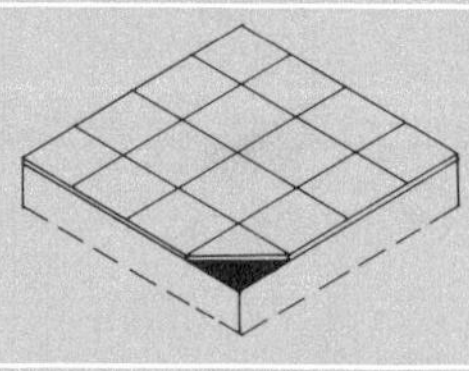 ⅛ inch cork tile floor installed in mastic on concrete slab	Good	Fair; needs frequent cleaning and waxing	Very good	Used primarily in libraries and kindergartens; floor is subject to indentations by chair legs; acoustically good	
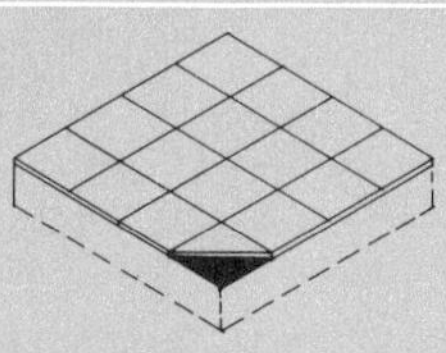 ⅛ inch rubber tile finish installed in mastic on concrete slab	Good	Fair; needs cleaning and waxing once a week	Very good	Subject to slight indentation by chair legs	
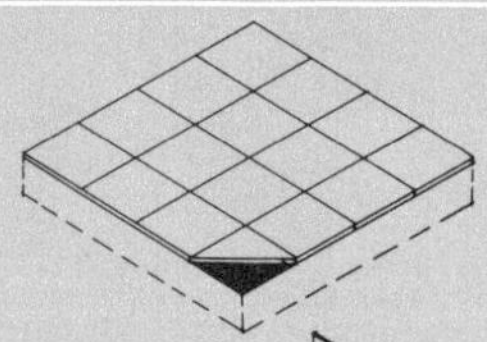 ⅛ inch vinyl tile finish installed in mastic on concrete slab	Good	Fair; needs a weekly cleaning and waxing	Very good	Subject to indentation	
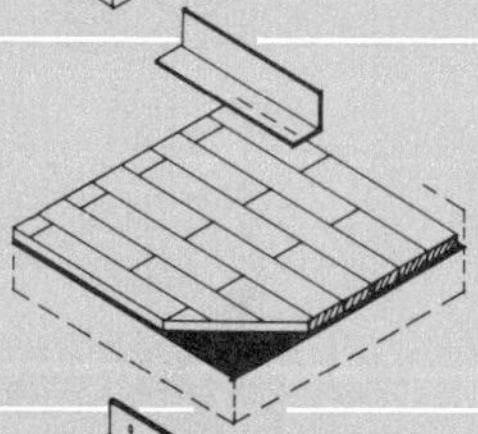 25/32 inch maple strip flooring set in ⅛ inch hot asphalt mastic on concrete slab	Very good	Good; requires monthly cleaning with steelwool and a wax finish	Fair	Steel angles necessary to cover expansion joint; used in gymnasiums and playrooms; not suitable for damp areas or climates	
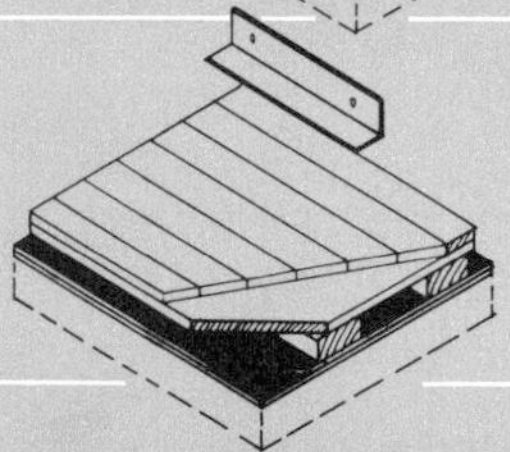 25/32 inch maple finish; 1 by 4 inch cypress sub-floor laid diagonally; 2 by 6 inch cypress sleepers, 12 inches apart, set in two ⅛ inch layers of hot asphalt mastic	Very good	Good; requires a monthly cleaning with steelwool and a wax finish; sand and re-finish every 2 years	Excellent	A deluxe gymnasium floor	

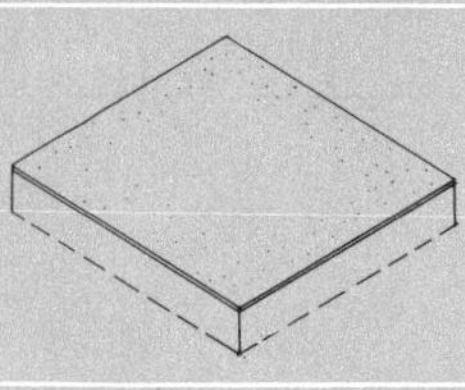

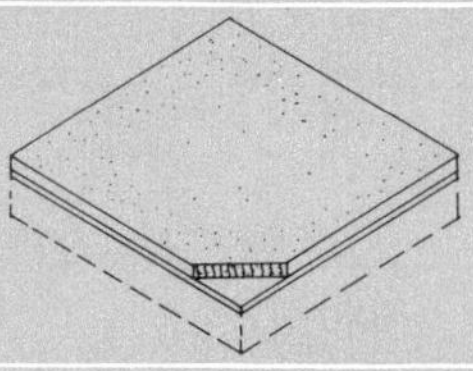

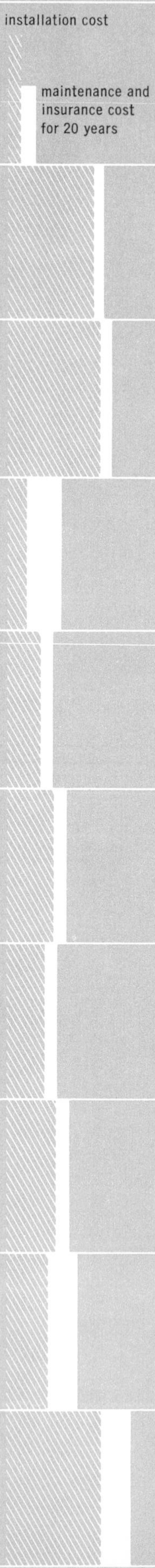

planks, and beams. In these concrete structural members, the concrete takes all the compressive stresses—the pushing together—but metal reinforcement has to be added to resist the tensile stresses—the pulling apart. To *prestress* concrete means simply to anticipate a load before it is applied by tightening up the metal reinforcing in advance; the load will stretch it slightly.

In the same way that the roof load is gathered by the roof framing and carried to columns to be transmitted vertically down to the foundations, so is the load of each floor gathered by its framing and carried to the columns. But something has to be added: a weight figure for the people and furniture. Most codes specify a minimum assumed live load of sixty pounds per square foot for classrooms. Because of this, as you move down closer to earth, the columns do become thicker, tree-like. And when they reach the ground they need roots—foundations.

The foundations depend upon the ground and climate. In soupy soil they may be piles driven 100 feet down. On rocks they may be little more than dowels to hook the building to the rocks. Whatever form they take, they must be adequate to distribute the weight of the building over a wide enough section of ground to support it without sinking. Any buildings are heavy. A single classroom can easily weigh 135,000 pounds, almost as much as thirty Cadillac limousines.

Whether the school has a basement or not, it is unlikely that it can sit directly on the ground. If it can, the foundation is part of the floor and must be well waterproofed. Another simple requirement of foundations is that they penetrate down below the frost line; the earth, when damp and frozen, can swell up like a sponge and crack buildings, just as it does sidewalks. Several common foundation types are diagrammed to the right.

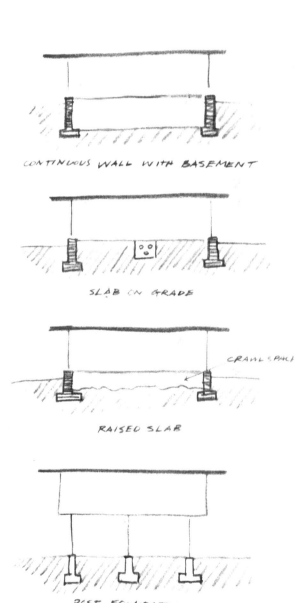

CONTINUOUS WALL WITH BASEMENT

SLAB ON GRADE

CRAWL SPACE

RAISED SLAB

POST FOUNDATION

2

1   3

This quick description of the structural frame has left out all intricacies, of course—the myriad details of structural practice that keep slide rules in motion late into the night. For instance, many engineering hours must be devoted to sideways bracing, especially in buildings with many openings and light spidery frames. For if a building sways too much, you can't keep the joints tight. On the West Coast, earthquake-resistant design is also a necessary specialty. Another detail in all buildings, especially big ones, is the uneven expansion and contraction of various materials. This can even affect the acoustics. There are some buildings which have a tendency to pop and crackle—not the best thing for a study hall.

In all structural design, theory must yield frequently to building practice. For instance, a beam which is entirely adequate to support a roof load may have to be made stiffer—thus bigger—if the ceiling under it is to be plastered. Plastering lim-its the flexing or bending to about 1/360 of the span, and this factor determines surprisingly many spanning specifications.

Beyond carrying the weight of the building, the structure has another responsibility—fire safety. There actually is no such thing as a fireproof building after it is finished and occupied; no school is fireproof after it is equipped with paper and pencils. The real danger, practically, that must be guarded against is collapse; the structure has to stand up even as it burns. Under the conscientious prodding of the fire prevention bureau and local fire chiefs, virtually all towns are very careful to demand the ultimate in fire-safe schools. One of the strongest reasons for the acceptance of the one-story school is the speed with which the occupants can be herded outdoors, of course.

So most schools are simply more substantial versions of the way most kites are built. They are

5

6

4

Sink the Battleship

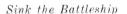

skins on frames, and beyond the frame, the quality of the skin is enormously important. Like human skin, a school's skin must remain healthy itself and it must resist Nature's assaults.

Some parts of the skin of schools are almost as flexible as human skin—roof finishes, for example, which are subject to tremendous wear. These must stretch and shrink constantly back and forth as the temperature changes; a variation of 60 degrees Fahrenheit in one day from the afternoon summer sun at 120 degrees to an evening storm at 60 degrees is not at all unusual.

For this reason most slanting roofs wear a number of small units—shingles or metal strips overlapped to spread the contraction and expansion. Flat roofs are usually finished with a flexible skin of asphalt over felt, topped off with imbedded gravel, metallic paint, or other hard substance.

For economy, the simplest geometrical shape of roof and walls with the fewest intersections and

penetrations is the best. Flat roofs have less area and less material in them—this is why you see so many flat roofs. Also, intersections and the seams between the various slanting planes must be lined with metal flashing, and if it is not installed right, it may eventually leak. A half hour's heavy rainfall on the roof of a building 200 feet long and 70 feet wide can easily total 9,000 gallons.

Although schools are not compelled to break the sound barrier, the aggressive forces to which their skins are subjected are not small. Air pressure is one of them. When a stormy wind blows a sudden fifty-mile-per-hour gust against the window wall of a school, it is not only *pushing* drafts and moisture at every crack and point, it is also actually being *sucked in* by the lower air pressure of the inside rooms, where the air is placid, protected from the storm. The difference in pressure between a strong gust and normal room pressure is substantial. The water comes in in those little streams which we have all seeen crawling across window sills as if they were seeking refuge from the storm outside.

Besides rain, the other great adversary of comfort and security is temperature. The problem before a school board is never *shall we insulate our building?* All good buildings are insulated. But what does well-insulated mean? And how much insulation is economically justified?

To answer these questions you have to begin with your weather. In Minnesota, for example, the temperature you must anticipate is 20 degrees Fahrenheit below zero, and the heating season is a long one. In Ohio the heating season is a third shorter than in Minnesota and the design temperature is about zero degrees F. (days colder than this do happen in Ohio, of course, but not often enough on the average to warrant the expense of assuming they are normal). Farther south, in Louisiana, the heating season is only half as long as in Ohio, and the design temperature is plus 10 degrees F. Another thing to consider: which surface of the building is being insulated? The roof, as we've mentioned, very likely has to insulate against heat and cold during the same twenty-four hours. Floors on grade, however, leak heat only at the edges. Exterior walls lose or gain heat in wide swings, depending on sun, wind, and air temperatures. Insulation should be applied to match the anticipated conditions.

How do you know how good an insulator any substance is? This is not difficult; the precise insulating characteristics of any building material or combination of materials are commonly described by its thermal conductance or "U" factor. A low U factor means that a material or a wall is a poor conductor, which means a good insulator. A high U factor means that heat pours out of the surface the way water does through a sieve. A single pane of ordinary glass (U, 1.13) conducts heat three times as easily as a twelve-inch brick wall (U, 0.36). A brick wall is no paragon, incidentally; the addition of a couple of inches of insulation to the brick can cut its conductance by two-thirds to a U of 0.12.

A few of the most common examples of walls used in schools are described in the charts on page 182, but hundreds of other combinations, of course, are built. Calculating the conductance of any wall is a simple matter to your architect and engineer.

The effect of the U factor on the economy of school operation is anything but mysterious. As an example, assume that a school in Ohio burns No. 2 fuel oil, bought in bulk for about ten cents a gallon, heating a classroom whose walls are built of brick, uninsulated. The yearly cost of heating this room would come to a little over five cents for each square foot of wall surface. If insulation were added to this wall, as mentioned earlier, cutting the U from 0.36 to 0.12, and the roof were beefed up similarly, the heating costs could be cut roughly by two-thirds, which would lower the fuel cost to about 1.7 cents per square foot. Before shrugging this off as pennies, remember that the exposed surface of one classroom may be as much as 1,500 square feet, bringing the savings possible by ordinary insulation in colder climates as high as fifty dollars a year *per classroom*.

To balance against the benefits of insulation is the cost of buying and installing it. There is a break-even point beyond which nothing is gained in fattening up the insulation. As the thickness of bulk insulation increases, the cost goes up, but the efficiency decreases. For example, in going from ½ inch to a full inch of one ordinary kind of roof insulation, the U factor decreases not 50 per cent, but about 31 per cent, while the cost increases 40 per cent. The limit of economical thickness of most bulk insulations is about 3½ inches.

Bulk is not everything. Although most of the many insulating materials on the market work on the same principle that wool does on a lamb's back —holding a layer of still, warm air around the body of the building—another category uses shiny aluminum foil to *reflect back* the escaping heat. This is the principle used also in the mirrored surfaces of a thermos bottle. Reflectivity, even in the matter of color alone, is of particular importance

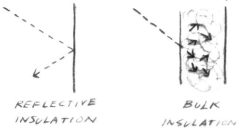

REFLECTIVE INSULATION

BULK INSULATION

in roofs. A dramatic example of its thermal effect: when Piccard first went up into the stratosphere, years ago, where the temperature is 70 degrees below zero, the gondola of his balloon was painted black. It shortly soaked up so much of the sun's rays that the scientist sweltered inside, at 100 degrees above zero. So on his second ascent he painted his gondola white. Result: he shivered in a temperature down about zero.

Another way to classify insulations is in chemical make-up. One group is made from the woody divisions of plant cells: cork, plant fiber, cotton batting, and wood fiber. Contrasting with these organic insulators are those materials that have an inorganic mineral source: foam glass, asbestos wool, glass wool, vermiculite, gypsum boards, and metal foil. Used correctly, all these insulations pay their way. Here are some questions to consider in picking one:

Is it fireproof? Some of the organic insulations char and give off smoke. Some of the inorganic

insulations have resin binders that will burn.

How strong is the insulation structurally? It probably will have to withstand rough handling and abuse during construction; it may well be walked on by workmen.

Is it rot and waterproof? Organic insulations are food for bacteria. By contrast, mineral insulations are "inedible." Some insulations break down under repeated drenchings. Others are impervious, shedding water.

Does it provide a vapor barrier?

To explain this last question, in the winter the air of most schools is humid and warm, compared with the outside air, and there is a forced exodus of molecules of water vapor from inside the school *through* the building construction to the outside. As a result condensation inside walls and above ceilings can bring serious deterioration. In a wooden building there is the chance of dry rot. In a steel structure there is rust. Where the condensation occurs above the ceiling of a lofty assembly room, a gentle rain may even fall indoors.

The best way of controlling this condensation is to provide natural ventilation in the attics above hung ceilings, the air spaces in walls, and the crawl spaces below floors, to carry off damp air before it can condense. But another essential safeguard is a barrier to prevent air-borne water vapor from ever reaching a cold condensing surface. In other words, vapor must be kept inside the warm zone of a building by a kind of dam. A thin skin of metal can do this. Other such vapor barriers: asphalt cement, certain paints, and some

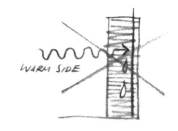

WARM SIDE

WARM SIDE

plastics. What architects have to remember in applying the barrier is to keep it on the warm side of the insulation. If it is on the cold side, wet air will penetrate the insulation, condense on the barrier and drip down inside the insulation, drying, but slowly. A beard takes longer to dry than a shaved face; bulk insulation is like a beard; and worse, some insulation rots if, enclosed within the walls, it is damp for a long time.

The cost of the structure of most school buildings, the frames, foundations, roofs and walls, and the finishes that these wear, generally accounts for 50 to 60 per cent of the plant cost, so it is an obvious place to try to save on the bond issue. One easy but eventually expensive way is to cut quality of materials (but take a look at the charts indicating long-term maintenance expenses). Another way is skimping on hours of workmanship, which is also risky.

Many people leap at what seems a very good method to save money—building *up*. Adding a second story to a building almost never doubles the structural burden, true. Structurally, a building is a rack of trays. The top one is a roof, then comes the ceiling, then the floor, then the basement floor or crawl space. Adding another floor merely means sliding another tray into the rack, raising the roof and bolstering up the structure. In schools, however, the structural economy of two or three-story construction is usually more than offset by two other complications: the exorbitant amount of extra space needed for stairways, and the more rigidly fireproof construction demanded by most codes in a multi-story school. Elevators, necessary in a number of city schools, are very, very expensive. So unless real estate costs are really staggering, multi-story schools seldom are money-savers.

The place where major savings should be made

in schoolhouse structures is in the thinking behind the structural design and working drawings. Through shrewd design the architect can save time and materials. The extra study he gives a design, the time he keeps it on the drafting board, can be multiplied in the workmen's time saved on the site later. This calls also for careful bookkeeping. Complete control and a tight, efficient scheduling of construction can tighten up any budget.

In the structure itself simplicity usually pays off, the kind of simplicity which substitutes a single fairly large part for several smaller ones, saving time and handling. The architect's alertness to new techniques for everything from spanning to waterproofing is very important to the client, and so is the architect's intimate knowledge of local variations in suppliers and supplies. Not only do prices of building materials vary considerably among general geographic areas of the United States, but even within the areas there is great variation. In building, things do not cost the same in Houston as they do in Dallas, and for sound reasons. And they do not cost the same this month as last.

In detail, it is up to your architect to save money in the specification and assembly of every small part. In general, there are several large strategic approaches generally agreed by architects and engineers to save building dollars in the

putting together of any structural design.

The first is standardization of the structural unit; that is, deciding and designing one part of the frame—frequently the columns and beams of one classroom—then repeating this same pattern over as much of the rest of the school as is possible. This means you have one basic set of beams and columns. These can be ordered cheaper by the dozen, and even more important, they go together on the job fast because the workmen are repeating themselves—once the loom is set it becomes simple to weave. (This does not mean that the school itself is standardized; it can still be full of pleasant spatial surprises, on a regular frame.)

This standardization of the frame also permits standardization of the walls that fill in the frame. If he knows the columns are going to be placed ten feet apart along the entire exterior school wall, the architect can design several different walls: one with big windows, one with small windows, and one with no windows—all size ten—and put them in where they are appropriate, like dominoes.

Because more and more schools are being walled with factory-made components delivered on the site, the question, *Why not a factory-built school like an automobile?* is legitimate. One answer to this, but not a complete answer, is that a car fits any highway, but a pre-fabricated school doesn't fit every site. Ideally, each school should be built to fit its own geography. Even more important, educational programs vary significantly from locality to locality and demand different solutions. One factor in pre-fab schools which many educators find depressing is seeing the same schoolhouse built over and over, without anyone trying to do better; this might mean flattening out of progress in school design, they think. True, this did not happen in the automotive field, but automobiles are not permanent—they are traded frequently;

automobile loans run three years, school bonds frequently are with a community for thirty years.

In putting schools together out of manufactured components, a further technical refinement leading to economies is "modular" construction. This is a system of standard dimensions which is intended to operate not only within the design of one building but in manufactured items for all buildings. The basic measurement is four inches, the width of a brick. Logically, if all designers used this as their basic domino, manufacturers could produce fewer sizes of everything from window frames to acoustical tiles, and everything would fit, just as all manufacturers' light bulbs fit the socket on your reading lamp.

The *order of attack* is a classical military specialty which the architect is very aware of in school construction, and this can effect economies too. For instance, if you can get the structural frame and the roof up fast, bad weather will not hamper the workmen doing the finish work—they will have an umbrella. The architect also saves labor with a design program that permits the various subcontractors' squads—plumbers, masons, metal-workers, etc.—to move in, perform their jobs, and move out, not waiting around for each other to get out of the way. (It is vital also not to rile local building unions by mixing their specialties carelessly. If you do, the only workman on your job may be a man with a sign, walking up and down in front of it.)

An American specialty in construction is extensive use of machines on the job, and the architect is aware of this. For instance, large sections of the school walls can be pre-assembled on the ground or roof or in a factory miles away and hoisted into place by crane, saving hours and scaffolding. If the floor is a concrete slab and the walls are metal and glass, the architect can have them fastened together by fast explosion—with a stud gun which shoots bolts into the concrete, eliminating boring. Just as your doctor has to keep up with medical science, your architect has his journals, manufacturers' literature, and professional meetings to keep up with; and the building manufacturers, like the pharmaceutical companies, fortunately are providing him with quite a few miracle cures these years. The precise point of practicality even in component prefabrication has yet to be established in building—that point at which it is better and more economical to build parts of the school on jigs in a shop, to be delivered to the site and assembled there. But, short of total prefabrication, certainly the factory's part is growing bigger every year.

This seems a logical time to point out a large architectural economy which is almost entirely strategic, not structural. What many people have forgotten is that building is a seasonal business, almost as seasonal as farming, yet the spring and fall of a building year in any one locality are not quite so easy to pinpoint as the farmer's seasons. Many architects more than earn their total design fees by the money they help save in letting the contract at just the right lull in the local building market, when numerous contractors are seeking work and competition is keen. This involves more than just knowing the total building conditions, of course; it means being ready to go out for bids with a complete set of blueprints when the predicted opportunity occurs, and it also means having the confidence of the competing bidders. All contractors, in the backs of their minds, have bitter memories of having lost money on jobs in the past in which there were unanswered questions at bidding time. If there are questions left in your proposition, even the most eager bidder will add a factor-of-ignorance cushion in his bid. (Another

professional tip: never go out for bids on the Monday of a short week.)

Basic for economy in building or anything else will always be the avoidance of waste. This villain wears various disguises—sometimes pious ones. He may appear in a design which calls for a carpenter to saw four different sizes of two-by-fours on the job where one pre-cut size might have been used (not only is the carpenter's time wasted but so may be the other ends of a lot of two-by-fours). Waste also may appear dressed like Hercules in the form of structural *over*-design. This means making a building *too* strong—stronger than the law or the loads require. This happens frequently. It is the quickest and easiest way to design, for one thing, because it avoids close calculating. An example: making the connections between beams and columns stronger than the beams or columns themselves—obviously it costs money and accomplishes nothing to put an oversized link in a chain.

But the most respectable clothing worn by waste is the blue serge of local law. Like the policeman at the school crossing, a building code is a wonderful, necessary institution, but some building codes seemingly want to allow only *old* building methods to cross the street. A code written in the 1920's probably is costing a school district a lot of money if it hasn't been rewritten recently.

Some state laws, for instance, require minimum ceiling heights in classrooms—ten feet, or higher. The original purpose of such a stipulation was to guarantee enough outside wall area to make sure windows were high enough so there would be enough daylight, and such a law may have made sense before today's techniques for daylighting and electrical lighting. But today it means simply that you have to build taller and more expensive schools than you really need. Another favorite minimum stipulation is the amount of outdoor air which must be delivered in the classroom per child per minute. Sometimes thirty cubic feet per minute is demanded, winter and summer. (An athlete, running hard, can only breathe 3.6 cubic feet per minute.) Pushing this lavish supply of air through the room in summer may be no problem (although the windows will be open anyway), but in winter the air has to be heated before it is released in the room, and this can be lavishly expensive in consumption of fuel.

In some states all schoolhouses, single-story or five-story, have to observe the same fireproofing measures despite the ease of escape from a single-story building. This fear of fire is a hard thing to argue against, of course; it has its base in panic. But your local fire chief can easily prove how much faster a single-story building can be cleared than a five-story one.

None of us can afford to build schoolhouses that are museums of outworn building beliefs or plumbing practices that were conventional a half century ago. Yet some towns are doing it—architects who practice nationally point out that there are thousands of school districts in which it is not *possible*, legally, to build a good modern school today.

The biggest structural economy in the school you are about to build—and all others to come—may actually be a re-examination of your building code. This is something which local architects may be able to help with, but they need support from citizens' groups. In the field of structure, a legitimate question for you or the building code to ask your architect at any point is *Why*. Save your architect the right to ask the code *Why not?* —this is a peculiarly American question. Any code reasonably should be expected to answer it, put to it reasonably.

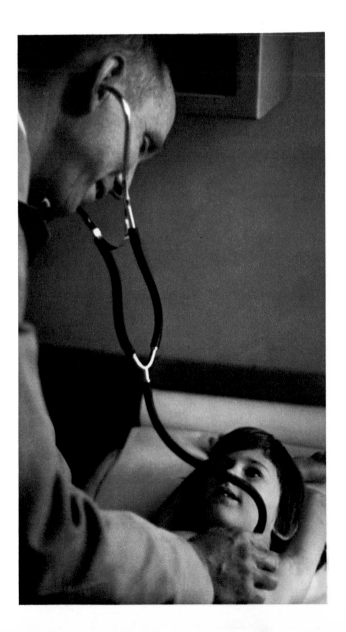

Acoustics

*"Penrod was doing something very unusual and rare,
something almost never accomplished except by . . .
a boy in school on a spring day: he was doing really
nothing at all. He was merely a state of being.*

*"From the street a sound stole in through the
open window and abhorring Nature began to fill
the vacuum called Penrod Schofield, for the sound was
the spring song of a mouth-organ, coming down
the sidewalk. The windows were intentionally above
the level of the eyes of the seated pupils; but the
picture of the musician was plain to Penrod,
pointed for him by a quality in the runs and trills,
partaking of the oboe, of the calliope, and of
cats in anguish; an excruciating sweetness obtained
only by the wallowing, walloping . . . palm of a hand
. . . The music came down the street and passed beneath
the window, accompanied by the carefree shuffling
of a pair of old shoes scuffing syncopations on
the cement sidewalk. It passed into the distance;
became faint and blurred; and was gone. Emotion
stirred in Penrod a great and poignant desire . . ."*

—BOOTH TARKINGTON, *Penrod*

If you ask almost any elementary school teacher what her biggest struggle is in the classroom, during any season of the year, she'll probably tell you control of the acoustical environment. She surely won't use those words, however, but will put it more personally—keeping the kids quiet and attentive. "They get worse every year . . . I don't know what their homes can be like," says Miss Rimstock, with a sigh.

What Miss Rimstock may not realize is that her struggle is not just with the kids, but with the classroom. Classrooms may be noisy, no matter who is in them, simply because of the way they are constructed and finished. Some of the handsomest new schools we inspected across the U. S. were surprisingly noisy. This is perhaps the most common fault in new schools.

It is a shocking fault, for the need to hear well is basic in education. Most education begins with the ear. Even before he knows individual words, a baby knows what a tone of voice means—and knows how to use it himself, eloquently. But soon words become the key to thought, so anything that interferes with the teacher's words is a particularly dangerous barrier in elementary years, when the first concentrative habits are forming. When a child is just beginning to listen effectively, it must not be made difficult for him to hear.

A world-famous neurologist, the late Dr. Foster Kennedy, said during the course of an official inquiry into noise in New York City:

"The fact that school children cannot concentrate so well under the influence of noise has a profound effect on their work. It often means that whole hours of the day are completely wasted, because if we do not concentrate well, we cannot remember—only those ideas on which we have trained the full searchlight of our conscious mind become clearly recorded in our memory. Children may sit all day in the noisy schoolroom never learning how to focus this searchlight upon the facts before them. They may finish their full years of schooling and never achieve any clear pictures in their memory."

There is more to classroom acoustics than just that, of course. We know that children feel two ways about noise. Sometimes it frightens them, but in addition many noises that make adults flinch can be fairly pleasant to the small fry. Because some elementary school children are still very little, really just peeping out of the baby's plump, personal, egocentric world, they still have an energetic curiosity about sounds, finding them interesting instead of annoying, welcoming their distraction. In really bad classroom acoustical conditions, it is not the children who are miserable; it is the teacher, trying to reach them.

This, then, extends the noise problem even beyond that of keeping the teacher's words intelligible. There must also be a minimum of distraction—shouts from the playground, giggles from the hall, mumbles from the ventilating fan.

The dual problem has to be solved in two steps, first by improving speech intelligibility within the room, then by concentrating on blocking the distracting noises from outside. It is because most people, including architects, seem to see only one of these two steps that so many of today's schools are annoying acoustically.

The first part of the acoustical problem is the

easy one, with the easy modern solution: *Noise originating inside the classroom* beclouds intelligibility. The children in the back cannot hear as comfortably as the children in the front. (Or, with today's easygoing furniture arrangements—movable chairs and tables, circle seating, etc.—it might be more realistic to ask whether the teacher can be heard well all over the room from any one spot. And when classes split into smaller groups for separate activities, does it produce bedlam within the classroom walls?)

When we were all in school ourselves, Miss Rimstock told us that sound travels like the waves from a pebble dropped in a pond. Also we learned from Echo Canyon that sound waves will bounce off a hard surface and return, ghostlike. We stood in empty gymnasiums or in tunnels and clapped our hands, then listened, delighted, for the sound to come back.

This unfortunately could also be done to some degree in some of our classrooms. A room which has hard, flat finishes on all its surfaces is a minor-league Echo Canyon; it is annoying acoustically because there are thousands of almost imperceptible echoes and overtones bouncing around from any little sound that is made. Actually the first sound keeps recurring, and produces a fog of distracting or covering noises through which the teacher's new words are not so clear as they ought to be. Acoustical experts call a room like this too *live*. It is so lively it talks back, makes its own nervous noises, rattles and blurs the teacher's speech. If someone drops a pencil everyone jumps.

But this part of the acoustical problem is easy; rooms which rattle in this way can be cured with the twentieth century's acoustical penicillin, materials with soft surfaces which soak up some of the sound that hits them, instead of bouncing it all back. There is a wide range of these wonderful sound-sponging materials available, from special kinds of coarse, porous plaster to perforated sheet materials backed up with loose glass fibers. They calm the room, deadening background noise so that the teacher's voice is dominant, without making it necessary for her to talk any louder. If anything, she can talk more softly without losing attention.

In the early days of radio, broadcasting rooms were improvised by hanging blankets on the walls to cut down on reflected noise. Echo Canyon doesn't work after a heavy fall of snow. Classrooms observe the same principle in their use of acoustical absorbents, but theirs also have to be selected to take long hard wear, unlike blankets or landscapes blanketed with snow.

The difficult part of the acoustical problem today is *noise originating outside the classroom,* which most people still try to solve in the easy, wrong way. This should be discussed more thoroughly before we return to noises which begin inside the classroom.

Noises from beyond the classroom walls

There are many people who think they can cure the noise of outside traffic by bandaging a room thoroughly on the inside with sound absorbing materials. This does not work. It is about as effective as trying to keep your hair combed in a high wind by taking aspirin; what is needed is a hat. Interior sound absorbing materials are not hats; they were never designed to stop sound from coming through a wall from outside, or from a corridor, or from the next classroom.

What does stop noise from outside? The answer is old fashioned: a good, substantial air-tight wall. Why? Because the invisible vibrations of the air which hit our eardrums and produce hearing simply are not capable of passing through anything really dense. When sound waves hit a wall on one side they make it vibrate, just like our eardrums. If the wall is flimsy, it vibrates easily and the sound waves are reproduced on the other side, drumlike. If the wall is substantial, it does not vibrate, and the sound waves are not reproduced on the other side. It is the difference between hitting a drum and a block of granite.

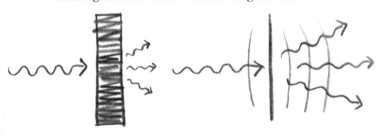

How quiet?

A classroom should not be any noisier than the quietest room of a suburban home. No annoying mechanical noises should intrude, such as the sound of truck traffic; there should not be too much noise from children playing outside (although a little of this is all right). Children leaving another classroom should never be so audible as to turn the class-bound child's thoughts yearningly to escape, away from Miss Rimstock's conversation on the Bill of Rights or the shape of Argentina.

The exact technical evaluation of any noise depends not only on the force of the original noise but on its pitch. High-pitched and high-frequency noises etch through low ones; a single oboe player can be heard through an entire symphony orchestra, especially if he plays a little sharp or flat. For most of us there are 120 noticeable different loudnesses, from silence to deafening noise. They are registered in decibels. Each increase of 3 decibels actually doubles the noise level.

Logically the first element in protecting the classroom from exterior noise is choice of the site where you put the school. But even if it is necessary to build in a noisy neighborhood, a large lot offers protection—and since neighborhoods change, acreage is always the best acoustical protection.

Zoning, of course, is another noise insulator, and is especially important on a smaller-than-ideal lot. A school design possibly might back away from traffic noises, crouching at its interior lot lines, then find a machine shop moving in next door. Another growing problem: aircraft noise.

Even before a good many long-distance noises reach the school, however, they can be muted partially by such devices as hedges, trees, earth embankments, and masonry walls outdoors, and also

by elevation. Shrubs and trees are not directly useful in reducing low-pitched noises like truck rumble, but they are good against high-pitched noises like young cries, and can be used to blur the character of any noise somewhat to a more anonymous general hum.

With planting, the efficiency varies by season, of course, but there are compensating factors for that too. When the classroom windows are open in spring and fall, the planting is leafy and dense, at its most effective as a noise muter; in winter, when most of the plants have shed their bulky leafage, the classroom windows are likely to be closed. In general, of course, non-shedding evergreens are the steadiest plants for acoustical purposes. The place to locate any of these external physical barriers is as close to the noise *source* as possible, not right up by the schoolhouse windows.

The classroom next door

In some schools the teachers actually are in competition with one another for children's attention, especially toward the back walls where the children may be closer to the teacher in the next classroom than to their own. A child's school day can seem slow. The game of distraction is always welcome.

Acoustically the ideal solution for inter-classroom noise might be to disconnect all classrooms from each other into separate buildings, arranging the classes in a row of little pavilions with air between them. There would be about sixty feet between kindergarten and first grade, narrowing to about fifteen feet between fifth and sixth grades, as age and a certain calm creep up on the inhabitants of the pavilions.

In actual practice this air space between classes usually has to be replaced by a single partition, which is obliged to serve as a concentrated sound barrier, doing the job of distance.

A partition's acoustical efficiency is not actually measured in feet of air space it replaces. Instead it is measured, technically, in decibels of noise reduction. As an example: if a sound at 90 decibels (a wail) hits one side of a partition, and a sound at 65 decibels (a whimper) can be *heard* through the partition on the other side, the partition itself has subtracted 25 decibels. Its noise reduction rating is the total of that subtraction (the N.R. is 25 db., in engineers' clipped speech).

Bulk and air tightness can be given one assist in stopping the flow of noise through a partition— an extra wall of air inside the partition itself. If a partition is built double, that is if it has two vertical layers entirely separated by a slice of air between them, from floor to roof, it can get away with being a little lighter than if both surfaces

were nailed to the same frame. But both surfaces still must be anchored firmly to floor and roof (or the floor above).

It is worth mentioning here again that up-holstering a partition with acoustical absorbent does not add significantly to the partition's noise reduction rating. If sound soaks into a substance easily, it also soaks through. A partition of plywood facings on a frame of two by four inch studs is both easy and cheap to build, but its noise reduction is only about 25 decibels. If the studs are staggered—arranged so that only every other stud touches one side of the wall and there is an interior cushion of air, the noise reduction goes up to 28 decibels, but it still is too low for most activities. Plaster or some other kind of facing must be added to the surfaces. The trick of pouring sand down the center of such a partition has been used in some places to add weight (and thus acoustical insulation) but this usually is impractical. Noise reduction ratings for a few common partitions, with comparative costs and data on upkeep, etc., are given in chart form on page 141.

Leaks

There would be little point in building an acoustical wall of solid lead five inches thick (noise reduction, 60 decibels) if you were going to put a single-panel wood door in it (noise reduction, 15 decibels). No partition is stronger than any five square feet of its surface. And if you include a door in a partition that shows light under the bottom edge, you may as well leave it open, acoustically; it won't stop much noise.

Another increasing practice is to top a partition wall between classrooms with a strip of glass next to the ceiling to give the rooms a feeling of spaciousness. Visually this is pleasant, but single glass is not a good sound barrier. If you want to use glass between classrooms, the conservative method is to use at least two thicknesses of ¼ inch glass, with at least four inches of air space between them, for sound insulation.

Hushing noises which originate inside

It has been suggested that so far as walls and ceilings are concerned, the ideal classroom would be one without any, outdoors under a tree on a grassy sward. Since the "walls" would be air, and the floor soft grass, there would be no echo or bounceback of sound waves, but instead there would be the effect of 100 per cent absorbency by the soft surroundings. The teacher's voice would go directly to the students, then fade on into space. Small noises made by the students themselves would die quickly.

But symphony orchestras seldom sound best outdoors, and perhaps schoolteachers don't either. Think back to the times you have sat in an outdoor class: in the army, or on a college quadrangle some spring day so giddy that the professor was touched,

INTERIOR PARTITIONS

DRAWING AND DESCRIPTION	FIRE-RATING	SOIL AND DAMAGE RESISTANCE	ACOUSTICS	REMARKS	COST COMPARISON
4 inch face brick, tooled joints; Actual thickness, 3⅝ inches; Weight, 40 lbs. per square foot of wall surface	Incombustible, with one hour fire-rating	Good	Very good; transmission loss, 45 decibels	Low maintenance, but limited flexibility; a good-looking wall, but poor light reflection	installation cost / maintenance and insurance cost for 20 years
4 inch concrete block, tooled joints, two coats of paint on each side; Actual thickness, 3⅝ inches; Weight, 30 lbs. per square foot	Incombustible, with one hour fire-rating	Good	Good; transmission loss, 40 decibels	Inexpensive; attractive if constructed neatly; frequently used for corridors, gyms, assembly rooms, etc.; no flexibility	
4 inch cinder block, ¾ inch layer of plaster on each side, 2 coats of paint on each side; Actual thickness, 5¼ inches; Weight, 30 lbs. per square foot	Incombustible, with two hour fire-rating	Poor	Good; transmission loss, 43 decibels	A smooth, dense finish; a good light reflector if painted a light color; no flexibility	
3 inch cinder block, ¾ inch layer of plaster on each side, 2 coats of paint on each side; Thickness, 4½ inches; Weight, 21 lbs. per square foot	Incombustible, with two hour fire-rating	Poor	Good; transmission loss, 39 decibels	A smooth, dense finish; a good light reflector if painted a light color; no flexibility	
4 inch structural facing tile, glazed on each side; Actual thickness, 3¾ inches; Weight, 40 lbs. per square foot	Incombustible, with a fire-rating of less than one hour	Very good	Good; transmission loss, 35 decibels	Used well in classrooms, corridors, also in toilets and showers; care must be taken with the design to avoid bright reflectivity; no flexibility	
4 inch concrete block, 2 coats of vinyl plastic spray over entire surface of each side; Actual thickness, 3¾ inches; Weight, 38 lbs. per square foot	Incombustible, with one hour fire-rating	Good	Good; transmission loss, 40 decibels	Sleek finish, but no flexibility	
2 by 4 inch wood studs, spaced 16 inches apart; metal lath and plaster, 2 coats of paint on each side; Thickness, 4¾ inches; Weight, 20 lbs. per square foot	Combustible	Poor	Good; transmission loss, 39 decibels	Good light reflector, not much flexibility	

DRAWING AND DESCRIPTION	FIRE-RATING	SOIL AND DAMAGE RESISTANCE	ACOUSTICS	REMARKS	COST COMPARISON
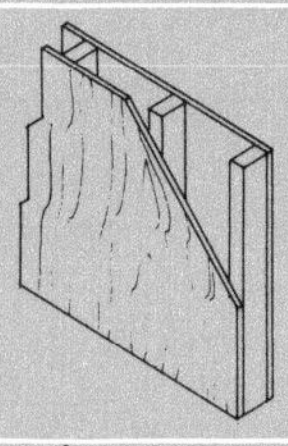 2 by 4 inch wood studs, spaced 16 inches apart; ⅜ inch fir plywood with rubbed paint finish on each side; Thickness, 4½ inches; Weight, 8 lbs. per square foot	Combustible, no time rating	Fair	Very poor; transmission loss, 25 decibels	Fairly flexible (often can be demounted and re-used)	installation cost / maintenance and insurance cost for 20 years
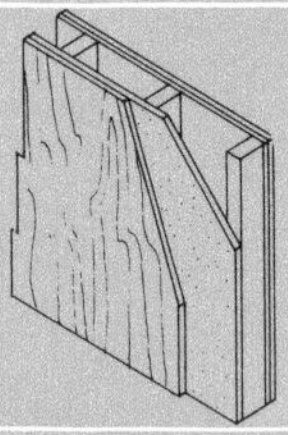 2 by 4 inch wood studs, spaced 16 inches apart; ⅜ inch rock lath, ⅜ inch fir plywood, with rubbed paint finish on each side; Thickness, 5¼ inches; Weight, 12 lbs. per square foot	Combustible, no time rating	Fair	Good; transmission loss, 38 decibels	Considerable flexibility through re-use of panels	
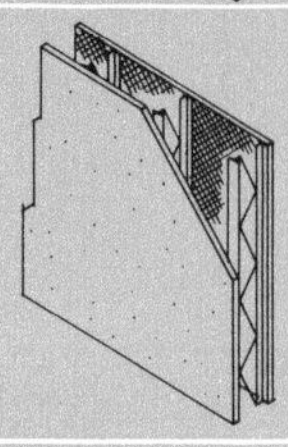 4 inch open web steel studs, spaced 16 inches apart; ¾ inch metal lath and plaster, 2 coats of paint on each side; Thickness, 5½ inches; Weight, 18 lbs. per square foot	Incombustible, with one hour fire-rating	Poor	Good; transmission loss, 40 decibels	Good light reflecting surface; little flexibility	
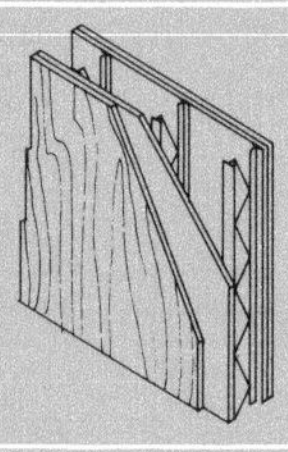 4 inch open web steel studs, spaced 16 inches apart; ⅜ inch rock lath backing each side, with ⅜ inch fir plywood finish; each side stained and waxed; Thickness, 5½ inches; Weight, 12 lbs. per square foot	Combustible, no time-rating	Fair	Good; transmission loss, 38 decibels	Limited flexibility	
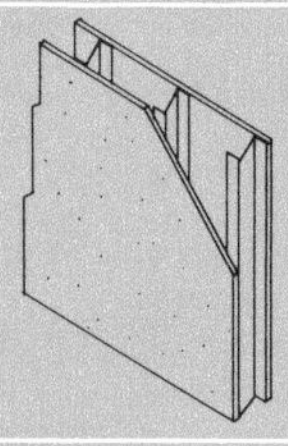 Z-shaped steel studs, spaced 16 inches apart; ½ inch rock lath with metal clips and taped joints; 2 coats of paint on each side; Thickness, 5 inches; Weight, 11 lbs. per square foot	Incombustible, with a fire-rating of less than one hour	Poor	Good; transmission loss, 35 decibels	Low initial cost	
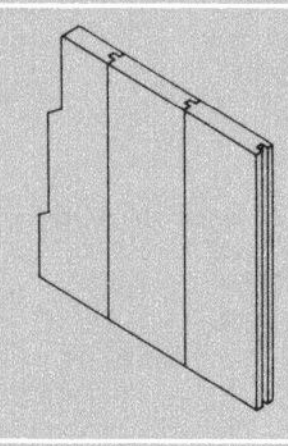 Prefabricated, movable partitions, with metal skin and mineral core, tongue-and-groove joints; 2 coats of paint on each side; Thickness, 2 inches; Weight, 5 lbs. per square foot	Incombustible, with a fire-rating of less than one hour	Fair	Poor; transmission loss, 30 decibels	Extremely flexible	
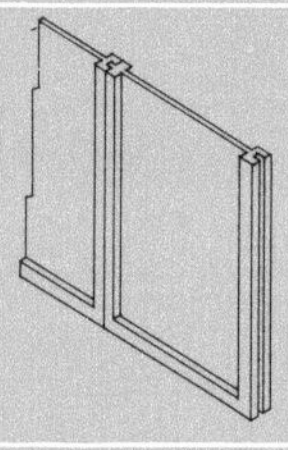 Prefabricated, movable partitions, with a locking metal frame on each side holding a metal or glass panel; Thickness, 2½ inches; Weight, 5 lbs. per square foot	Incombustible, with a fire-rating of less than one hour	Fair	Very poor; transmission loss, 25 decibels	Extremely flexible	
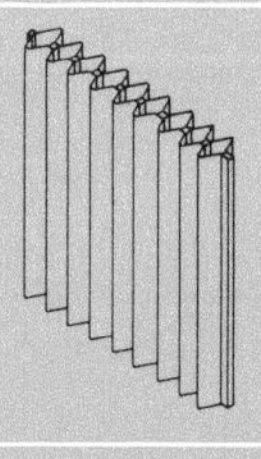 Folding partitions suspended from ceiling track, made of glass fiber material with plastic coating; Thickness, 4 to 8 inches; Weight, 1 to 2 lbs. per square foot	Combustible, no time rating	Fair	Very poor; transmission loss, 20 decibels	Practical use is limited	

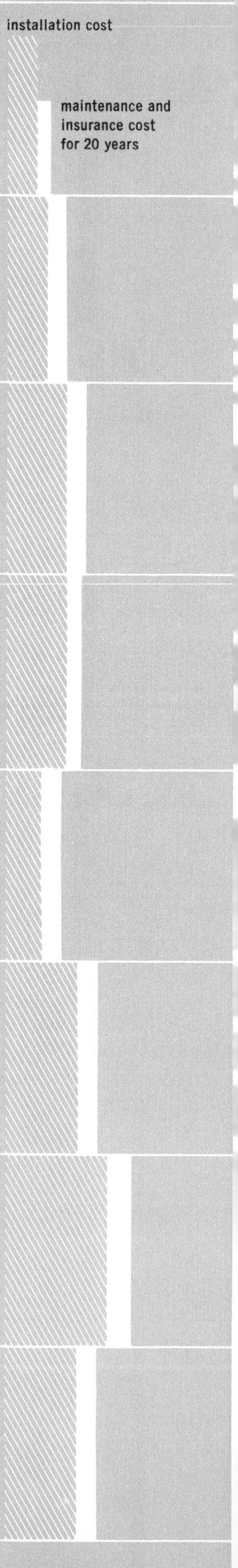

DRAWING AND DESCRIPTION	FIRE-RATING	SOIL AND DAMAGE RESISTANCE	ACOUSTICS	REMARKS	COST COMPARISON
Sliding door partitions, suspended from ceiling track, with wood surface and mineral core; Thickness, 2 inches; Weight, 4 lbs. per square foot	Combustible, no time rating	Fair	Poor; transmission loss, 28 decibels	Very flexible	
4 inch structural glass block partition; Thickness, 3¾ inches; Weight, 18 lbs. per square foot	Incombustible, with a fire-rating of less than one hour	Very good	Good; transmission loss, 40 decibels	Particularly useful for "borrowing" daylight for interior room from exterior room	

ROOFDECK AND ROOF CONSTRUCTION

DRAWING AND DESCRIPTION	DECK SPAN	FIRE-RATING	INSULATING QUALITY	REMARKS	COST COMPARISON
5 ply built-up roofing / 2 inch rigid insulation with vapor barrier / 7½ inch steel decking, painted on ceiling side	28 feet	Incombustible, with a fire-rating of less than one hour	Good; U value— .15	Very easily erected; poor acoustically unless underside receives at least ½ inch acoustical treatment; wiring for lighting fixtures can be run through cavities in deck	installation cost / maintenance and insurance cost for 20 years
5 ply built-up roofing / 2 inch rigid insulation with vapor barrier / 4½ inch steel deck, painted on ceiling side	16 feet	Incombustible, with a fire-rating of less than one hour	Good; U value— .15	Very easily erected; poor acoustically unless ceiling receives at least ½ inch acoustical treatment or deck is perforated	
5 ply built-up roofing / 2 inch rigid insulation with vapor barrier / 1½ inch ribbed steel deck, painted on ceiling side	8 feet	Incombustible, with a fire-rating of less than one hour	Good; U value— .15	Very easily erected; poor acoustically unless ceiling receives at least ½ inch acoustical treatment	
5 ply built-up roofing / 2 inch rigid insulation with vapor barrier / light weight, reinforced concrete fill on corrugated steel deck, painted on ceiling side	8 feet	Incombustible, with a fire-rating of less than one hour	Good; U value— .13	Speed of erection is fair; concrete fill process will slow down completion; underside can be left exposed, but this is not general practice unless it is acoustically treated	

DRAWING AND DESCRIPTION	DECK SPAN	FIRE-RATING	INSULATING QUALITY	REMARKS	COST COMPARISON
5 ply built-up roofing 2⅞ inch wood fiber-and-concrete composition board roof deck on steel subpurlin supports	8 feet	Incombustible, with a fire-rating of less than one hour	Good; U value— .16	Very easily constructed; underside can be left exposed or painted with joints concealed by the supporting subpurlins; Very good acoustically	installation cost maintenance and insurance cost for 20 years
5 ply built-up roofing 2 inch rigid insulation with vapor barrier 2 by 6 inch tongue-and-groove wood deck, stained, painted or waxed on ceiling side	4 feet	Combustible	Very good; U value— .12	Easily erected; deck underside is frequently left exposed, but further acoustical treatment is recommended	
5 ply built-up roofing 2 inch rigid insulation with vapor barrier 2 inch gypsum plank with metal edging, painted on ceiling side	4 feet	Incombustible, with a fire-rating of less than one hour	Good; U value— .13	Easily erected; deck can be left exposed, but further acoustical treatment is recommended	
5 ply built-up roofing 2 inch rigid insulation with vapor barrier gypsum deck (poured in place) on acoustical form-board with reinforcing steel wire and steel subpurlin supports	8 feet	Incombustible, with a fire-rating of one hour	Good; U value— .15	Fairly easy construction (the poured-in-place deck will delay completion of roof); deck can be left exposed as ceiling; good acoustically	
5 ply built-up roofing 2 inch rigid insulation with vapor barrier 2 inch concrete slab poured on galvanized steel wire with waterproofed backing attached	2 feet	Incombustible, with a fire-rating of one hour	Good; U value— .15	Erection speed is fair, the poured deck must set before being roofed; needs a hung ceiling for finish	
5 ply built-up roofing 2 inch rigid insulation with vapor barrier 2 ¾ inch nailable concrete plank with tongue-and-grooved joints, painted	8 feet	Incombustible, with a fire-rating of one hour	Good, U value— .15	Erection time is good; can be drilled and sawed; ceiling can be left exposed, but some further acoustical treatment is recommended	
5 ply built-up roofing 2 inch rigid insulation with vapor barrier 8 inch long-span, hollow core, concrete plank deck, painted	28 feet	Incombustible, with a fire-rating of two hours	Very good; U value— .10	Good erection time; deck can be left exposed, but further acoustical treatment is necessary	
5 ply built-up roofing 2 inch rigid insulation with vapor barrier, supported on aluminum roofdeck steel subpurlin supports, spaced 2 feet apart	8 feet	Incombustible, with a fire-rating of less than one hour	Good; U value— .15	Erection speed is good; deck can be left exposed, but needs acoustical treatment	
5 ply built-up roofing 2 inch rigid insulation with vapor barrier 5½ inch concrete slab, poured in place	16 feet	Incombustible, with a fire-rating of four hours	Good; U value— .13	Slow erection time; slab needs setting time; the under side of slab is frequently left exposed (painted), but further acoustical treatment is required	(cost does not include slab)

or at camp. How good was it? Didn't the professor's voice somehow flatten and seem insignificant, even if he was talking so loud that he grew hoarse (as he probably was)?

The usual answers to these questions indicate that a classroom with 100 per cent absorbent walls, ceiling, and floor would be oppressive acoustically, either inherently or through our habits of hearing —not quite so bad as an Echo Canyon, but not good either. Something in between should be about right, and fortunately this compromise can easily be reached by discreet application of any of a number of industrially produced sound-absorbent materials to walls or ceilings.

The amount of acoustical absorbent you may need in a classroom depends, of course, on how noisy the room is, and how good the absorbent is. A kindergarten needs more than the fifth grade, a music room just as much as the kindergarten. When a classroom is to be used frequently for instructing the class in small groups rather than in one constant group, additional absorbent is needed to avoid confusion (and a good big classroom is appreciated by everyone too, of course). Fortunately, children themselves have a capacity for absorbing sound that compensates for some of their famous capacity for emitting sound. It is one of Nature's nice (although incomplete) balancing acts. Their woolly clothing soaks up sound especially well in winter.

But on the other hand, the minimum of sound absorbent is recommended more as a measure of economy than anything else. Don't worry much about over-upholstering the classroom with an absorbent that you want for another purpose, such as cork pin boards. If you have an ordinary floor and include the hard reflective surfaces of the normal chalkboards and windows, you are not likely to deaden the room's atmosphere too much.

Room shapes

Because sound travels in a room in somewhat the same way a billiard ball bounces off its cushions (in the reverse from its striking angle) the shape of the walls and roof of the room bears directly on the acoustical environment. Some broadcasting studios recognize this by having adjustable walls of large wood vanes; by shifting the pitch of the vanes the room can be tuned almost like an enormous violin.

School architects are more and more going in for classrooms with roofs pitched at various angles; there is no acoustical reason why not except in one case, the arched roof. This curved shape has the unfortunate effect of reflecting sound waves into a central spot, focusing them downward toward the center of the room. Because acoustical absorbent often cannot entirely cure this, avoid arched ceilings for classroom use.

these are excellent acoustically because they do not "contain" sound. One whole side of the speaking tube is missing, and the teachers in these schools are generally enthusiastic about their feeling of complete isolation—*if* there are good partitions between classrooms.

In schools which do have interior halls, with classrooms opening off both sides, place the classroom doors so that they don't face each other across the hall. Even if doors are closed, transoms will frequently be left open, so that one classroom eavesdrops on another.

Halls can also be quite useful acoustically. In a noisy neighborhood, they can sometimes be placed between the classrooms and the outdoor noise, to function as a kind of gigantic hollow partition.

It would be less than fair to some architects and educators not to point out, as they do, that acoustics is not a perfected science; it involves a great deal of psychology too. In the Southwest, particularly, there are some "open plan" schools which do not even run the partitions between their classrooms all the way to the ceilings. This practice evolved after their architects had noticed in other schools that all doors and windows were left open much of the year because of the heat—a bigger potential area of discomfort in that climate than sound—and that the classes seemed to adjust to this lessening of sound barriers. A trick used to help classes adjust to this acoustical openness is the introduction of a low level of background music throughout the school, which seems to absorb (psychologically, if not actually) some of the distracting noises. The call for flexibility and convertibility for future classrooms is another very difficult demand to reconcile with the stubbornly bulky (and therefore permanent) partitions demanded by pure acoustical utility.

Halls

Neglected in the acoustic design of a school, a corridor becomes a huge speaking tube, down which every footstep or cough echoes and resounds. The sound of a group of pupils leaving a classroom for recess interrupts everything. The slam of a door can startle people all over the building.

So it is especially important to install as much absorbing material as possible on ceilings and walls of halls and corridors. A good solution is to cover the top several feet of the walls and the entire ceiling. Durable materials should be specified for this rough wear: cylinder block or perforated plywood, hardboard or asbestos-cement board facings with sound absorptive backings. Resilient hall floors are also important, to soften the sounds made by impacts.

In some parts of the country outdoor corridors have come into use to save money on schools, and

Music lesson

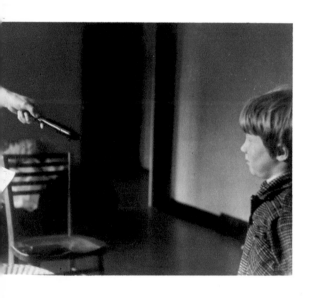

Extreme situations demand extreme solutions. If you cannot avoid building your school on a site near one of these, the situation is extreme:

—a railroad switching yard.

—a main truck route.

—bus stops, corners, or hills where much stopping or gear changing occurs.

—air fields.

—manufacturing plants which use high-pitched saws, or make other piercing noises.

—airplane or engine manufacturing plants which test airplanes in run-up operations or check engines in test cells.

Here are some of the measures you probably will have to take:

Windows will have to be sealed and double glazed. The use of a standard, fixed sash with the addition of storm sash having at least four inches of air space between the two panes would be recommended.

Ventilation will have to be obtained through a central ventilating system with sound traps and acoustical lining of the duct work. Air conditioning might be a necessity.

Entrances will have to be equipped with vestibules having two sets of doors which perform the function of a sound lock.

You will need an acoustical engineer in any such situation. His professional consulting fee will save you headaches in the end. The measures he tells you to take to sound-insulate your school in the planning stages need not always be expensive, but ignoring them can be. In one thirty-room school which had to be built near an airfield recently, the extra acoustical measures, added after completion, cost $25,000. Remember this when you go shopping for a school site, and if you are in doubt on any particular site, have your architect call in the acoustical engineer to make a sound survey before you buy.

Auditoriums and gymnasiums also should have the attention of a professional acoustics engineer. Working within the limitations the architect sketches, he can quickly calculate the correctional measures needed to make the room a good one, without ever seeing anything but drawings. This is especially important if the room is to be used both as gymnasium and auditorium, a frequent necessity today.

In general the important things to remember in planning a conventional auditorium are these:

In plan, walls should be slanted back from the stage, widening the room.

Ceilings should also be slanted up from the stage.

Concave wall shapes, or concave ceiling shapes, should be avoided. They focus the reflected sounds.

Sound-absorptive material should be put on surfaces *away* from the stage, toward the rear wall, rear ceiling, and rear side walls. The surfaces nearer the stage have to be reflective, so people in the back can hear. Don't put any acoustical absorbent on the under side of a balcony or mezzanine. If you do, anyone sitting beneath will be leaning forward straining to hear, or dozing.

A number of ingenious schemes have been devised by architects to keep noise from accompanying fresh air into classrooms, especially in the warm Southwest. These include sound chambers between classrooms which do permit air to pass through, while damping sound, and baffles outside the walls. Our consultants' tests indicate fin walls generally are a doubtful investment. Measurements of baffle walls on roofs indicated that they too are rarely necessary at that level unless the roofs have very long overhangs.

Don't expect too much of an acoustical absorbent—this bears repeating as one final warning in this section. Suspended acoustical ceilings are daily being improved and made less costly. They are excellent when used right, but not when they are taken as excuses to cut partition walls short. This is happening too frequently, with this result.

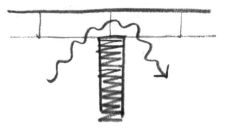

The partition must be carried all the way up to the structure, made secure and solid, even if it is a movable partition. If it is just a fence, noise will hop it.

Some decibels:

Mouse — .02 decibels

Ventilation needs are closely tied to acoustical needs, generally contradicting them. Frequently you want to close a building up for acoustics, but open it for air circulation. In planning, this means that central courtyards with classrooms arranged around them must be spacious, or the classes may disturb each other (each other's teachers, anyway—the classes may delight each other). Long rows of classrooms should not be too close, or should face away from each other. If you can separate classrooms with closets and offices, do. (But remember that a typewriter's voice is very penetrating.) The mechanical noise generated within the classroom itself is also a factor to be considered; don't install a noisy ventilator.

Hippopotamus — 100 decibels
Hemingway — 10000 decibels

How loud?

An index to some approximate sound levels:

Hamlet — 500 decibels

quiet garden	20 decibels
average background level in house	40 decibels
ordinary conversation	65 decibels
ordinary background noise in street	70 decibels
heavy street traffic	80 decibels
pneumatic drill	90 decibels
riveting machine	95 decibels
boiler shop	100 decibels
nearby thunder	115 decibels
nearby jet airplane	140 decibels

Rosencrantz & Guildenstern
— 800 decibels
(~400 decibels each)

Alas, poor Yorick
— alas, no decibels

alas:

1. 27503 decibel point

plus:

"One nation, indecibel, with liberty and justice for all"

"SUH! Your conduct with my daughter is absolutely indecibel!"

150

The first time a young girl goes out
in the evening calls for an early
start. She wavers between childhood
and adolescence all afternoon.
And when she appears, finally, in the
new dress, ready to embark—then
is when her parents' own mental picture
of _themselves_ begins to waver
between middle youth and middle age.

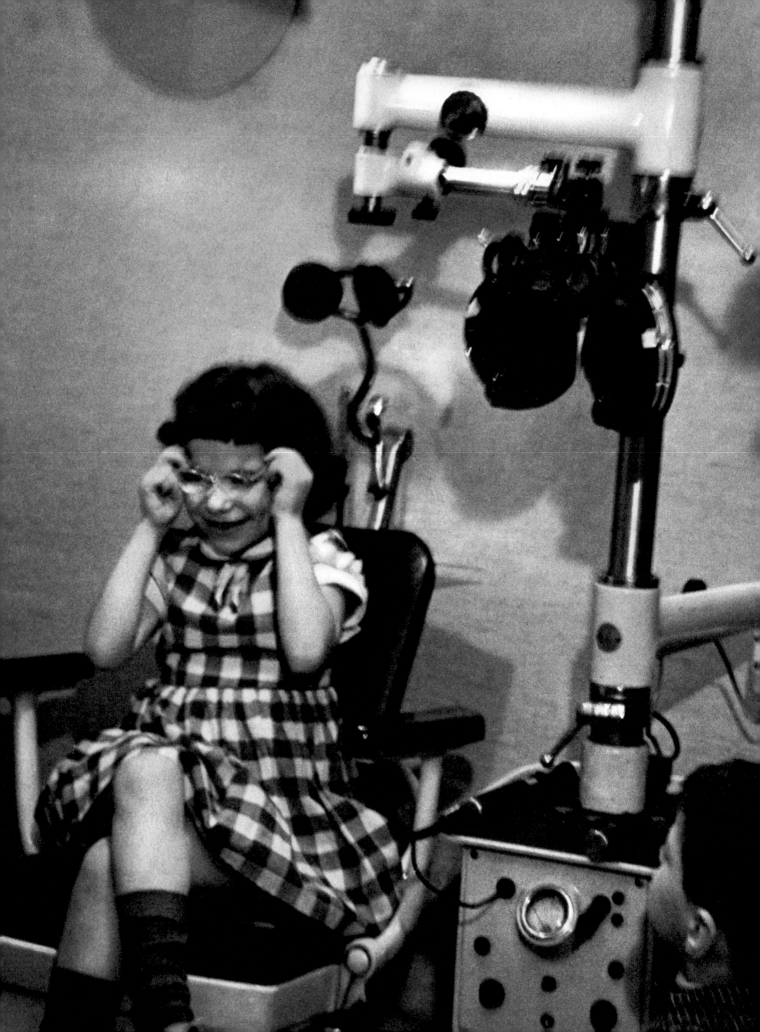

Lighting and wiring

*"There is a consumption of a quarter of the bodily
energy in the processes of seeing. When vision
is normal, the ease of seeing is controlled almost
entirely by sufficient and proper lighting. However,
when the illumination is improper or inadequate,
and when the vision is poor, then the consumption
of bodily energy is increased . . ."*

—DR. CHARLES SHEARD,
The American Journal of Optometry, July, 1936

Most of us can agree that the eye is one of the
incredible possessions of man. It can read small
type or scan a distant horizon; it performs well at
the end of a microscope or under water, in a dim
cave or on the Sahara. It is so versatile that many
people wonder why school men worry so about
lighting. The reason, as pointed out by the late
Dr. Charles Sheard: the marvelous flexibility of
the eye has its price in bodily fatigue—not just
headaches or burning eyelids, but exhaustion.

It is true that the eye passes its problems on to
the rest of the system so successfully that few people are aware of what has happened. But think of
the last time you had to drive a car a long way on
a dark night, and remember how tiring it was—
how much more tiring than by daylight.

The car seat was soft, little muscular movement
was required, the headlights of your car probably
provided pretty good lighting in just about the
right place on the road ahead, unless you were

driving so fast you were outrunning their range. What then was so tiring?

You were pushing the flexibility of your eyes. Probably in addition to your own headlights there were also other headlights coming *at* you at intervals, exploding the soft darkness into glare. At one moment you were forcing your sight to penetrate darkness, then suddenly cringing, blinking into brilliance. This is "an inadequate lighting situation." A night that is not only dark but rainy, with road reflections, can be even more demanding on the eyes. A poor TV picture also is annoying, and *annoying* in seeing means *exhausting.*

Yet most people do think that it is the amount of lighting that counts, the quantity of illumination falling on a surface—that you buy foot-candles like bananas. Actually, many experts are coming to believe that foot-candles are no more important than horsepower is to a car engine—given enough power to do the job, it is the way the power is geared or applied, its *quality*, that matters most.

How much lighting power is enough?

There are various expert recommendations. The Illuminating Engineering Society now advises having enough wattage to produce a level of 30 foot-candles at desk top height in the classroom. Special tasks, such as sewing, should have 50 foot-candles, and raising the light level even above these standards is of particular benefit in the case of subnormal eyesight. (About 20 per cent of our school children's vision needs correcting.)

But even in classrooms whose total lighting "horsepower" meets high standards, students sometimes are not able to see questions quickly and accurately on worksheets on their desks or on chalkboards across the room, and their marks—and vigor—suffer. Again, a large quantity of light is nothing to feel smug about. More important is

how the light is used, for the pupil or against.

The light should be directed where it is needed—on the work—and it should be strong enough for the most difficult task. On classroom desks there should be enough light for reading *small* type. On the chalkboard there should be enough light for seeing from the *back* of the room. (This almost always calls for special chalkboard fixtures, incidentally; a general high level of room lighting rarely suffices.) The areas surrounding the task should be somewhat less bright than the task, but not too dim. More than anything else there should be no glare—from the sky, from exposed lighting fixtures, or from shiny desk tops. Ideally there should never be more light on the eye than on the task—and this is the biggest problem in school lighting today, just as it is in night driving.

In measuring glare—and all other aspects of lighting—instrumentation is very necessary; you can't do it just by looking. The human eye cannot provide numerical readings of lighting conditions, of course. But also the eye is too adaptable, too anxious to accommodate, to be trusted. It will flat-

ter the facts. Until recently this has been a handicap to the people who have been pushing the significance of brightness in lighting. Foot-candles—quantity—have been easy to measure for a long time, using a device resembling an ordinary photographic exposure meter. Foot-candles are not what you see, however, any more than you see a breeze blowing.

What you *see* is the effect of the breeze stirring a flag and the effect of foot-candles brightening a flag. It was only about five years ago that Karl Freund invented his Spectra Brightness Spot Meter, which does provide a simple method of measuring this brightness, the *effect* of lighting, giving a reading in *foot-lamberts*, measuring conditions of the surface, not the source.

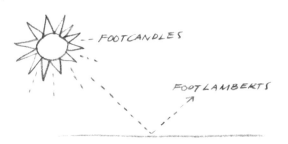

For instance, when 100 foot-candles strike a sheet of black velvet, the velvet remains quite dark, absorbing about 95 per cent of the illumination; the foot-lambert reading is only 5. But when 100 foot-candles strike a light tan tile floor, the floor appears quite bright because it reflects back about 40 per cent of the foot-candles, perhaps 40 foot-lamberts.

The differences in reflectivity of desk tops usually don't compare with the differences between velvet and tile, but they still can be significant. A matte-finish desk surface may have a 50 per cent reflection factor; under an illumination of 50 foot-candles it would register 25 foot-lamberts on the brightness meter. Under the same illumination a piece of white paper would register 40 foot-lamberts. So the difference between the reflectivity of the paper and the desk top would not be serious. But if you varnish that desk top, you will have trouble: it actually might reflect the full brightness of the light source directly into the pupil's eyes and compete seriously with what he is trying to read.

As an example of the dangers of open skies and open lamps, here are some approximate readings on self-luminous sources, which also can be read directly from the Spectra Brightness Spot Meter:

FOOT-LAMBERTS

clear-azure-blue sky 1,000
sky with high haze..............1,000 to 6,000
white clouds ....2,000 to 10,000
sunlight on green trees............75 to 1,000
sunlight on white building ....5,000 to 9,000
green grass 1,200
dry grass 2,400
bare dry ground 1,500
concrete paving 3,300
macadam paving 1,080
fresh snow 6,000
desert sand 5,000
bare 200 watt filament lamp............65,000
opal glass globe ....800 to 1,200
white ceiling above indirect-
　　incandescent fixture:
　　500 watt—30″ from ceiling ....110 to 130
　　500 watt—42″ from ceiling ....60 to 80
　　750 watt—48″ from ceiling ....95 to 120
　　1,000 watt—48″ from ceiling ....120 to 160
bare T-12 fluorescent lamp ....1,400 to 1,900
louvered fluorescent fixture ....300 to 1,700
luminous indirect fluorescent fixture...200 to 400
luminous ceiling.....................100 to 200

It is obvious that all seeing is accomplished by contrasts, by dark print on white paper or a bright rocket against a dark sky. But contrasts, if they are too sharp, can be more confusing than helpful. If the light is behind someone, you can see him in silhouette but you can't make out his face. Also, contrasts and reflections within the "task" can be disturbing. Sometimes it hurts your eyes to look at a neon sign.

To define these contrasts and describe how to use them best, lighting specialists use two jaw-breaking terms: *brightness-difference-within-the-task* and *brightness-difference-between-the-task-and-surround*. The first might describe a piece of paper and the words printed on it. The second widens to include the desk top and the floor (the immediate "surround") and also the rest of the 360-degree view, the more remote "surround." Brightness is balanced well, minimizing fatigue, when contrast *within* the task, the words and the paper, is high, but differences *between* the task, the piece of paper, and surrounding areas are low; where there is enough light and contrast for speed and accuracy, but no useless glare. Here are several general lighting objectives for a classroom (the general task illumination level is assumed to be 30 to 50 foot-candles with a 70 per cent reflection factor on a horizontal working surface) :

—ideally the task confronting the student should be at least as bright as the surrounding visual environment; slightly brighter is better.

—but this first objective is very difficult to attain, and usually it is necessary to settle for less: practically speaking, when a child looks up from his desk in the classroom, he shouldn't be confronted with anything more than *ten* times the brightness of his task. If he is, the pupils of his eyes immediately must start closing in, a process that consumes a lot of energy over the course of the many glances of a day.

—but the surfaces in view from any normal sitting or standing position should not be too dark, either, no darker than one-third the brightness of the task. If they are, the eye's pupil has to adjust too much in the opposite way, this time opening (which, however, is not so much of a strain as adjusting down against glare).

—the closer the surrounding surface to the child's task—his desk top for instance—the more essential it is that the surface not be too bright. Never, under any conditions, even if you cannot approach the ideal balance, should you permit these close surfaces to exceed three times the brightness of the task—the book on the desk, for instance. A glossy desk top sometimes will do this.

—a general harmony of brightness in the room is good, without too much contrast anywhere. Again speaking ideally, adjacent surfaces should be as close as they can to the same brightness. But carried to the extreme, this can make a very bland, flat environment. In a practical sense the lighting objectives need not inhibit an architect from using accents to liven the classroom and make it a cheerful place for the children and teacher.

The implication of this list is clear. The big point, again, is avoiding glare. Good lighting involves not only electricity and daylight, but the whole design and furnishing of a classroom as well. The reflectivity of all surfaces from the floor on up has to be brought into adjustment. The old style blackboard makes too grim a contrast. The old "schoolroom tan" or "poisonous green" paint is only a rudimentary solution to coloring the surfaces of a classroom.

Note that this lighting list is one of objectives, not standards. In school lighting, as in ventilation and fire safety, there are all too many laws stipulating not only what the final conditions should be but *exactly how* to achieve them. Charles D. Gibson, a widely respected lighting expert, comments pungently on this situation:

"It usually is faster and easier for the designer to hack out a solution from a list of standards, but this way solutions become stereotyped, progress rots in the doldrums, students and teachers live and work under minimum conditions, and those paying the educational bill are robbed. Lighting is by no means simply a matter of cost, but rather a matter of interest and technological know-how. Many poor lighting jobs cost more than a good job would have cost."

There are other costs, too, in poor lighting; many teachers have pointed out that it contributes generously to a child's learning difficulties and his subsequent dislike of school.

The easiest comment on school lighting today is: "Why worry about daylight? The teachers are going to leave on the electric lights anyway."

It is true that in our travels around the country looking at schools, we found that teachers often did have the electric lights on when they didn't really need them, when the sky was beaming down plenty of free lighting power. Many times, however, this superfluous lighting was being used, consciously or unconsciously, to obtain visual comfort by creating better balance between indoor light and "unconditioned" outdoor brightnesses. Gibson points out, "if a teacher is in a classroom that has 50 foot-candles of daylight, but looks out directly into a 5,000 foot-lambert sky, she may not *know* she has a 1 to 143 brightness ratio, but she *feels* it—and turning on the electric lights helps some. Adding 50 foot-candles of electric light doesn't bring indoor-outdoor brightness into recommended balance, but it does reduce the 1 to 143 ration to about 1 to 71, which helps out."

Electric light still cannot match daylight in force or in clarity. Even on an overcast day the sky dome is loaded with illuminating power (and dangerous brightness). Data gathered by the armed forces during World War II indicates that daylight is sufficient for lighting a school anywhere in the continental United States. But in the past, daylight was seldom controlled properly or distributed well in a classroom. The kids who sat near the window were overwhelmed by glare, while the kids on the hall side sat in dimness. It still is not easy, but designers recently have used a number of ways to bring in daylight through two or more walls—*not* depending entirely on the vision

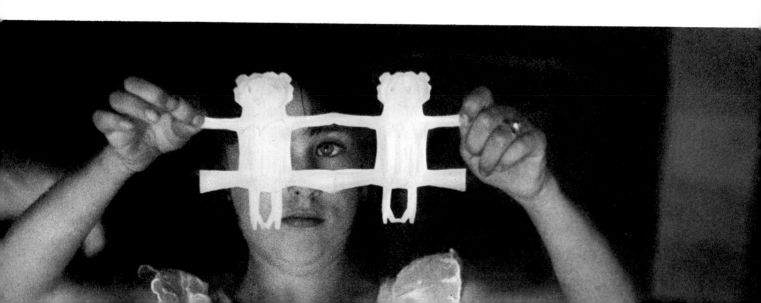

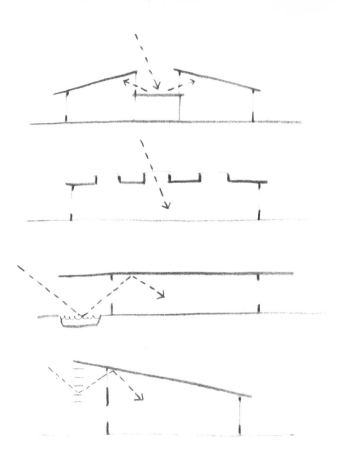

windows. This can also be done by means of a reflecting pool or a band of white concrete on the ground outside the wall carefully placed to bounce light up into the classroom. (But using concrete, you will bounce a good deal of heat up at the windows too.) Direct sunlight is seldom invited in. Nurseries or kindergartens sometimes make good use of sunshine, but in general it is too hard to handle and its germicidal powers are minor by the time it has passed through glass.

To block the excessive brightness from either sky or sunlight which develops during parts of most days, windows commonly wear many different mantles. The old standard shield, white or green interior shades, can control ordinary sky brightnesses, but if the sun strikes the shades, they light up and become sources of glare themselves, besides blocking ventilation. Adjustable horizontal venetian blinds are the conventional method today, although they have some of the same disadvantages as shades, notably blocking ventilation. Vertical blinds are coming in, too. They generally have bigger vanes than the horizontal blinds so they do not seem so enclosing; they work best on east and west exposures. Horizontal venetian blinds, however, do retain the advantage over the vertical kind of being able to bounce light up to the ceiling, dimming the glare, "conditioning" it.

Both horizontal and vertical blinds have to be adjusted carefully, of course, to cut off direct view of the sky, or they will be ineffectual in brightness control. Non-adjustable blinds, baffles fixed in place, can be quite efficient, especially when used in windows high in a wall, and horizontal louvers, properly designed and hung *outside* the building a short space away from the windows actually are the most effective deflectors in many situations. Because glare generally accompanies heat, most of

the climatizing devices used on the exteriors of buildings—overhangs, trees, louvers, and reflective screening—are also good for lighting, unless they are very dense. Some long overhangs, for instance, should have skylights in close to the windows. Another method: reflective aluminum screening, which can also assist in a subsidiary problem of shading—the need for partially darkening classrooms for showing films and slides. Fortunately, the visual aids manufacturers are developing machines which don't call for total darkness but are satisfied with dimness.

A few mechanically marvelous schools in the United States control daylight with motorized vanes actuated by delicate electronic controls, filtering the daylight differently at different hours of the different seasons, and keeping direct sunlight out. These are buildings which can depend almost entirely on the sky for year-round illumination, with little use of electrical lighting. Some of

them demand a mechanical marvel as janitor, however; their value is still mostly experimental. An easier-to-use advance has come recently from the glass industry, which has provided architects with many different tones and colors of glass, which can be used in windows to cut brightness contrasts from outdoors. Too much color in the glass can create a somewhat ghoulish atmosphere indoors, but it is surprising how nearly imperceptible a neutral color glass, for example, can be in a room if *all* windows are equipped with it.

Most schools mix daylight and electricity for a lighting solution. There is no doubt that electric light is easier to maintain. (Some daylighting skylights and windows are difficult to get at for cleaning, for instance.) Electric lights also lend themselves to easy control and do not make such demands on room shapes. But you can't simply wire in any available fixture and hope to meet the con-

ditions sketched earlier in this chapter.

There are three basic kinds of electric light sources in use today:

A *spot source,* which is man's imitation of the sun—concentrated, giving direct light and throwing hard shadows. A bare electric incandescent bulb is an example.

A *line source,* which is like a long white cloud—not so glaring as the sun, throwing softer shadows. The fluorescent tube is the electric equivalent, throwing shadows only in one direction, parallel with the tube.

A *plane source,* which is like an overcast sky when the sun is hidden—throwing a lot of light, but from a big source. There are no sharp shad-

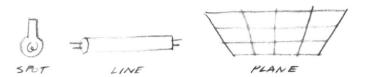

SPOT   LINE   PLANE

ows. This diffused, enveloping kind of light is produced electrically at present by "luminous" ceilings made of glass or plastic—or a metal honeycomb—with incandescent or fluorescent lamps above them, or by indirect lighting which makes the ceiling into the source. Experimental work is also quite far along toward developing a plane source that will glow by itself without any lights behind it.

Fixturing can clothe any one of these light sources in the attributes of another. For instance, an incandescent bulb can be lensed to become more like a line source, or can be pointed upward to the ceiling to become indirect, more like a plane source. Fluorescent can be banked, reflected, or lensed, changing its characteristics.

Other comparisons: the intrinsic color of incandescent generally is rather yellow, or warm, while that of fluorescent is rather blue, or cool (but phosphors and glass housings can alter the source in tone). In the variety of atmosphere it can produce, incandescent still has the edge over fluorescent. Incandescent, in a spotlight, can be

hard, concentrated, and demanding; or, used in shaded lamps, it can be soft, a pool of friendly, mellow light. Incandescent is a cheerful light; a little of it on a cloudy, sullen day helps even if there actually are plenty of foot-candles about. Fluorescent is a bland bath of light, a practical imitation of daylight.

Fluorescent fixtures consume less power than incandescent for the quantity of light produced, and last longer, but are usually more expensive to install and maintain. (The chart on page 162 gives a few comparative costs for fixtures in original price and maintenance, priced in one city on one day.) In selecting fixtures for a classroom, and in installing them, remember the list of general objectives on page 156: no fixture should be selected that has a brightness more than ten times that of the children's tasks—or, if such a fixture is unavoidable, it should be masked. Also, if the fixture is an extra powerful one, delivering 100 or more foot-candles at desk height, this ratio should be cut to *seven* times task brightness. The prescription is not so limiting as it may seem; there are many ways a clever designer can mask the source of brightness of a light bulb or tube without losing its illuminating efficiency.

One of these ways, of course, is by making the light indirect, reflecting it off the ceiling. If this is the method selected, however, be careful not to make the ceiling itself too bright. Sometimes a perfectly suitable indirect fixture is hung on too short a stem, and produces ceiling brightnesses actually in *excess* of fixture brightnesses. It is best, incidentally, to have ceiling brightnesses as uniform as possible, not spotty, which is why it may be better to use twelve 200-watt fixtures in a classroom than six 400-watt fixtures.

The problem of controlling electric lighting in classrooms is well understood by many manufac-

WINDOWS

OPERATION	VENTILATION	REMARKS	COST COMPARISON
			installed cost / maintenance and insurance cost for twenty years
Double-hung window: upper and lower sections slide vertically to open; spring balance; lock at meeting rail	Substantial airflow, but not directed well; drafty without a shield	No parts project even when open; sometimes difficult to open if schoolroom has usual shelving at sill level; usually a glass deflector is installed to prevent drafts	ALUMINUM / GALVANIZED STEEL / STEEL / WOOD
Casement window: with fixed glass section at bottom, two swing-out sections at top; crank-operated	Substantial airflow, but not directed well; drafts are difficult to avoid	Easily operated; shades can be drawn without obstruction when window is open (but they will billow in breeze); these windows must be placed carefully—there is danger of children running into them outdoors if open; rarely used in schools	A / G / S / W
Projected window: with fixed upper section of glass, vent (hopper type) at bottom opening in; crank-operated	Adequate airflow in most climates; well directed, not drafty	Easily operated, can be used with shades or blinds closed over most of its area; view is unobstructed, even when window is closed	A / G / S / W
Projected window: with sections opening out at top, in at bottom; crank-operated	Very good airflow, both in quantity and quality (not drafty)	Easily operated; does provide some ventilation even when partially shaded; view through this type is almost unhindered with few obstructions at eye level	A / G / S / W
Awning window: four horizontal sections project out; crank-operated	Large quantities of airflow are easily controlled, with fairly good draft control	Can be opened quite wide even during rainstorms; is easily operated; shades can be drawn without obstruction; framing does obstruct outdoor view somewhat whether window is open or closed	A / G / S / W
Sliding window with lower fixed section	Substantial airflow, but hard to control, drafty	No parts project either inward or outward when open, but window is sometimes difficult to slide with the usual schoolroom shelf at sill level	A / G / S / W
Combination window: upper section is of glass block, supported on angle and channel girts attached to columns; lower section is half fixed glass, and half hopper (crank-operated)	Adequate, well directed air flow for most climates	Some types of glass block refract light to ceiling, providing good light distribution across classroom and eliminating need for shades or blinds; however, designer must take care to use properly; this type does not always meet brightness tests for good schoolroom lighting	A / G / S / W

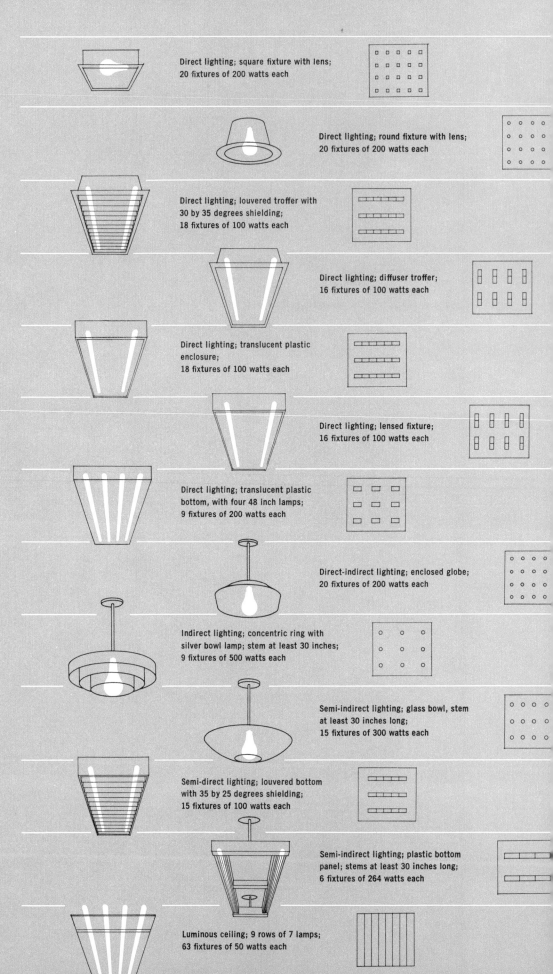

Direct lighting; square fixture with lens;
20 fixtures of 200 watts each

Direct lighting; round fixture with lens;
20 fixtures of 200 watts each

Direct lighting; louvered troffer with
30 by 35 degrees shielding;
18 fixtures of 100 watts each

Direct lighting; diffuser troffer;
16 fixtures of 100 watts each

Direct lighting; translucent plastic
enclosure;
18 fixtures of 100 watts each

Direct lighting; lensed fixture;
16 fixtures of 100 watts each

Direct lighting; translucent plastic
bottom, with four 48 inch lamps;
9 fixtures of 200 watts each

Direct-indirect lighting; enclosed globe;
20 fixtures of 200 watts each

Indirect lighting; concentric ring with
silver bowl lamp; stem at least 30 inches;
9 fixtures of 500 watts each

Semi-indirect lighting; glass bowl, stem
at least 30 inches long;
15 fixtures of 300 watts each

Semi-direct lighting; louvered bottom
with 35 by 25 degrees shielding;
15 fixtures of 100 watts each

Semi-indirect lighting; plastic bottom
panel; stems at least 30 inches long;
6 fixtures of 264 watts each

Luminous ceiling; 9 rows of 7 lamps;
63 fixtures of 50 watts each

FIXTURE BRIGHTNESS (in foot lamberts)			BRIGHTNESS AT DESK LEVEL (in foot candles)	LAMP LIFE (in hours)	POWER REQUIRED (in watts)	REMARKS	COST COMPARISON
75°	60° to 45°	22½°					
400	800 to 2200	3400	29.5	750	4000	The brightnesses of these fixtures are generally high; operating costs are also high; a suspended ceiling is required to house these; the heat they radiate may also be a problem in warm weather	installation cost maintenance, relamping and power for 20 years
400	800 to 2200	3400	31	750	4000	The brightnesses of these fixtures are generally high; operating costs are also high; a suspended ceiling is required to house these; the heat they radiate may be a problem in warm weather	
500	700 to 1250	1800	32.3	7500	1800	Fixture brightness is high; ceilings are dark; installation costs are high (a suspended ceiling is required); this fixture creates reflected glare problem; eggcrates like these are difficult to clean	
600	800	800	29	7500	1600	Fixture brightness high; ceilings dark; installation costs are high; brightness high in direct glare zone	
800	800 to 1300	1400	28	7500	1800	High fixture brightness; overly contrasting ceiling patterns	
600	1600	2000	33.8	7500	1600	High brightness values; initial cost of fixture is high, but operating costs are low	
1000	1200 to 1250	1250	30	7500	1800	High fixture brightness, especially in glare zone; if two lamps are used in this fixture, brightness is reduced but twice as many fixtures are required	
to 2000	1000 to 2000	1000 to 2000	29	750	4000	Brightness excessive and varies considerably, depending on size and shape of globe; rarely used in modern classrooms	
to 250	5 to 250	5 to 250	25.8	1000	4500	Low fixture brightness; good brightness patterns on ceiling; high wattage and operating costs, but with lowest initial cost; lamp life is low; easy maintenance; difficult to use this fixture on a low ceiling	
300	300	300	30.5	750	4500	If a relatively dense diffuser is used, brightness of fixture can be lowered; maintenance is difficult—the bowl is a dust catcher	
300	550 to 1500	1700	33	7500	1500	Ample light, but with excessive brightness (unless shielding is better than usual); poor pattern of light (unless supplementary lighting is provided); reflected glare is also bad	
225	325	350	30	7500	1600	Excellent brightness patterns; high efficiency; a relatively new type of fixture, developed to utilize new high-output lamps; becoming increasingly popular	
Brightness from various angles ranges from 0 to 200 foot lamberts in this continuous fixture (if lamps are at least 2 feet above plastic ceiling)			60	7500	3150	Excellent brightness patterns; difficult to maintain, requires frequent washing to remain effective; very high initial cost	

The History of Light

At first, every night was Dark.

Primitive Man was safe only during the day.

Then the Home was invented...

...and man was in the Dark during the Day, also.

This made Man angry.

Thus was Fire invented.

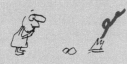

Fire meant LIGHT.

But Fire was unpredictable.

Then, several Eons later, Thomas Alva Edison was born.

He had an Idea,...

...& the Electric Bulb was Born.

The Bulb grew Popular...

...& More Popular..

...until Today there is No Night...

there is only LIGHT.

THE END

turers and architects, although such things as lowering ceilings to cut construction costs can sometimes raise new problems. But the crucial part of the lighting process, that of balancing brightness both inside and *outside* the classroom, remains difficult; again, it cannot be solved just by buying foot-candles. It needs care and study.

The unseen part of the lighting system (and an increasing number of other elements in schools) is the wiring buried in the structure. At the end of subtle ties of metal thread are such lively participants as clocks, signal buzzers, telephones, intercom systems, and fire alarms, all feeding on the elixir of the twentieth century, electricity. For economy a number of these are sometimes combined. For instance, with a little ingenuity in use, the intercom can transmit signals and alarms as well as the principal's voice. The teacher, by setting the volume of her receiver, can control the intimacy of its use if it is located at her desk. Most administrators do feel the necessity for communication with all classrooms, particularly as school plants continue to sprawl out horizontally.

The central console of such a public address system can also include radio amplifying equipment and a record player. From kindergarten to sixth grade a single-channel console, transmitting one selection, is generally adequate, but in the higher grades a two-channel console which can pipe two different programs to different classes may get good use. (The extra channel currently costs about $800.)

It is wise to leave space in the conduit runs (as pointed out in Chapter III) for TV cables too. Two other electric items to remember: put a pay telephone booth somewhere in the school, particularly if it is a high school; and in classrooms which may be used for motion picture projection, build in

a conduit from the front to the back, or from the projecting end to the screening end, to get that long electrical cord out from underfoot.

The simplest of the usual fire alarm systems, but one which is not approved by the insurance underwriters, is an open circuit, non-supervised system. The major objection: if wiring becomes defective, it may not be discovered until too late. To overcome this disadvantage, most fire alarm systems are under constant electrical check. If any wire breaks or any station becomes defective, a trouble bell rings and a pilot light goes on.

Getting the electricity into the building to feed all the circuits is a job for the electrical engineer, of course. But one important over-all decision, particularly in putting up a large building, is the practicality of stepping up from the regular voltage system. In some places codes discourage the move up to high voltage for schools, it is true, but many office buildings and numerous commercial installations have found it pays, so it may be worth a question to your professionals.

Furniture

"But fidgety Phil,
He won't sit still;
He wriggles,
And giggles,
And then, I declare,
Swings backwards and forwards
And tilts up his chair,
Just like any rocking horse—
'Philip! I am getting cross!'"

—DR. HOFFMAN,
Der Struwwelpeter

To America's biggest group of adults—those who received their high school diplomas to the uplifting strains of *Pomp and Circumstance* in the years before the end of World War II—there are many fascinating recent changes in the new schoolhouses. On the exterior, of course, there is much less pomp and a good deal more economic circumstance—fewer colonial cupolas, Greek columns, and Gothic battlements, more metal and glass. But it is indoors, particularly in the elementary schools, that the differences may be most striking. Teaching has changed, and so the equipment has changed too.

Fifty years ago education was more passive. The way to learn something was to sit quietly in a bolted-down seat, pay attention to what the teacher told you, and copy down the things she wrote on the blackboard. Needless to say, real learning is just as hard work as it ever was. But today a child is expected to learn not so much by being good as by being interested—less by sheer memory, and more by curiosity and initiative. One consequence is that a classroom today, like an efficient office, is supposed to be physically pleasant: comfortable, stimulating, and adaptable to the work of its young tenants. If the children are consistently restless it is no longer assumed that what they need is a stern talking to. Perhaps what they need is furniture that fits them—and their work—better. Perhaps they need a less monotonous atmosphere in general. Perhaps they simply need action.

Learning today is full of action. The class will write and perform a historical playlet. Or it will divide up into teams to study the industries of a country, with each team making an oral classroom report. This constant re-grouping has meant unscrewing the chairs and desks from the floors, and once that was accomplished, the way was clear for other innovations in flexibility. Today few really good classrooms have formal fronts or backs anymore except perhaps for high school lecture rooms.

The basic furniture still, of course, is chairs, tables, working surfaces, play equipment—things to sit on, to work at, to climb on—and storage to hold coats and wet galoshes and to keep teaching supplies within easy reach. Some notes on each:

Chairs

In the younger classrooms, especially kindergarten, first grade, and second grade, chairs must keep pace with the dynamos who push and pull them around. As important to a five-year-old as the shape of his seat and comfort of the back is its mobility and durability in maneuvers. Those little squarish wooden chairs popular for the past thirty years may be almost indestructible, but they are heavy to move and hard to get really out of the way. Lighter weight stackable chairs are more useful; they come in molded plywood, also in polyester plastic and glass fiber pigmented in bright colors. Some can be piled neatly on top of one another, freeing floor space for games, marching, or naps. In addition to this kind of chair, teachers point out that kindergartens should also include a few stools, a bench, a rocking chair, an easy chair or couch, some cushions, and ideally some kind of chair you can take apart and put back together.

There is confusion over the question of size in chairs. Some teachers have pointed out that it is annoying when the chairs in a class are not all the same size; there is rivalry over the bigger ones and you have to check to see if they are taken to tables of corresponding height. On the other hand, some children are bound to get the wrong size chairs if they are all identical, and this makes for fatigue and bad posture. One teacher pointed out a crying need for a chair that is small but *looks* big. If desks are used, this need is partially satisfied by the pedestal type of furniture, which has slip fittings for height adjustments. However, you can't move these around easily; and where are the children going to put their feet? Very few children of any age are capable of yogi immobility. Chair legs, in the opinion of many designers, are for wrapping human legs around, and for resting restless shoes on (if not quite so easy for cleaning men to sweep under).

One type of seating for higher grades, junior high on up—the tablet armchair—is a favorite because of the small bites it takes into budgets and classroom space. It also has been criticized on the grounds that its occupants tend to lean on the affixed tablet off-balance. In some cases shoulder distortions have been noted in children using these chairs. To avoid any such hunching and its aftereffects, a few manufacturers are now making the combination chair-writing surface with full-width tablets across the front. This also makes it easier to take care of the 11 per cent of youngsters who are naturally left-handed.

Squirming, and discomfort at sitting quietly, persist all the way through high school and beyond. Seats seem very hard. With younger children it is sometimes a matter of wrong proportions. Chairs for them should be extra long in the seat because compared with adults their thighs are long, their calves short. But partly it is just that inborn craving for action, for motion, that children

possess, which cannot be assuaged even by the most action packed curriculum. One fourth grader spoke highly of the movable furniture in her classroom because "When the teacher says to stay in your seat you can still move around a lot and she can't say you are out of your seat."

A further suggestion of the experts: if possible provide classrooms of eleven- and twelve-year-olds with a few big, soft, upholstered armchairs in an alcove to sprawl and lounge in while reading—at this age children have a way of working so furiously at things, with such intensity and enthusiasm, that they often suffer great fatigue.

Tables

Professionals call them "horizontal work surfaces" and include under this heading such equipment as a sandbox, a water trough, a laminated wood workbench for carpentry, and an asbestos-

stone composition laboratory counter. But tables and desks still remain the basic units.

Perhaps the main thing to shop for here is flexibility. Children in schools today work in large groups, in small groups, and singly, each experience having its particular values, and the surfaces they work on should be able to adjust to these changes. Of all the geometric shapes available the trapezoid seems most adaptable. A single table can be used by several children (or of course by one) ; a pair may be set up as a parallelogram or wing shape to take a group of as many as eight. Back to back, two trapezoids make a perfect six-sided unit. L-shaped tables are also useful—either singly, for small groups, or joined into U formations for larger groups, or combined to become a large rectangle. Circles are nice friendly shapes but harder to arrange.

A movable table means a light-weight one, but like most other good things this can be overdone: sometimes all a little boy has to do is scratch his mosquito bites and his table begins to slide. This ailment can usually be cured if the table's legs are tipped in rubber or some other soft material. The legs themselves these days more and more are made of hollow tubular metal to keep the weight down. The top of the table might be a honeycomb panel type of construction. First used in aircraft, these sandwiches of plywood or metal surfaces on a core of paper or aluminum honeycomb are very strong and warp resistant.

From the intermediate groups on up, individual tables with open storage beneath and flat—not angled—tops are both the cheapest and the most flexible—easy to push together into larger work surfaces and in many cases stackable for storage (soon everything in the schools will be stackable but the children). To cut the price further one manufacturer is putting out a double desk, but as usual there are arguments on all sides. Double desks are harder to move around and unpopular with some age groups because they lack a feeling of privacy. Some experts point out that a sloping surface may be less flexible, and more expensive, than a flat one, but the child who uses it doesn't have to hunch so much. Hinged-top desks are apt to be frowned on these days; fingers get caught in them, they are more expensive, and in the hands of the high spirited can turn into ideal noise-makers, a kind of semi-legitimate firecracker.

For upkeep and longevity, today's favorite surfacing materials are the melamine-impregnated veneers, not too richly figured to be distracting. Writing on such hard surfaces has its trials, however; pencil points break and finger muscles tire easily. In the upper classes where there is lots of paper work, linoleum or hardwood works better. The main thing about a writing surface is that it should be soft enough, but smooth (some kinds of wood develop ruts that ruin the painstaking efforts of children just learning to write), and for visual reasons, not too shiny. Also for visual reasons, pale colors are usually prescribed, but this can be carried too far too. An utterly blonde room soon gets drab and lifeless, too bland—like eating cream cheese sandwiches on white bread for breakfast, dinner, and supper. Some warmer birch tones pass the reflectivity tests and warm up the atmosphere of the classroom at the same time.

Vertical teaching surfaces

This means writing space and display space—and nowadays the two are likely to be combined, with the stimulation of color and texture thrown in for good measure. The demand for this kind of wall never goes down in schools. All of us, especially children, grow by seeing the things we do.

Hanging their work on the walls around them gives children a chance to step back and get a perspective on where they've been yesterday and may want to go tomorrow, and since children can be mighty productive, it takes a whole lot of wall to accommodate the paintings, spelling papers, book reports, diagrams, maps, and the endless variety and number of things they turn out in the course of a school day. It is an elementary but sometimes neglected fact that the smallest child should be able to reach the chalkboard comfortably—which means the bottom must not be more than two feet six inches from the floor. A truth more commonly overlooked is that the average child under eight actually cannot see so very well. Muscularly speaking, his visual powers are not fully developed, so he needs to be close to what he looks at. He needs movable chalkboards that are big, with big writing on them. Big portable easels are useful, too.

The old blackboards once standard in school-rooms have faded. They are gray, or green, or some other tone that will contrast with chalk but not too much and that will clean well but won't look so deadly. The cost of these writing surfaces ranges from a few cents per square foot for paint that will cover hardboard and can be written on with chalk (and must be maintained meticulously), up to several dollars per square foot for porcelainized metal writing panels (which aren't so expensive as they sound, if used floor-to-ceiling—you save money on frames). Another panel is silicate glass; its dull surface takes chalk well and wipes clean easily. Two new chalkboards: clear acrylic plastic, edge-lighted so that figures written on it pick up luminosity, and milk-white opaque glass. Dark crayons are used on the glass (cleaned with ordinary floor wax), which may also be used as a projection screen. And of course there is the standard slate as a chalkboard.

A few display surfaces that can take thumb tack punishment gracefully are (in approximate order of cost, starting with the least expensive): fiber board; coarse burlap, colorful felt, or vinyl plastic mounted on fiber board; rough cork; soft natural pine; and finely grained cork. This last is particularly handsome. It looks almost like suede (smudges can be cleaned with sandpaper) and it holds tacks better than rough cork. Walls of perforated metal panels with golf tees as pegs are fine for display and they can also be loaded with acoustical absorbent. Another handsome wall covering consists of fabric with a quarter inch layer of foam rubber behind it, for sound absorption. Incidentally, a detail, but one of those little ones that can make a big difference in the end both in cost and in use value, is the design of the wood or metal strips used as a finish to cover the seams on display panels—if these are prominent enough to get in the way when very large murals or exhibits have to be hung, it sometimes is better to leave them off.

A complete vertical teaching wall system designed by a New England architectural firm is now on the market. In this setup panels of various sizes and materials—including bulletin boards, chalkboards, even screens for film projection—are mounted on tracks fastened to the wall. They can be shifted and interchanged quite easily to conform to the needs of the particular class. Less elaborate track systems are also available.

Storage

The better equipped the classroom, the more acute the storage problem. Fortunately, storage is one area where both the manufacturers and the school designers shine. In fact the problem is not finding good storage units in the first place, but fitting them into the classroom without cutting down on teaching space. Ordinary ingenuity is one answer: for example, unit ventilators—the kind that go under classroom windows—can now be bought in sets with metal shelving to fit in the spaces between them, spaces that might otherwise be wasted. Another answer is what is called dual usage: the combination of storage with display, or storage with chalkboard, into what is known as a working wall. Custom built, but of standard components, these walls can be set up permanently to assist as sound buffers between classrooms, or for that matter, within a single classroom where certain group activities noisier than others have to be allowed for.

Still a third answer is, again, flexibility. Some of the more sensible new storage pieces come on wheels so that they can be rolled to the part of the room where they will actually be used, then rolled out of the way (perhaps into their place in the working wall) when they are finished with. One such wagon can be outfitted with audio-visual devices, projector, tape recorder, etc., and travel from room to room when needed. Naturally, these days storage stacks too—again, for flexibility.

A "flexible" classroom, incidentally, does not mean that every half hour or so everyone gets up and moves all the furniture around. Not to mention the trouble involved, nobody can work in an atmosphere of utter impermanence. So-called flexible school equipment is often flexible not so much from hour to hour or even day to day, but from room to room. In other words it is produced in standard units for the budget's sake, but in units that can be combined to suit the special needs of an individual room and its occupants. Stackable storage is a case in point. It can be low for six-year-olds, high for twelve-year-olds. It can be used to create alcoves in a kindergarten, say, where children oppressed by the mob (and to a five-year-old, a group of twenty-five others sometimes does seem like a mob) can get off with maybe two other children and relax. Also, since each child learns best at his own pace, today's classroom can sometimes seem like the three rings of the old circus tent. In a fourth grade class one "ring" may have a group of advanced spellers doing fifth or sixth grade work while a different group which has trouble with spelling is being helped with phonetic sounds in another "ring"; the third may have youngsters who are clipping and pasting magazine pictures which illustrate the meanings of the words they are studying (and humming to themselves while they're at it). All this goes on at the same time! Flexible storage units that can be used for partitions are very valuable here to keep distractions at a minimum.

Space-saving is a major aim in classroom storage but by no means the only one. Storage should be geared to the children—that is, low enough for them to reach, with hardware that they can operate easily. Sliding doors, for instance, are fine space savers but unless they are well designed they tend to stick and fingers are likely to get caught. Especially with younger children, storage should be organized simply enough so they can find what they need by themselves—though not so simply that it is all automatic. Making small choices is an important, if rather interior, part of learning in the younger grades. A five-year-old, playing Indian, may drag a piece of lace out of a scrap box, put it over his head and give out with a fine realistic war whoop. But a year later he will know enough to select feathers for his headdress. He knows this because he has had experience in making choices. For this reason storage in general in the lower grades should not all be massed in one place. It should be distributed through the room so a child can explore its resources—sifting over

different materials to find what he needs.

Storage in schools should include both open shelves and closed cabinets. Having things on view naturally lends a certain gaiety and stimulation to the atmosphere—and of course some kinds of storage are really display anyway, particularly in fourth and fifth grades when children are at the height of the "collecting" phase. But too much equipment on view is confusing—and sometimes less fun. A take-apart airplane that comes out of hiding now and then is an exciting event for a six-year-old—especially if you have to unlock a door to get it. Keys and locks have a kind of magical appeal for the very young. Covered storage is of course easier to keep clean too.

Special storage—for music rooms, print shops, science labs, etc.—is difficult, even dangerous, to generalize about. This calls for specific programming with the teachers who are going to direct the space. Only the conductor knows how many saxophones, bassoons, and harps are likely to be lurking in the shadows, and he should be asked.

Another special problem—coat storage—has no easy solution because what is needed is not only security but ventilation, especially on rainy days. Louvered doors are an answer but only if air is pushed toward them and pulled through them. Open-sided storage in hallways works fairly well, though it sometimes look sloppy. Incidentally, very young children have better luck putting on their galoshes from a low platform than from a chair. They are likely to fall out of a chair.

Play equipment

Old-fashioned swings, slides, and seesaws are still favorites throughout elementary school, but they do have limitations. They are a little monotonous. Many children may want to swing in a swing every day—but not for more than ten minutes.

There are many ways of playing, and they tend to go in and out of fashion according to the age of the child. In lower elementary school, play is apt to be both inventive and repetitive—involving dolls, "dressing up," toy cars, and the like. For sheer exercise, hitting a ball with a bat has little appeal as yet; they much prefer climbing, crawling, jumping, and the other more massive maneuvers. Games are often informal, with simple rules created on the spur of the moment and easily changed. For these reasons, the new sculptural playground equipment is very popular with younger children. They also like a little house on the playground—and indoors, too, for that matter.

In upper elementary school, children begin to get interested in competitive athletics—baseball and football become terribly urgent at ten or eleven —but they still in their own way enjoy the simpler pleasures, including climbing on a jungle gym type of structure if it is a challenging enough one, or the more creative efforts involved in making something or other (perhaps unrecognizable to an adult) out of an old tire, a piece of rope and some cast-off boards. At this age the child adores junk, his romantic imagination is set afire by it, and what he would really like on a playground is an enclosed space full of it, as described in Chapter II.

Some pieces of play equipment can be made light enough to come indoors for rainy day use. And of course some strictly indoor materials are convertible to the same purpose. The metal framework of a working wall, stripped of writing and display boards, makes a fine jungle gym. Telegraph pole rungs can be attached to a column.

Not for play, but special in their own way, are two other pieces of equipment that teachers consistently ask for. One is a sink in the classroom—considered essential in lower elementary school

and useful through sixth grade. The best kinds are free-standing and circular so that eight or ten children can use them at once. The other is something to cook on; a stove or hot plate. Elementary school children love to cook, boys as well as girls, and their enthusiasm creates an opportunity for learning which goes beyond mere culinary techniques. Cooking involves reading, mathematics, and nutrition as well.

A final word on equipment and furnishings: they are as endless in their variety as a toy shop combined with a housewares department. And they provide a wonderful opportunity to make an environment for children that is warm, friendly, and instructive at the same time. But sometimes it is overdone. The purpose of classroom equipment is to help a child develop and extend his abilities and resources—not to do all the work for him. For this reason, an old wind-up phonograph might be better in lower grades than hi-fi. In one kindergarten, a well equipped and realistic doll house lost favor when a few of the children set up a scrap of felt and an old prune box on the edge of a platform and brought their dolls there to play. The new site was better, at least temporarily, because they had made it themselves.

And don't overdo at the cost of the teacher. Remember that although she—or he—is not charged actually with cleaning and vacuuming the classroom, she does have to keep it in order. She will be harassed and unhappy if it is so gimmicky that this is impossible. This is why the best furnishings and equipment must be a part of the school concept—the programming and design—not thrown in later.

Heating and plumbing

"If I were a bear,
*   And a big bear, too,*
I shouldn't much care
*   If it froze or snew."*

Furry Bear, *Now We Are Six*
                    A. A. MILNE

There are many ways to describe hot and cold situations; the most emphatic emphasize not just the physical pain of the freeze or scorch, but the agony of mind it produces. Heating scientists know this; although they use musty words—thermal situation, environmental condition, and physiological behavior—they recognize the urgent inner nature of comfort and the outer effects it produces.

"If the environmental conditions are not optimum, they [children] do something about it," L. P. Herrington, a leading environmental physiologist, has pointed out. "Not practically, but in terms of physiological behavior. That is, to a far larger degree than adults they boil over with restlessness in a cold room, daydream in hot rooms, seek the light in dark rooms, whisper in an ultra-quiet room and compete with noise in an environment with high acoustic level. In short, in contrast to the adult, they 'optimize' the environment more directly and with less regard for schedules and the requirements of a prescribed activity."

Pity the teacher in a hot or cold classroom. The class may *pessimize* her. Comfort—their comfort and hers—is not a luxury, but a physical and mental requirement.

Awkwardly enough, there is a definite difference in thermal comfort between the children and the teacher herself, especially in the lower grades. Because of their higher metabolic rate, children are happier in a somewhat cooler climate than adults—usually about 5 degrees cooler. Why? Because they burn energy faster, producing more heat, and have less skin surface with which to dispose of the heat. As they grow older (and possibly become teachers) this changes, especially in the case of females; physiologically, women, especially elderly ones, want warmer rooms than males. Nor can adults tolerate thermal extremes as readily as children can. A little boy can run a 104 degree fever with ease—all he needs is to be tucked into bed for a day or so; if the teacher hits 104 degrees the doctors will tuck her into the hospital.

And there is still another point about school heating that is sometimes forgotten: even when the thermometer plunges in cold weather, classrooms in most parts of the U. S. may still need to be *cooled* more than *heated*. People are furnaces; when thirty-five children enter an empty classroom whose heating equipment has brought it to a comfortable 72-degree temperature, the kids, each with a temperature of about 98.6 degrees, go warmly to work themselves. In an hour the room is going to be definitely warmer—in fact, hot, if nothing is done about it. A well-known heating consultant, Henry Wright of New York, several years ago ran an experiment on a classroom in Moline, Illinois, on a cold day. He found that the room needed heat put into it only from 7 to 8:30 a.m. and again between 12 and 1 p.m. Heat had to be *removed* the rest of the day.

Basic, of course, is the ability to provide the right kind of warmth in the school at those times when warmth is needed. An empty classroom, in the early morning, presents the same challenge, thermally, as an empty theater in the early evening; although the audience itself takes over a large part of the heating job after it arrives, the room must first be made pleasant to come into. Even if a heating system has to pour on the thermal units for only two hours in a day, the

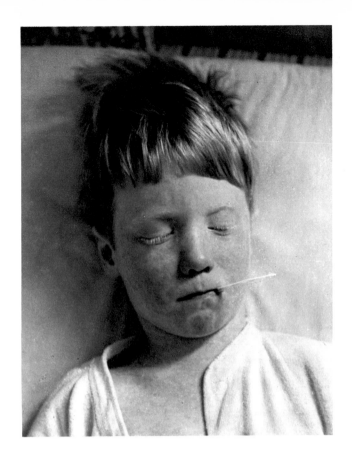

hour in the morning before the kids arrive and the lunch hour (when they are off heating up the cafeteria), it is this rush hour "design peak" that dictates the size of the heating plant. The right kind of warmth implies also air which is not too humid, too dry, or stale, for the liveliest teacher can't make up for a really stuffy atmosphere.

So the heating engineer, frequently taken for granted, carries a heavy load—including a large fiscal responsibility. Indoor climate costs a lot of money in most parts of the world. In recent years, Architect John Lyon Reid points out that mechanical services in schools in his locale, the West Coast, used to amount to about 28 per cent of total cost, but by 1954 they had crept up to 36 per cent and by 1957, in one school, to 41 per cent. Furnaces, fans, and other equipment are not only a major budgetary factor in building a school, but their maintenance and fuel cost is the heaviest fixed annual expense over most of the U. S. A school of 20,000 square feet, costing $300,000 to build, may well have an annual $3,000 heating bill.

Heating starts with choosing a fuel. This in

turn may determine the apparatus which will convert this fuel to heat, and may also heavily influence the method of distributing the heat throughout the building. In some areas, of course, the fuel chooses the school. A school district standing in the midst of a group of gas domes has very little need to exercise choice of judgment. Similarly, coal, oil, and direct electric current are sometimes the only conceivable choice because of their availability or because of the climate.

Most school districts, however, are in overlapping areas of available fuels, where choosing the wrong fuel may raise the heating bill by as much as 50 per cent. At that, the right decision cannot really be made merely by picking the fuel with the least cost. A number of other factors conflict, and must be weighed professionally by the architect and his consulting engineer in a process sometimes called a *fuel survey*, involving heating plant, school shape, construction, labor costs, availability of technical supervision, insulation, glazing, ventilation, automatic controls, and boiler efficiency.

For an example of one of the many factors affecting fuel choice, if your school is large enough to be considered a heavy fuel consumer, you will pay less per unit of fuel than a light consumer. However, bulk buying at lower cost implies two conditions: accessibility and storage, which both add initial expense. You must consider such innocent details as whether access roads can support heavy delivery trucks. (Electricity and gas, of course, need no storage.)

Another point: heating value of the fuel must be taken into account. A gallon of fuel oil, for instance, will produce about 140,000 B.T.U.—enough to heat an average classroom forty minutes. A cubic foot of manufactured gas will produce about 400 B.T.U., which will heat the classroom about five seconds; a cubic foot of natural gas will produce about 1,200 B.T.U., about eighteen seconds of heat. A pound of coal will produce about 12,000 B.T.U., heating the classroom about three minutes. A kilowatt-hour of electricity is enough energy to heat it about two minutes.

The favorite fuel for schools today probably is oil, which is available everywhere in one grade or another. Each grade of oil dictates its own heating plant, however, which by a sorry but familiar law of economics varies inversely as the cost of the fuel. The cheapest grade of fuel requires a plant of abounding complexity and expense.

To burn No. 6 fuel oil, which is thick, viscous, and cheap, you need this array of apparatus: large tank, expensive burners, tank heating system, fuel pumps, and complicated ignition, including a gas pilot lighter. And to ride herd on this jumble of equipment you need a diligent and technically trained janitor. At the other end of the scale is No. 2 fuel oil, light, distilled, comparatively expensive. But all it needs is a simple low-cost domestic type burner.

Your fuel survey may well surprise you by strongly favoring that "old-fashioned" fuel, coal, which is still a steady and reliable workhorse. Coal is available in many areas at a relatively low cost. Disadvantages: storage bunkers are essential and are even bulkier than fuel tanks; equipment may also be even more complicated than for No. 6 oil, and maintenance is more difficult.

Your engineer's study may very possibly recommend natural gas over coal or oil—not manufactured gas, but the "hotter" natural gas. Like coal, this is a "found" fuel; like electricity, it needs no fuel storage tanks; like oil, most packaged furnaces and boilers can be adapted to it. Coal, strictly on the basis of fuel cost, may be the most economical fuel, but for most large schools the usual *overall* annual cost calculations for economy today will still favor No. 6 oil or natural gas.

Electricity remains something of a question mark for school heating. Although it may own the future, especially when atomic generation comes down in cost, there are only a few areas where it is feasible economically today. Even in mild states like Florida, whose heating demands are so minor that the low installation cost favors electricity in theory for all fuel, there are sometimes electricity shortages to take into account.

When you have a line on fuel, then you begin thinking in terms of furnaces to turn it into heat. Here you will enter the realm of codes and regulations. Because of the hazards connected with combustion, a number of authorities—the National Board of Fire Underwriters, fuel associations, and municipal and state units of government—will advise you and watch you. Fortunately your engineer can choose among many good furnaces.

Cleanliness may help him to decide. Gas and oil are clean fuels and quite efficient, averaging around 75 per cent. Electricity is 100 per cent efficient. Coal can be another matter; even handled by motor-driven stokers, bunkered below ground, and with skilled operators, coal seldom exceeds an efficiency of 70 per cent. And even when a conscientious operator can keep a coal burning system fairly clean, he must also contend with ash removal and disposal, which is probably the heaviest maintenance job in the whole school.

The most widely used oil burners in schools are the *pressure atomizing,* the *horizontal rotary cup,* and the *air atomizing burner.* The pressure atomizing type (the service man will call it a gun burner) is mostly limited to light No. 2 oil and will usually serve economically only in small schools. The rotary cup burner can handle all grades of oil. The air atomizing burner, generally used with "packaged" steam generators, includes a small integral air compressor to assist in atomization, and also can burn all grades of oil. Dual fuel burners are available for burning either gas *or* oil, and can be switched if shortages should develop in either fuel, or if either should become a better buy locally.

If you select gas as your fuel, you will find that an additional agency, the public utility, will want to approve its burner system and controls. One caution: some gas burners employ high-speed blowers, which can be peculiarly noisy.

Choosing a central heating plant, the next element in most heating systems, involves another decision: what medium—hot water, steam, or air—is going to transmit the heat to the rest of the building? If steam or hot water is chosen, a family of roughly similar boilers may be used. These range from the *cast-iron sectional boiler* through the *Scotch marine* (a boiler developed originally for use in ships), the *packaged steam generator,* the *fire tube steel firebox,* and the *water tube steel firebox.* Your architect and engineer will go about choosing from these on the basis of cost, compactness, and capability.

Warm air, as a medium for heat, implies bulk; warm air furnaces are probably central heating's biggest space-gobblers. The reason: air, unlike water or steam, is not a compact vehicle for carrying heat. The trade winds are warm, but coffee is hotter. An institutional type warm air furnace, which is what a school has to use, needs a wide, slow-moving centrifugal blower and capacious channels, or it will be noisy. Also, unlike boilers, air furnaces seldom come in pairs, and so they seldom possess standby capacity. Other conditions: there is a practical limit to the size school in which warm air can be used for heating; a separate water boiler is needed for making hot water; and small boilers by their very nature cannot use heavy (and cheap) oil.

But warm air heating plants have unique advantages too. Like the trade winds, the warm air furnace can, with certain modifications, ventilate as well as heat. Even better, with a few more modifications and enlargements to a warm air heating plant a cooling system can be added.

So far we have selected a fuel, and a fuel burning system. The heat, at this stage, is packed into steam, hot water, or warm air. Now the problem is moving the heat from the furnace room to the classroom.

Steam, by definition, is water that is hot enough to turn into a vapor, and it is not too difficult to pipe to the classroom. There it will drop its cargo of heat and, in doing so, revert to water, or as engineers call it, *condensate*. Thus an additional problem arises: how to return the condensate to the source of heat.

One of the simplest, and cheapest, ways of accomplishing both tasks is by means of the *one-pipe steam system* in which the steam drops its passenger, heat, and travels back to the furnace in the same pipe. The one-pipe steam system is simple and inexpensive to install, durable and easy to maintain. But, alas, it can only be controlled in two ways: full-on, shut-off. It is rarely installed in a modern school.

Next to the one-pipe steam system in simplicity and low cost is the *two-pipe, open circuit, pumped return system: two-pipe*, because it has a separate piping system for detouring the condensate back to the boiler; *open*, because the condensate is open to atmospheric pressure and flows back to the boiler by gravity; and *pumped return*, because a pump gathers the returned condensate and forces it back

into the boiler, to be loaded with heat again and sent on its way. Unlike that of the one-pipe system, its heat output can be controlled in each classroom within certain limits.

More complex, but usually worth it, is the *two-pipe vacuum steam system*. This variation adds a vacuum pump to the return system, which puts the system under complete control at all times. It is capable of handling low temperature steam of 160 degrees as well as steam at 240 degrees. And although it does add to the initial building budget, careful operation can eke out long term fuel economies over the course of a few years.

Hot water, as a vehicle for carrying warmth around the school, is a great deal like steam in principle, but it can be handled more simply. Small air vents replace the steam system's complicated steam traps. The hot water circulating pump is cheaper than steam condensate or vacuum pumps. And the temperature of the circulated water can be varied widely (and rapidly), enabling a good operator or a good system of automatic controls to save a lot of fuel.

At present, the first cost of a good hot water heating system is about the same as that of a two-pipe vacuum system, the only steam system that can match it in over-all performance. Total long term costs usually favor hot water over steam because maintenance is cheaper, but the most important feature of hot water systems really is the fine control possible. A range of water temperatures from as low as 90 degrees Fahrenheit to 210 degrees can be ordered and delivered.

To get back to the trade winds, the inherent advantage of a warm air system is in the combination of all the required climate control functions it can provide: heating, cooling, humidity control, ventilation. Indoors, there are two usual ways to move the air from the furnace room through its ducts and on to the classrooms.

One choice is to provide a twin air-duct system —one duct carrying *heated* air from the furnace, and the other cool *unheated* air throughout the school. At each classroom a mixing box with dampers is provided, which can draw air from either the hot or the cold duct; the mix is regulated by a thermostat in the classroom.

The second method (really no more than a modification of the first) is a kind of octopus arrangement of ducts; all the air for each room is heated, humidified, and mixed at the furnace itself, and the network of ducts runs from the central furnace directly to each classroom. In effect, the mixing chamber for each class is exiled to the boiler room, in a central assembly.

The first scheme is more logical for big schools, while the second is limited to smaller ones.

By one means or another we've got heat to our classroom. The heat may be "loose," in air itself, or "packaged" in steam, hot water, or possibly in electric current. If packaged, the heat now has to be unwrapped in the classroom. An engineer calls this is a problem of *heat exchange*—from one medium to another. This can be done by convection (normal air movement over heated surfaces—hot air rises) or by radiation (the "glow" of warmth). Some of the familiar devices used: cast-iron radiators, convectors (cast-iron or finned tubes), warm air vents or diffusers, unit heaters, unit ventilators, and radiant heating surfaces.

To make this explanation less simple, engineers

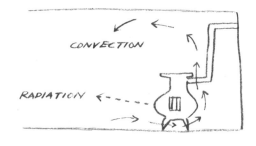

point out right away that the common *radiator* actually distributes 80 per cent of its heat energy *not* by radiation, but by convection. Air passes the radiator's surface, is warmed, rises, moves across the room, cools, drops, and moves back to be warmed again. Although misnamed, the standard radiator remains a good basic device for some uses. Its initial cost is in the middle range and its durability is little short of amazing. Radiators outlive men, buildings, perhaps civilizations. However, they are awkward looking objects, take up a lot of valuable floor space, are hard to clean, and are architecturally inflexible. They are also hot to touch and may be a "bump hazard" to active children in classrooms.

Convectors come in five types—steel, copper, aluminum, stainless steel, cast-iron—all of which wear metal fins. Architecturally they are very flexible because they can fit any plan, and can be recessed and concealed easily with grilles, or even set into the floor near doorways.

The real radiators are *radiant heating surfaces* —whole floors, ceilings, or walls warmed by buried piping, ducts, or electrical resistance wires. These surfaces provide silent, still heat of a very comfortable kind; they heat the occupants of the room not by heating the air first, but directly, as the sun does on the ski slopes of Sun Valley. In the usual radiant heating system, hot water is run through continuous coils of flexible piping imbedded in a floor slab. This is particularly popular for kindergartens. The floor is nice to play on in winter— even to dry socks on.

Hot water piping can also be run in ceilings to radiate heat downward. This is usually a little more expensive than floor slab installations (more skill is needed in completing concealment), but because no one actually touches the ceiling, the radiating surface can be hotter, and thus more

SCHEMATIC DRAWING	DOES THIS SYSTEM:	VENTILATE AND FILTER AIR?	CONTROL TEMPERATURE?	CONVERT TO SUMMER COOLING?	REMARKS	COST COMPARISON
Unit Ventilator (with finned tube extensions) under windows; pulls outdoor air through louvers, heats, and disperses it about room with fans; exhaust air is carried out by ducts above corridor ceiling; a two pipe hot water or steam system		Yes	Very good in all seasons; quick and sensitive	No, except for forced air circulation	Occupies considerable space in classroom, but little in central heating room; if not carefully maintained, fans may get somewhat noisy	installation cost / operating, power and fuel cost for 20 years
	Unit ventilator, similar to one above with addition of chilled water lines to central compressor room for summer cooling	Yes	Very good in all seasons; quick and sensitive	Yes	Occupies considerable space in classroom, but little in central heating room; if not carefully maintained, fans may get somewhat noisy	
Finned baseboard convector, extending across exterior wall near floor level; Air is warmed by convecting surfaces, rises, crosses room; central duct for ventilation and air supply is in corridor; a two pipe hot water or steam system		Yes	Fair in all seasons	Yes, but only if ducts and piping are insulated and special drainage system is provided in original installation	A quiet system; requires little classroom area but considerable central fan room area	
	Finned tube convector, hung on wall under windows; air enters through window, is heated, rises in convection pattern, and is exhausted through ducts in corridor ceiling; a two pipe hot water or steam system	No	Fair in spring and fall, poor in winter (except in mild climatic areas)	No	A quiet system; requires little classroom area and moderate central heating room area	
Metal pan radiant ceiling; prefabricated metal units make up ceiling and contain pipeways for two pipe hot water system; heat radiates downward; air is supplied and exhausted by ducts		Yes	Good in all seasons	Yes, but only if ducts and piping are insulated and special drainage system is provided in original installation	A quiet system; requires no usable space in classroom and moderate area in central heating room; pan ceiling may also include acoustical treatment	
	Forced warm air, delivered into room through grills under windows; air is mixed in fan room, sent through floor ducts and exhausted through corridor ceiling ducts	Yes	Very good in all seasons	Yes, but only if ducts and piping are insulated and special drainage system is provided in original installation	A quiet system at normal velocities; requires moderate space in classroom, but considerable area in the central heating room	
	Hot and cold air, delivered by ducts to mixing box beneath floor of room; mixed air is introduced into classroom through grills under windows and exhausted through corridor ceiling ducts	Yes	Very good in all seasons	Yes, but only if ducts and piping are insulated and special drainage system is provided in original installation	A quiet system; requires moderate space in the classroom, but considerable space in the fan room	
	Radiant floor slab; contains pipe coils through which hot water (a two pipe system) is circulated; air is supplied and exhausted through corridor ducts	Yes	Good in all seasons	Yes, but only if ducts and piping are insulated and special drainage system is provided in original installation	A quiet system; requires no usable space in the classroom and moderate space in the central heating room; needs careful temperature control; heat lag is sometimes a problem	

SCHEMATIC DRAWING		DOES THIS SYSTEM:	VENTI-LATE AND FILTER AIR?	CONTROL TEMPER-ATURE?	CONVERT TO SUMMER COOLING?	REMARKS	COST COMPARISON
Direct fired unit; ceiling-hung, it heats the room air which, after circulating, is exhausted through ceiling ducts; natural gas fired			No	Good in fall, fair in spring and winter	No, except for fan effect	Noisy; occupies considerable space in the classroom, but no space in the central heating room; seldom used in classrooms	installation cost / operating, power and fuel cost for 20 years
Electric panels, set in ceiling, radiating heat downward; air is supplied and exhausted through corridor ducts			Yes	Good in all seasons	No, unless complete system is added to utilize ductwork in the corridors	A quiet system; requires no space in the classroom and little space in the central fan room	
Cast iron radiator; roof fan exhaust; two pipe hot water system			No	Fair in spring and fall, poor in winter	No	Roof fan might become noisy; radiators take up considerable space in the classroom, are difficult to keep clean, and are hazards unless enclosed	

EXTERIOR WALL CONSTRUCTION

DRAWING AND DESCRIPTION		FIRE-RATING	INSULATING QUALITY	MAINTE-NANCE	REMARKS	COST COMPARISON
8 inch concrete block, water-repellent paint on exterior 2 inch foam insulation applied with cement mortar to concrete block ¾ inch layer of plaster, painted thickness, 11 inches; weight, 50 lbs. psf		Incombustible, with a fire-rating of three hours	Very good U value—.14	Fair, soils somewhat	Weightbearing; expensive for framing windows; very good condensation control	installation cost / maintenance insurance cost for 20 years
8 inch concrete block, 1 inch cement stucco on exterior ¾ inch layer of interior plaster, painted thickness, 9¾ inches; weight, 52 lbs. psf		Incombustible, with a fire-rating of four hours	Poor U value— .48	Some problems with soiling and weather-resistance	Used only in mild, dry climates because of conden-sation problems; weight-bearing; expensive for framing windows	
4 inch concrete block, water-repellent paint on exterior 2 inch cavity (air space) 4 inch concrete block, painted thickness, 10 inches; weight, 46 lbs. psf		Incombustible, with a fire-rating of three hours	Fair U value— .28	Fair, some soiling	Limited weightbearing capacity; expensive for framing windows; good in-terior acoustical finish	
4 inch exterior face brick 2 inch cavity 4 inch common interior brick with ¾ inch layer of plaster, painted thickness, 10¾ inches; weight, 48 lbs. psf		Incombustible, with a four hour fire-rating	Fair U value— .27	Fair	Limited loadbearer; expensive for framing windows	

DRAWING AND DESCRIPTION		FIRE-RATING	INSULATING QUALITY	MAINTE-NANCE	REMARKS	COST COMPARISON
						installation cost
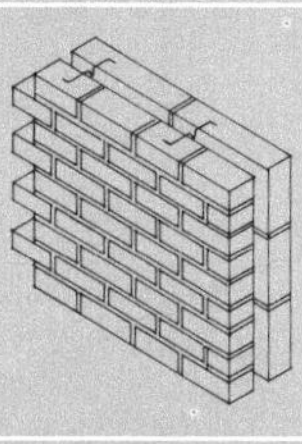 4 inch exterior face brick 2 inch cavity 4 inch concrete block, painted thickness, 10 inches; weight, 46 lbs. psf		Incombustible, with a four hour fire-rating	Fair U value— .28	Fair	Limited loadbearer; some-what expensive for framing windows	maintenance, insurance cost for 20 years
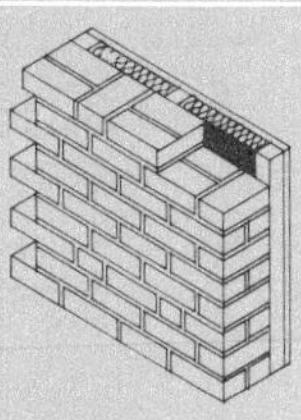 8 inch face brick, damp-proofing 2 by 2 inch furring strips, spaced 16 inches apart metal lath and plaster, painted thickness, 10¾ inches; weight, 52 lbs. psf		Incombustible, with a fire-rating of four hours	Good U value— .15	Fair	Weightbearing; good conden-sation control; somewhat expensive for framing windows	
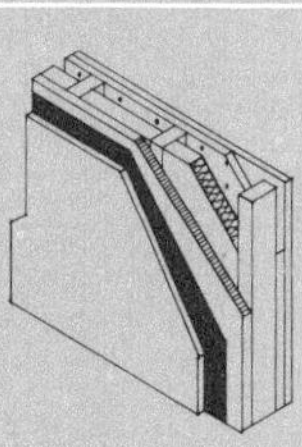 1 inch cement stucco on lath and building paper ¾ inch composition board sheathing 2 by 6 inch wood studs (spaced 16 inches apart) with 4 inch mineral insulation layer between gypsum rocklath and plaster, painted thickness, 8½ inches; weight, 30 lbs. psf		Fire retardent, with a fire-rating of about ¾ of an hour	Very good U value— .10	Poor, some soiling, poor endu-rance	Limited loadbearing; easy for framing windows; very good condensation control	
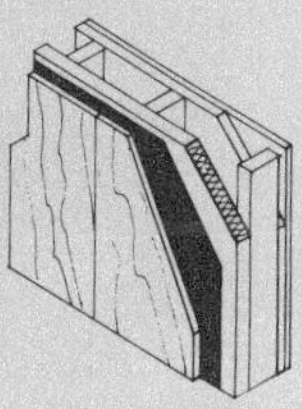 ⅜ inch waterproof plywood, stained, and building paper ¾ inch insulation board 2 by 6 inch wood studs, spaced 24 inches ½ inch composition board ¾ inch interior grade plywood, stained and waxed thickness, 8 inches; weight, 15 lbs. psf		Combustible	Fair U value— .24	Fair	Limited loadbearing; easy for framing windows; a fast wall to build	
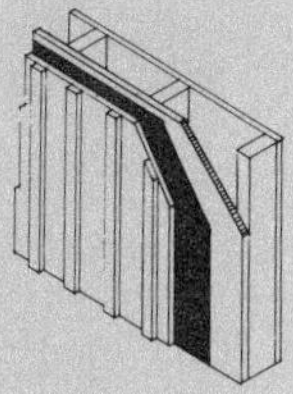 ⅞ inch wood board-and-batten, oiled or stained finish, and building paper ¾ inch insulating board 2 by 6 inch wood studs, spaced 16 inches ½ inch wallboard, with taped joints, painted thickness, 8 inches; weight, 15 lbs. psf		Combustible	Good U value— .20	Fair	Limited loadbearer; windows are easily framed; a fast wall to build	
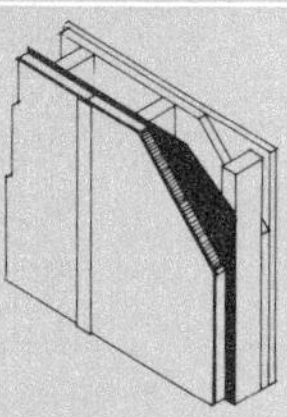 2 inch asbestos-cement composition panels, held in aluminum grid, and building paper 2 by 6 inch wood studs, spaced 24 inches ½ inch wallboard ⅜ inch composition panels, painted thickness, 8½ inches; weight, 14 lbs. psf		Combustible	Good U value— .15	Good	Limited loadbearer; win-dows are easily framed; asbestos-cement is somewhat brittle to handle, but wall can be built quickly	
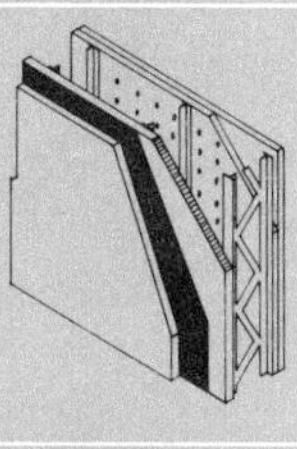 1 inch stucco on self-furring lath, and building paper ¾ inch composition board sheathing 4 inch nailable steel studs, spaced 24 inches apart gypsum lath board and plaster, painted thickness, 7 inches; weight, 32 lbs. psf		Incombustible, with about a ¾ hour fire-rating	Fair U value— .22	Fair	Limited loadbearer; easy for framing windows	
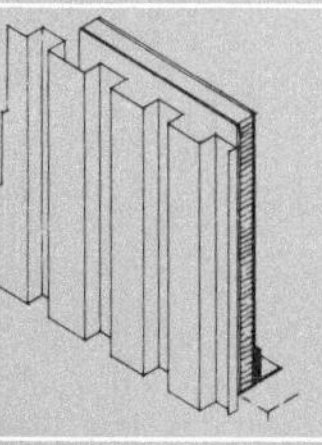 16 gauge extruded aluminum sheathing "sandwich" panel of 1½ inch rigid insula-tion, clad in 18 gauge steel (primed and painted) thickness, 3½ inches; weight, 6 lbs. psf		Incombustible, but still not rated in many building codes	Good U value— .15	Good	Nonloadbearing; these pre-fabricated components become a "curtain wall" hung on framing; very light, can be built quickly; unlike most of the other walls, the price **with** windows will be lower than that for solid wall (given right)	

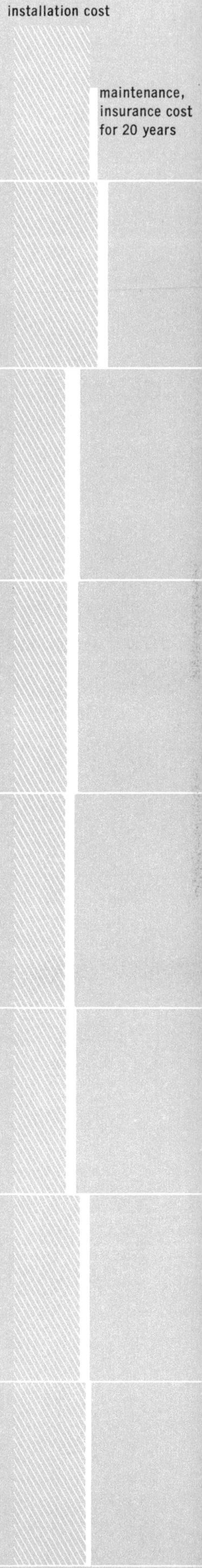

DRAWING AND DESCRIPTION	FIRE-RATING	INSULATING QUALITY	MAINTE-NANCE	REMARKS	COST COMPARISON
"Sandwich" panel with 2 inch glass fiber core clad in 16 gauge galvanized steel, to be installed in steel frame with plastic gaskets, primed and painted, inside and outside thickness, 2½ inches; weight, 5 lbs. psf	Incombustible, but still not rated in many building codes	Good U value— .18	Good	Only fair provisions for condensation; easily demountable, wall can be built quickly; windows can be inserted with ease; price (psf) **with** windows actually will be lower than price for solid wall, given at right	installation cost maintenance insurance cost for 20 years
Ventilated "sandwich" panels with 2 inch glass composition core plus air space, clad in porcelain-enameled aluminum or steel facing interior galvanized steel facing panels installed in aluminum frame with glazing beads and plastic gaskets thickness, 2½ inches; weight, 5 lbs. psf	Incombustible, no time-rating	Good U value— .15	Good	Can be made to bear load by strengthening frame; a prefabricated component, it facilitates construction, and can be removed easily to revise building; cost of wall **with** windows will be less than cost of solid wall shown at right	
"Sandwich" panel with core of foamed plastic or composition glass, 2 inches thick, sheathed in aluminum or steel porcelain enamel exterior finish installed in aluminum frame with glazing beads and plastic gaskets thickness, 2½ inches; weight, 5 lbs. psf	Incombustible, but still not fire-rated in many areas	Good U value— .15	Good	A prefabricated panel, it is easily mounted when building, demounted when remodeling; frame can be strengthened to become loadbearing; cost of walls **with** windows will be less than cost of solid wall shown at right	
⅞ inch clapboard siding, finished with primer and paint, and building paper ¾ inch Insulation board 2 by 6 inch wood studs, spaced 16 inches 3 inch mineral wool insulation between studs ½ inch wallboard with taped joints; painted thickness, 8½ inches; weight, 16 lbs. psf	Combustible	Very good U value— .12	Fair	Limited loadbearing; easy for framing windows	
Natural stone, 12 inches thick vapor barrier 2 by 2 inch furring strips metal lath and plaster, painted thickness, 15 inches; weight, 125 lbs. psf	Incombustible, with a fire-rating of four hours	Poor U value— .30	Good	A handsome wall if the right mason is chosen and given enough time; load-bearing, permanent, inflexible; difficult for framing windows	
4 inch exterior face brick 6 inch concrete block, and vapor barrier 1¾ inch metal lath and plaster, painted thickness, 11¾ inches; weight, 54 lbs. psf	Incombustible, with a fire-rating of four hours	Poor U value— .30	Good, soils somewhat	Loadbearing; expensive for framing windows; good condensation control	
Window-wall with one thickness of "double-strength B" glass in a 4 inch wood frame, with an operating hopper at top or bottom thickness of glass, ⅛ inch; weight, 2 lbs. psf	no rating	Very poor U value— 1.14	Poor	A good wall in moderate climates, but one which demands careful shading from heat and glare; poor condensation control; poor acoustically	
Welded, double-glazed window wall, with two layers of "double-strength" glass separated by partial vacuum in 4 inch wood frame, with hopper at top or bottom thickness, ½ inch; weight, 4 lbs. psf	no rating	Poor U value— .67	Poor	A handsome wall if used appropriately in moderate climates; needs shading; good condensation control; fair acoustically	

efficient. Sometimes warm air is used with radiant systems and released into the classroom after being moved through channels in the floor or ceiling.

In schools radiant heating installations do have two disadvantages: they usually need supplementary heating—convectors or radiators—at the windows to kill cold downdrafts sliding off the glass; they are sometimes slow in reacting to changes in the weather. A radiant slab, for instance, heats up slowly, and after it is warm it is not easy to cool if the sun suddenly swims from behind rain clouds and raises the general temperature. Recently, however, this disadvantage has been offset by the development of aluminum pan radiant ceilings, which lack the phlegmatic bulk of slabs. Radiant pan heating also has the economies of mass fabrication; it is a school heating system with considerable economic promise.

The problem of air movement and ventilation is large in schools, particularly if you use a warm air system; in delivering air from the ducts, you can't just dump it into a room. It used to be that you could let it rise—hot and dry—through registers from room to room, but today's buildings have abandoned that primitive pattern. Today it is accepted that the air coming into a room must be mixed with the air already there to prevent drafts and currents—chill or hot. This mixing is done with baffled or vented diffusers manufactured by a number of companies.

Standards for air movement are not yet based on rigid scientific findings, but at least this much is known: air movement at a rate of less than fifteen feet per minute causes a feeling of stagnation; at more than sixty-five feet per minute loose papers will flutter on the desks. Another related problem is that cool drafts are less tolerable than warm ones, which means that cool air must be circulated at lower velocities than warm air. All high velocities (more than twenty-five to thirty-five feet per minute) must be kept above or to one side of the occupied area.

The ventilation of classrooms is a favorite subject of many city and state codes. These codes usually prescribe in great precision the number of air changes for a given space, or the amount of fresh outside air which must be supplied to persons within a given space. For example, a classroom of twenty-five pupils must, according to one typical code, provide at least ten cubic feet of fresh air per pupil per minute (no matter how the room is heated—by hot water, steam, or air). The same code requires at least six changes of air per hour for a locker room, although twelve changes are recommended. In the opinion of engineers, architects, and medical men, many of these demands, based on outmoded principles, are excessive; the codes stipulate arbitrary air quantities, where they should concentrate on how much air is required for cooling and eliminating smells. Much more important than these general high ventilation requirements, but less discussed, is the matter of relating the thermal environment to the type of activity for which the space is designed, from gymnasium to sewing room.

There are two self-contained systems for creating and distributing climate inside the classroom. One is like a truck, powerful but rough; the other is as smooth as a new car. The first is the *direct fired unit heater*, frequently a safety hazard in the classroom, a noise-maker, and an architectural wart. However, it is cheap.

The other, the *unit ventilator*, is a packaged individual room unit with fans, filters, coils, and controls. Steam or hot water lines bring its basic heat from the furnace room, but it can be prescribed precisely to fit each room's climate. Usually delivered in a trim looking metal cabinet, set in under the classroom window, its fans control the ventilation pattern of the room, even when the windows have to be closed and darkened for showing slides. Unit ventilators are not cheap and they require alert maintenance because they do contain motors; if you don't take good care of them they sometimes get noisy. But they have another advantage. It is not hard (although it *is* expensive) to turn the newest models into effective air conditioners by adding a chilled water line leading to a central compressor in the central mechanical equipment room of the school.

This brings us to a big, sometimes embattled field of the school thermal situation. Many business firms actually figure they save money by investing in air conditioning equipment—their employees do better work if they are comfortable. In the same way, efficiency in learning may be the pay-off for cooling schools. Advocates also insist that air conditioned schools will make the twelve-month school feasible, and point out that the twelve-month session could yield the equivalent of a 25 per cent increase in classroom space, although it creates problems too—in family vacation schedules, for example. Further, since an adequate school ventilation system is usually required by codes anyway, and a system of ducts adequate for forced warm air needs very little enlargement to become adequate for complete air conditioning, air conditioning may actually cost less in school buildings than in many other building types.

The conventional air conditioning system in a building as sizable as most schools centers in a compressor, roughly equivalent to the furnace used in winter. This produces a cold liquid, a refrigerant, which may be pumped in pipes to fan units or used directly to cool air which is then sent through ducts throughout the building. The refrigerant can also be pumped through radiant pipe systems, but here normal summer humidity usually raises condensation problems.

The easiest kind of air conditioning is by evaporation, but this is practiced only in dry areas like New Mexico. Its simplest mechanism is a wet bale of hay with a fan blowing through it, but even the most complicated evaporative cooler is less complicated than complete air conditioners. The most intriguing air conditioning apparatus, one which is becoming very popular, is a device which pumps well water out of the ground as the source of comfortable coolness in summer. More surprising, it uses the same stable well water as a source of warmth in winter, when heat is literally pumped out of the ground. Hence its name—the heat pump.

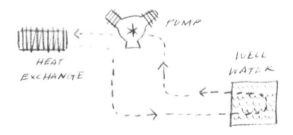

It would not be worth the trouble to heat and ventilate (and maybe cool) a school, and then abandon it entirely to the whims of the machines and their operators. In addition to the constant barrage from the sun and wind outdoors, a building's temperature faces constant internal insurrection from changing population, lighting loads, and room uses. The answer? Automatic controls, which not only rule the indoor weather impartially, within the reasonable average of comfort, but as a dividend may also save fuel—as much as 20 per cent per heating season.

Automatic controls have three main elements: a sensing mechanism, such as a thermostat; a communications system, wires or tubes which transmit the findings of the sensor; and an actuating unit, to do something about it. The simplest systems are self-contained, but these are rarely used. Electrical systems (found sometimes in smaller schools) are sensitive, but often a little cranky. Pneumatic systems are both sturdy and sensitive. And recently, electronic systems have been introduced which extend the range and degree of control even further by combining the best parts of several of the other methods.

Controls begin in the area to be heated (or cooled) and end in the furnace room. The highest degree of automatic control is achieved in schools by making each classroom an independent zone with one or more coordinated thermostats—an ideal arrangement, but an expensive one. Another, lesser, degree of control is achieved by taking all the classrooms on a single exposure (west, for example) and zoning them together on a single control. This method is cheaper than doing it room by room, and it does average comfort out on the warm and chilly sides for most of the classrooms. (Not infrequently the sunny side of the building needs cooling and the shaded side heating at the same moment.) Some schools use a single control for an entire building. This method can only be described as averaging out the discomfort.

Controls can also include such modifications as automatic operation of ventilating equipment and automatic reduction of room temperature at night and during weekends. Frequently thermostats are posted to stand guard outdoors to anticipate changes in heating demands by noticing fluctuations in the weather. These are particularly important in radiant systems.

Heating pipes compose only a part of the school's piping. Other basic jobs are to supply drinking and washing water, to dispose of water and waste from all fixtures, and to take care of basic fire protection by keeping water available on tap at sufficient pressure.

Like heating, plumbing sometimes seems routine because it is regulated thoroughly in both methods and materials: local codes, state codes, and the recommendations of engineering societies, manufacturers, and the United States Chamber of Commerce combine to guard against a number of common perils, such as back-ups of sewer gases, build-ups in water tank pressures, and release of scalding water. (Methods include traps, vents, relief and mixing valves, and many other protective devices.) As in all other legislated building fields, some codes do go beyond the function of intelligent protection to muffle the inventiveness of plumbing designers. If your community has no code of its own, most engineers recommend nothing more finicky than the National Plumbing Code, an intelligent, safe guide sponsored by the American Standards Association.

The basic worry in all plumbing systems is contaminated water, and this danger is by no means an antique threat, to be shrugged off. The board of health in a very civilized eastern state found in a survey not long ago that of 740 of their schools examined, fewer than half had pure water supplies. As school sites get larger and larger, more and more districts build on farmland away from convenient utility lines, and the danger rises.

About thirty gallons of water per pupil per day must be available in schools (flushing a toilet uses from four to six gallons), so the problem of supply is not simple in terms of quantity, either. The usual methods for obtaining water, if you cannot simply connect a pipe to a city system, are wells, springs, cisterns, sometimes even surface streams. Of these methods, a deep well is usually the safest —and most expensive, of course; most frequently it is drilled down through a layer of rock or clay to get at its pool, and the dense strata overhead act as a covering shield against impure surface water. Generally a deep well also has the most consistent and predictable yield.

Few wells, deep or shallow, can simply be turned on and off, however. The school day has strong peak demands for water (the highest is at lunch hour), and water usually has to be stored to be available in sufficient quantity when the faucets are opened. There are two ways: the gravity system, which perches a water tank on the roof of a tower, pumps water up into it, and then lets it flow down into the school upon demand; and the pneumatic, or pressure, type which pumps both air and water into a tank to push the water uphill, if necessary. Controls are essentials for each type, especially the latter; too much air pressure can blow a tank apart if there is no safety valve.

Many state and community health departments require treatment of well water for school use. This is not complicated. A chlorinating injector pump can usually be installed for under $500. Don't plan fluoridation, of course, without community approval; its equipment, incidentally, for a 300-pupil school would probably run about $750.

In some areas where the water table is sinking, schools use one prime supply for drinking and shower water and a less perfectly potable source for general washing and flushing. This sounds good, but demands careful policing of the plumbing in years to come so that no careless connections cross circuits. This method will also mean an increased first cost for piping; you need more lines. In general, the safe economies in plumbing design can be put quite tersely: use the right materials, consolidate pipe runs and insulate them well, try to avoid excavation, don't over-design, keep the layout compact. (To do this designers try to place toilets, showers, etc., back to back on two sides of a plumbing wall.)

Besides water, you need hot water, and usually hot at two different temperatures, 180 degrees for washing dishes and 130 degrees for washing pupils. Both degrees of hot water are often a product of the over-all heating plant in the school. If not, a number of good packaged hot water heaters are available. The danger of scalding is met in two ways. Some schools keep the water at 130 degrees for general safety, and for special uses like dishwashing send it up to 180 degrees by means of separate booster heaters located near the kitchen. Others use the higher temperature water in conjunction with tempering valves, a system which costs far less than separate heaters. However, tempering valves are not infallible; lime, which is present in most water, sometimes forms a coating on a valve and makes it stick, letting scalding water through.

In most states and municipalities there are specific minimum standards for toilet facilities in schools, calling for nothing more than centrally located, well aired rooms containing minimum numbers of fixtures. As far back as Mark Twain's day, however, the refusal to be satisfied with the minimum in bathrooms seems to have been a dominant American trait. A conducted tour of a friend's new house, according to Twain, always began with the gleaming bathroom.

Tours of many new U. S. elementary schools today reveal small individual toilets and lavatories attached to a number of the classrooms, and there are stronger reasons than pride for this. It is easier on both teacher and children; the seven-year-old doesn't get lost wandering down the hall, and the teacher doesn't lose time finding, or convoying, him. Also, at seven, children have been observed by psychologists to have a strong feeling for privacy, preferring a single small, homelike bathroom; and at eight, a stepped up bladder frequency, which fortunately relaxes somewhat after a year or so.

After about third grade embarrassment sets in, and some psychologists say it might be better to have bathrooms slightly more remote—down the hall. Still later, the problem of supervision sometimes changes to one of outwitting children; the amount of tampering, up to and including vandalism, that takes place in toilet rooms of many schools is astonishing. Plumbing fixtures in schools are more expensive than in most houses because they have to take harder wear, frequently abuse. Wall-mounted fixtures are favored, rugged ones with as few projections as possible (it is also easy to swing a mop under them).

Vitreous china seems to wear the best in fixtures; sheet metal and some plastics have joined ceramic tile as standard wall and stall surfaces. One thing that seems to help a good deal in maintenance of bathrooms is a flood of electric light— the warmer tone fluorescents, combined with a colorful wall or two in the room, make it look pleasant, make the children look nice in the mirror, and so they seem to act better too.

It is easy to match children's sizes in toilet equipment; water closets, for instance, come in sizes ten and thirteen inches high as well as the standard fifteen inches, and it is simple to set sinks lower than adult height. If water pressure is good (at least twelve pounds) most engineers recommend flush valves for water closets and urinals instead of the older type tank systems. These flush valves are noisier, but more efficient, and

noise reducers for them can be bought for about one dollar a fixture. These are recommended because the fury of flush valves frightens some young children; so do black toilet seats.

According to the Public Health Service, the best way to get rid of sewage, if you lack an easy link to a public sewer line, is by way of an adequately sized septic tank, and a field system. Bacterial action reduces the sewage in the septic tank to a less noxious condition, and the end products are a sludge which settles in the tank and a liquid effluent which flows out in the field in a network of loose-joint tile piping which permits its cargo to seep out and percolate into the soil.

Some of the important considerations in locating the disposal field are:

—allow ample area for the tile field, plus a margin of safety to the nearest property line.

—be sure the ground is porous enough, fairly level, and relatively free from rocks, boulders, and danger of settling or sliding. (Soil porosity is determined by a standard percolation test.)

—place the field, if possible, below the septic tank to encourage gravity flow, and near enough to preclude extensive sewer lines.

—keep away from large trees or shrubs. Roots can grow into the tile pipes and destroy them.

—double-check the danger of contaminating nearby wells or other sources of water supply.

If local conditions are really bad—non-porous soil and a high water table—the disposal of the effluent can be a problem. Sometimes the only answer is a small sewage disposal plant; fortunately for the taxpayer this situation is relatively rare with schools. If you use a septic tank, don't forget to have the septic tank itself inspected and cleaned every year or so; contrary to widespread faith, it is not a bottomless pit.

Heating notes

For a year after the construction is completed and the school is occupied, there is a proper period of adjustment, of *tuning,* for the mechanical system, which corresponds to the breaking-in period for an automobile. During this period the architect's and engineer's services, advice, and consultation should be available quickly.

In first and sixth grades (ages five and a half to six, and about eleven) physiologists have noticed a particular lability of internal temperatures in children. Says Dr. Frances Ilg, "Everything is rapidly shifting, blowing hot and cold, expressing extremes. In the first grade you can observe this with the sudden pulling off of a sweater, especially with the girls during an arithmetic period. I have known their body temperatures to rise to 102 degrees during the intense intellectual demands of the arithmetic process . . ." For this reason it may be particularly wise to try to provide separate room control of heating in the first and sixth grades, to meet this extra thermal problem when addition class begins.

To heat the scattered buildings of a campus type school, two courses are open: an individual heating plant for each building; or central heating. For the central system, which pipes its heat to each of the "campus" buildings, steam is the commonest medium, although high temperature hot water is a growing competitor. Individual heating units for each building can eliminate the expense of pipe tunnels and trenches and the transmission network of insulated pipe. Nevertheless, central heating usually works out better because fuel can be burned more efficiently (and purchased more cheaply), less janitoring is needed, and first cost of the single central plant is usually considerably less than the sum of the individual plants.

Architects and engineers (and janitors) frequently complain that schools still seem to expect nice old janitors, beloved by small children, to operate, regulate, adjust, and maintain complex heating and cooling systems which rightfully should get the attention of cold-hearted specialists. Sometimes, as a result, operating costs are high and maintenance deplorable. To help prevent this the very least that should be done by the architect and engineer when such a system goes in is to provide the operator with a full set of instructions and diagrams; better, a brief training course should be run off for the school's custodial personnel. The school system should free the personnel for this process; manufacturers generally are glad to help instruct too.

In certain heating plant work the real cost is hidden because the work is performed by a contractor of another trade. For example, excavation for a buried fuel tank is usually included in the general contractor's charge, but is really the result of what heating system you choose. Awareness of these hidden cost items can lead to sub-stantial savings. Here are other examples:

For a one-story building, a steam heating system, because it requires a crawl space or trench for the condensate return mains, means you must lower the boiler room floor. (Digging this trench can be expensive.) If, however, a hot water heating system is chosen instead, the return piping may be run overhead, with the boiler room on a level with the classrooms.

Natural draft chimneys, generally included under masonry work, require foundations and brickwork. A mechanical draft fan may effect a saving in this "hidden" cost.

Here is a sample comparison for one school:

Natural draft chimney
Chimney and foundation,
36" x 30" x 40' high . . . . $2,000.
Boiler room excavation,
20' x 25' x 10' deep . . . .   600.
Fan, including wiring
and controls . . . .   ———
                            ————
                            $2,600.

Induced draft fan and low chimney
Chimney and foundation,
28" x 24" x 20' high . . . . $1,000.
Boiler room excavation . .   ———
Fan, including wiring
and controls . . . .   900.
                            ————
                            $1,900.

Preparing a class of little children
to face the weather can be a staggering
task. The invention of the zipper
did not solve it.

Design

Everything must finally come together. All the aspects of school building discussed in earlier chapters in the end must be assembled, fitting the budget, the program, the children. The tailor for this job is the architect, and eventually, after all the conferences, directives, outlines, and programs, he must take his shears off into the cutting room, cut the pattern, and send it to the contractor to be stitched together. Your school district should get a good fit out of it and if you're a rapidly growing young district, future alterations should not be too difficult.

You may get something even more if your architect is a master tailor, a man whose imagination is a constant pull toward fulfillment of what made him an architect in the first place. It isn't just pride or ambition that makes people work in the PTA or run for the school board; chances are that it wasn't just the choice of a clean, dry way to make a living that made him into an architect. An architect properly is not a pure artist, but an artist of utility. Yet, when all the practical aspects of the program have been met, when all the coat closets and thermostats, and chalkboards and ductwork are figured, the most deeply utilitarian thing the architect can do for a community of parents, administrators, teachers, and children is give them a school building they like, perhaps love.

This is more than difficult; it calls for much more even than concentration and labor or deep knowledge. It calls for a cross between sculpture

School for Delinquent Children

FREE
ROOF PARKING
kiddies !

COME TO SCHOOL
AVOID PARKING
PROBLEMS

JOHN PAUL JONES SCHOOL

BOYS   GIRLS   VEHICLES

Detroit School

Detroit School Bus

PS 7-11
BIGGEST LITTLE SCHOOL IN THE WORLD

PS 7·11

BOYS GIRLS

NO COVER MINIMUM

TRY YOUR
LUCK
WIN AN
A+

Reno School

ST. EMILIA SCHOOL

GOOD
BOYS

GOOD
GIRLS

BAD
BOYS   BAD
GIRLS

Gothic School:
The Little Red Cloisters

P.S.8 P.S.8 P.S.8 P.S.8 P.S.8 P.S.8 P.S.8

BOYS GIRLS LIONS FRIENDS ROMANS COUNTRY MEN

Roman School:
The Little Red Colosseum

P S 8

Greek Revival School
The Little Red Parthenon

School Chariot

and poetry. This may sound starry-eyed, but, for a moment, recall how you may have been stirred into a kind of passive pleasure by certain buildings you have visited—a receptive state of being interrupted mentally in all the ordinary grocery-getting routines of thought. Perhaps you have stood in a cathedral and felt this aloneness with a building, sensed peace and security from the walls and their unity with the space and the idea they enclose. There are certain schools that can give you a little of that.

Do you remember loving a tree-house when you were a child? Have you stood in a barnyard and drawn pleasure simply from looking at the rich power of the beams of the barn? Have you sat in a living room with glass walls and sensed the sympathy of the house for nature—and the seeming reciprocal sympathy of nature for the house and for you?

Architecture is something that most people are not aware of in a primary sense. It is confused often with nostalgia, sentimentality, or awe, because these are a few of architecture's most blatant tools. A building is silent and still while its users talk and move; so sometimes we think we are reacting to them, not to it.

Yet the community that has a great building in it, or even a good building, gradually becomes aware of the fact, although it may take years. And because we all move in a man-made world, one of

these fine buildings, belonging to everyone, should yield a sense of great personal reassurance of man's eventual success in whatever it is we are all trying to do.

Schoolhouses are a wonderful opportunity for this. They belong to all of us, of course, and those who use them most—the children—are a wonderfully aware, unprejudiced group. They are very responsive. Most of the man-fashioned world into which they must grow is extremely ugly. If they can learn what is good by being sent to school in a pervasively good building, it may not be too much to hope that they may form standards that will help them improve some other surroundings which they will reach later.

So give your architect a fair site and a fair budget; he may improve your community the way nobody else can.

Following is a collection of photographs and a number of details from schools by a number of architectural firms. These are "successful" schools but they are by no means represented here as a group judged the continent's best. Other architects have perhaps done better ones (the same architects may also have). These pictures were selected after some months of search because we admire them and because they assemble reasonably well into a tour of the physical and visual satisfactions good schools can offer.

New York City School Bus   Oklahoma School Bus

From the air

Wilbert Snow Elementary School in Middletown, Connecticut, is the campus type. Small four-room schoolhouses are dispersed among the saplings and taller trees on this beautifully wooded slope, avoiding complicated foundation problems. The gymnasium, lunch facilities, and other central functions are concentrated in larger buildings. Architect: Warren H. Ashley.

Loft-plan school—Hillsdale High School, San Mateo, California— borrows an industrial pattern for economy and great flexibility. Skylights, not windows, are the primary source for daylight, and some interior classrooms get along fine with no windows at all. Partitions are lightly built and completely movable. Architects: John Lyon Reid and Partners. (In the background, a smaller school, Abbott School, by Architects Falk and Booth).

School-within-a-school — Syosset High School, Syosset, New York— divides a large building into neighborhoods of age groups, each in its own wing of classrooms grouped around a central high-roofed multi-use room, all sharing cafeteria, auditorium, and gymnasium (the bigger building blocks). Junior High School will be built across green to the rear; meanwhile these younger classes will be accommodated in two of the high school wings without getting lost. Architects: Eggers and Higgins.

Perhaps none of the photographs in our cross-country tour better illustrates the sociology of school building in the United States since World War II. This community is in one of the newer suburban areas of New York City. In the background (west, toward the city) lie new housing developments. Still holding out in the foreground is farmland. To the left: the commuting route, the Long Island Rail Road. Several years ago the Syosset School Board fortunately foresaw what was going to happen; they bought 55 acres of farmland for this school site, and so still have room to expand.

Underwood Elementary School in Andrews, Texas, looks out at the wide, level stretch of its native landscape from under long overhanging eaves for sun shading, and looks inward into a pleasant courtyard. Skylights admit daylight to the interiors of classrooms. Smaller wings are gymnasium and locker room. Architects: Caudill, Rowlett, Scott and Associates.

City school—Fox Point Elementary School—in Providence, Rhode Island, is bounded by commerce, industry, and heavy traffic, but nevertheless has ample play space and a large secluded central court. Gymnasium and auditorium are placed nearest heavy traffic to be an acoustical buffer for classrooms, which crouch behind. Architects: Cull, Robinson and Green.

Phillis Wheatley Elementary School in crowded New Orleans neighborhood is perched up on stilts so children can play under it during recess, sheltered in season from Louisiana's rains. Classrooms are second-story; lunchroom, etc. are in lower building to right. Architects: Charles R. Colbert and Lowrey, Moschella, Dent, Associates. (A block away, a typical older U. S. schoolhouse.)

New wing added to Alta Vista Elementary School in Sarasota, Florida, is simply a double row of classrooms with a central corridor, linked by a covered walkway to older school (built way back in 1954). Each classroom continues outdoors, under shaded, winglike overhang. Architect: Victor A. Lundy (architects for earlier section, Sellew and Gremli).

Finger-plan school — Acalanes Union High School in Lafayette, California—divides rows of classrooms with open-ended corridors of greenery, to achieve good ventilation, sound isolation, and a remarkable California-like architectural comfort. This kind of school also has proved easy to expand; it simply sprouts new wings of classrooms. Franklin & Kump & Associates, Architects.

Suburban Crow Island School in Winnetka, Illinois, near Chicago, separates classrooms by intervening outdoor spaces. One of the pattern-makers of modern schools, this was built in 1940. Roof of new wing, lowest in photograph, indicates how insulating techniques have advanced in recent years. Heat does not leak through to melt snow as it does in older roofs. Architects: Eliel and Eero Saarinen, and Perkins, Wheeler and Will.

Rural school—Tantasqua Regional High School in Sturbridge, Massachusetts—nestles between forest and field. Large amphitheater is used by organizations from many miles around for many events. Wings of building furnish fine example of how to fit interestingly into a hilly site, without much benefit of bulldozer. George H. Stoner was the architect.

Cluster-plan school—Tower Street School in Westerly, Rhode Island —is a collection of small schoolhouses linked together by enclosed hallways, a very popular current prototype. Easy to expand, it creates numerous pleasant, personal spaces on a flat, unwooded site. Architects: Alonzo J. Harriman, Inc.

From inside

Rooms should not be traps, especially school-
rooms. They need not be. They can enclose without
imprisoning—and if they succeed in this, they usually contain livelier classes, better learners. There
are some people who actually have come out in
favor of austere, barracks-like schools—in some
cases of actual discomfort. But these people include few children and no teachers we have met on
our travels in assembling this book.

What is the purpose of an imaginative schoolroom? Is it just the general happiness of the children, the teachers, or the architect? Not really.
Like a factory or office building, a good school is
designed for certain specific, highly practical ends
—to increase efficiency, to make a process convenient, to keep the children interested, to bring them
to learning. As such, good design is not a luxury,
and in most cases, it, like good teaching, does not
wear a high price tag anyway. It is an idea. Here
are some rooms for learning.

NEIGHBORHOOD CHURCH NURSERY SCHOOL
PASADENA, CALIF.
SMITH & WILLIAMS, ARCHITECTS

1. PETER PAN ELEMENTARY SCHOOL, ANDREWS, TEX.
   CAUDILL, ROWLETT, SCOTT & ASSOCIATES, ARCHITECTS

2. CORONA AVENUE SCHOOL, BELL, CALIF.
   RICHARD J. NEUTRA, ARCHITECT

3. PARKWAY SCHOOL, ST. LOUIS, MO.
   HELLMUTH, OBATA & KASSABAUM, INC., ARCHITECTS

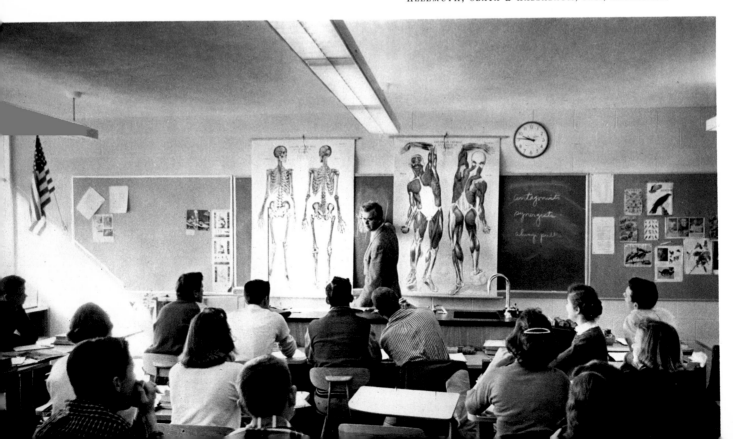

PETER THATCHER JUNIOR HIGH SCHOOL
ATTLEBORO, MASS.
THE ARCHITECTS COLLABORATIVE,
ARCHITECTS

5. PUYALLUP JUNIOR HIGH SCHOOL, PUYALLUP, WASH.
ROBERT B. PRICE, ARCHITECT

Classrooms

Classrooms today, like living rooms, have the freedom of movable furniture, but there are other freedoms too: lightly-framed, movable walls; freedom of view; and most of all, freedom of use for new teaching techniques. Some diverse approaches: (1) a split level classroom; (2) a classroom where moving outdoors is easy, not a big trek; (4) a corridor wide and pleasant enough to take overflow from a classroom; (5) a more formal lecture room, but a wide one, with good visibility; (3) a convenient lab classroom; (6) a classroom landscaped by virtue of its clear wall.

6. HEATHCOTE ELEMENTARY SCHOOL, SCARSDALE, N. Y.
PERKINS & WILL, ARCHITECTS

1. WHITE OAKS ELEMENTARY SCHOOL ANNEX
   SAN CARLOS, CALIF.
   JOHN CARL WARNECKE, ARCHITECT

2. A & M CONSOLIDATED HIGH SCHOOL, COLLEGE STATION, TEX.
   CAUDILL, ROWLETT, SCOTT & ASSOCIATES, ARCHITECTS

3. ALTA VISTA ELEMENTARY SCHOOL ADDITION, SARASOTA, FLA.
   VICTOR A. LUNDY, ARCHITECT

Classrooms

The open plan moved into the classroom from the modern factory and house, bringing along a great opportunity for flexibility. It can mean (1) walls that open up; (2) classrooms without doors, open to a common hall (in a climate where the biggest element of comfort is plenty of ventilation); (4) a *really* open classroom, a glade preserved in the site; (3) the openness of partitions that admit light from a corridor skylight; (5) the simple, free flexibility of plenty of unencumbered space.

4. OLIVIA ELEMENTARY SCHOOL, PORT CHESTER, N. Y.
SHERWOOD, MILLS & SMITH, ARCHITECTS

5. MEADOW DRIVE ELEMENTARY SCHOOL, MINEOLA, N. Y.
KETCHUM, GINA & SHARP, ARCHITECTS

1. SYOSSET HIGH SCHOOL, SYOSSET, N. Y.
   EGGERS AND HIGGINS, ARCHITECTS

2. MC GRATH ELEMENTARY SCHOOL, BRENTWOOD, MO.
   HELLMUTH, OBATA & KASSABAUM, INC., ARCHITECTS

3. ALTA VISTA ELEMENTARY SCHOOL ADDITION, SARASOTA, FLA.
   VICTOR A. LUNDY, ARCHITECT

Corridors

Hallways, in a school, are more than just links between rooms. They also form the social backdrop, comparable to a small town's main street, against which students meet and mingle many times during the day. And compared with the hallways in most buildings, they have to be highways, accommodating a lot of traffic all at once, when each period ends. Corridors frequently key the entire personality of a school, with window-walls (1 and 2), a skyline ceiling (3), a trip across a gorge (4), or a breath of fresh air, perfumed by growing things (5).

4. WALNUT CREEK ELEMENTARY SCHOOL, WALNUT CREEK, CALIF.
JOHN LYON REID & PARTNERS, ARCHITECTS

5. NORTH HILLSBOROUGH SCHOOL, HILLSBOROUGH, CALIF.
ERNEST J. KUMP, ARCHITECT

1. NORMAN HIGH SCHOOL, NORMAN, OKLA.
   PERKINS & WILL, AND CAUDILL, ROWLETT, SCOTT & ASSOCIATES, ARCHITECTS

2. POCANTICO CENTRAL SCHOOL, POCANTICO HILLS, N. Y.
   PERKINS & WILL, ARCHITECTS

3. PUYALLUP JUNIOR HIGH SCHOOL, PUYALLUP, WASH.
ROBERT B. PRICE, ARCHITECT

Corridors

Schoolhouse hallways, indoors or outdoors, also serve other functions. Their walls are frequently used for storage and display (1 and 2)—and note the glass partitions in the latter, to bring the corridor's daylighting into the classroom too. Outdoor corridors (3 and 4), simply sheltered from above in mild climates, become friendly anterooms and porches. In the case of climates which go beyond mildness to become too warm much of the school year, the porch roofs—as porch roof always have been—are fine sunshaders for the walls of the schoolhouse.

4. RAYMOND AVENUE SCHOOL, FULLERTON, CALIF.
SMITH, POWELL & MORGRIDGE, ARCHITECTS

1. MANCHESTER HIGH SCHOOL, MANCHESTER, CONN.
    EBBETS, FRID & PRENTICE, ARCHITECTS

2. LINCOLN-WAY HIGH SCHOOL, NEW LENOX, ILL.
    CHILDS & SMITH, ARCHITECTS

3. GREEN ACRES SCHOOL, MONTGOMERY COUNTY, MD.
DAVIS, BRODY & WISNIEWSKI, ARCHITECTS

Big rooms

Whether this kind of schoolhouse space is designed as a gymnasium (with great sliding walls for subdividing, 2), as a specialized place like a swimming pool (1), or as foyers or multi-purpose rooms (3 and 4), these big rooms have a major use which does not show here. They belong to the entire community, not just the students, and usually get heavy patronage from clubs and other adult groups.

4. THE COUNTRY SCHOOL, WESTON, MASS.
HUGH STUBBINS & ASSOCIATES, ARCHITECTS

1. MC GRATH ELEMENTARY SCHOOL, BRENTWOOD, MO.
   HELLMUTH, OBATA & KASSABAUM, INC., ARCHITECTS

2. WEST COLUMBIA ELEMENTARY SCHOOL, BRAZORIA COUNTY, TEX.
   DONALD BARTHELME & ASSOCIATES, ARCHITECTS

3. DE ANZA SCHOOL, EL SOBRANTE, CALIF.
JOHN CARL WARNECKE, ARCHITECT

4. PARKWAY SCHOOL, ST. LOUIS, MO.
HELLMUTH, OBATA & KASSABAUM, INC., ARCHITECTS

Multi-purpose

All the many uses that these larger spaces are put to in schools likely never have been listed. One shown here is frankly auditorium-plus-playhall (1), another, a home economics suite that opens up by sliding wall to social or assembly use (5). But frequently such spaces can be used temporarily in many ways, as in the gymnastic photograph (4), while the school is waiting to complete its intended building program. And eating spaces, outdoors (3) or indoors (2), are endless in their function, if only the tables are not bolted down.

5. ALAMITOS INTERMEDIATE SCHOOL, GARDEN GROVE, CALIF.
RICHARD J. NEUTRA & ROBERT E. ALEXANDER, ARCHITECT

1. CARMEL HIGH SCHOOL, CARMEL, CALIF.
ERNEST J. KUMP, ARCHITECT

2. WESTCHESTER HIGH SCHOOL, WESTCHESTER, CALIF.
HONNOLD & REX, ARCHITECTS

3. NORTH EAST PUBLIC LIBRARY, SEATTLE, WASH.
PAUL A. THIRY, ARCHITECT

Special purpose

Shops (1), theaters—indoor (4) or outdoor (2)—and home economics rooms (5) work by day for students and by night for parents in many schoolhouses. It is in these big spaces, such as the nicely scaled library (3) and the lunchroom-meeting-room-library (6) that structure is most frequently left exposed. A basic purpose of this is economy, of course, in leaving out extra applied finish ceilings, for example. But it can make for handsome rooms, too, as shown in the photographs on these pages. Most architects today will resist the tendency to smother the structural frames of their buildings, unless it is necessary to follow fire regulations. From indoors as well as from outdoors, the structure is the story of modern architecture, to a great degree.

6. HOLLOW TREE SCHOOL, DARIEN, CONN.
KETCHUM, GINA & SHARP, ARCHITECTS

4. WILLIAM CHRISTMAN HIGH SCHOOL, INDEPENDENCE, MO.
MARSHALL & BROWN, ARCHITECTS

5. PARKWAY SCHOOL, ST. LOUIS, MO.
HELLMUTH, OBATA & KASSABAUM, INC., ARCHITECTS

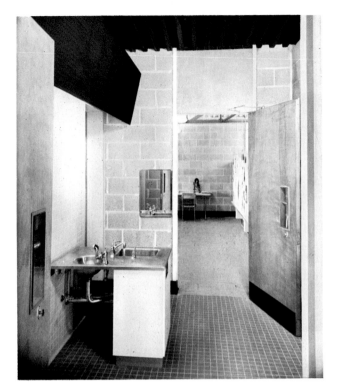

1. HOLLOW TREE ELEMENTARY SCHOOL, DARIEN, CONN.
   KETCHUM, GINA & SHARP, ARCHITECTS

2. TOKENEKE ELEMENTARY SCHOOL, DARIEN, CONN.
   O'CONNOR & KILHAM, ARCHITECTS

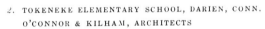

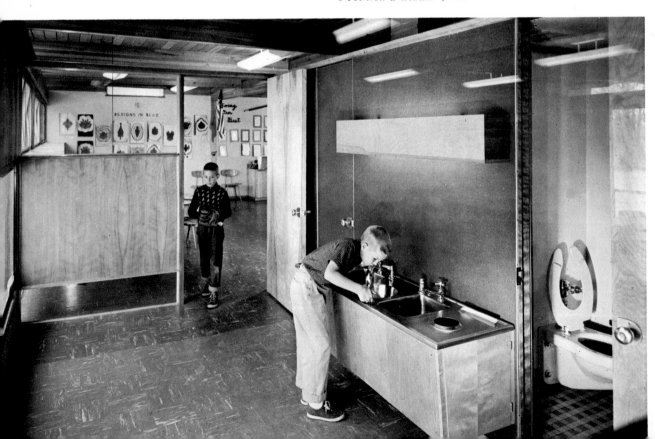

3. NEWFIELD SCHOOL, STAMFORD, CONN.
SHERWOOD, MILLS & SMITH, ARCHITECTS

Washrooms

Washing facilities in schools borrow both from industrial installations (circular washstands, 3) and from new design trends in houses; i.e., the "three passenger" bathroom, which partitions off the water closet and the washing facilities so both may be used with privacy simultaneously (1, 2). The beginning of this practice probably was the placing of washbasins in the classroom itself, which is now quite usual (4). Notice in these wash facilities the use of full lighting and natural materials to avoid an imposing institutional look.

4. NORTH EAST AUBURN ELEMENTARY SCHOOL, AUBURN, WASH.
VICTOR N. JONES & ASSOCIATES, ARCHITECTS

1. PARAMOUNT PARK ELEMENTARY SCHOOL, SEATTLE, WASH.
YOUNG, RICHARDSON, CARLETON & DETLIE, ARCHITECTS

2. HOLLOW TREE ELEMENTARY SCHOOL, DARIEN, CONN.
KETCHUM, GINA & SHARP, ARCHITECTS

4. SAN JACINTO ELEMENTARY SCHOOL, LIBERTY, TEX.
CAUDILL, ROWLETT, SCOTT & ASSOCIATES, ARCHITECTS

5. NORKIRK ELEMENTARY SCHOOL, KIRKLAND, WASH.
WALDRON & DIETZ, ARCHITECTS

3. MEDINA ELEMENTARY SCHOOL, BELLEVUE, WASH.
NARAMORE, BAIN, BRADY & JOHANSON, ARCHITECTS

Play areas

Protected, covered play areas (1, 2, 3, 4, 5, 6) are necessities in many parts of the country, where open ground churns into mud in spring and fall, and they are a boon anywhere, permitting outdoor play even in poor weather. They are an economy too—sometimes replacing gymnasium facilities, but without the costly necessity for heating. Coats, sweaters, and activity do that job.

6. THE COUNTRY SCHOOL, WESTON, MASS.
HUGH STUBBINS & ASSOCIATES, ARCHITECTS

2. PLAY SCULPTURES, INC.
AT SUN VALLEY SWIM CLUB
FLORHAM PARK, N. J.
LEO FISHER, ARCHITECT

1. EAGLE ROCK PLAYGROUND CLUB HOUSE, EAGLE ROCK, CALIF.
RICHARD J. NEUTRA, ARCHITECT

3. OLIVE AVENUE SCHOOL, NOVATO, CALIF.
JOHN LYON REID & PARTNERS, ARCHITECTS

Play areas

The basic play equipment is a good ground surface, with open space and some sunlight. Children will take it from there. But equipment helps. It may be time-tested (1), a newer approach (2), or improvised by the architect (4). For the young ones: space and country-side (3) to let off steam at recess. For older ones: games to unknot tension between exams (5).

4. WESTOVER ELEMENTARY SCHOOL, STAMFORD, CONN.
WILLIAM F. BALLARD, ARCHITECT

5. PUYALLUP JUNIOR HIGH SCHOOL, PUYALLUP, WASH.
ROBERT B. PRICE, ARCHITECT

In detail

Lacking the fancy trademarks of older styles of architecture such as Greek Revival and Regency, it is sometimes difficult to distinguish real quality in contemporary detailing, to recognize or judge the architectural craftsmanship with which the parts of a building are designed and assembled. There are some visual guides, however, and clarity is the foremost one. Look for an expressive use of materials, whether hand-hewn or factory-made, revealing how each part of the structure and finish is related to the next, making it very clear where the job of one part stops and the next begins. A successful modern building (especially one designed under the gun of economy, as most schools are) not only *looks* simply put together, but *is*. Its components, of course, must be complicated enough in their assembly to defy the cleverness of the weather, but today's best schools usually are direct in appearance, beauties without mascara. An accomplished architect, like a fine piano-player or cook, makes his accomplishment look easy.

SONOMA ELEMENTARY SCHOOL, SONOMA, CALIF.
MARIO J. CIAMPI, ARCHITECT

1. BRIERCREST ELEMENTARY SCHOOL, SEATTLE, WASH.
YOUNG, RICHARDSON, CARLETON & DETLIE, ARCHITECTS

2. SCHAUMBERG ELEMENTARY SCHOOL, SCHAUMBERG, ILL.
SCHWEIKHER & ELTING, ARCHITECTS

3. ALTA VISTA ELEMENTARY SCHOOL ADDITION, SARASOTA, FLA.
VICTOR A. LUNDY, ARCHITECT

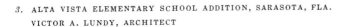

4. PHILLIS WHEATLEY ELEMENTARY SCHOOL, NEW ORLEANS, LA.
CHARLES R. COLBERT, ARCHITECT; M. P. LOWREY, J. T. DENT, S. C. MOSCHELLA, ASSOCIATES

5. NORTHEAST ELEMENTARY SCHOOL
WALTHAM, MASS.
THE ARCHITECTS COLLABORATIVE
ARCHITECTS

6. LENNOX TEST SCHOOL, DES MOINES, IOWA
PERKINS & WILL, ARCHITECTS

Construction

The neatness and trimness of modern architecture need not eliminate visual excitement. For witnesses: these imaginative structures, all fined down to eliminate wasted structural effort, but all lively in feeling. In all of them the framing that holds the building up is the thing; whether made of metal or timber, these buildings show their bones. Their materials, including the stones of this round and charming chimney (2), are used eloquently.

7. TOKENEKE ELEMENTARY SCHOOL, DARIEN, CONN.
O'CONNOR & KILHAM, ARCHITECTS

1. RAYMOND AVENUE SCHOOL, FULLERTON, CALIF.
   SMITH, POWELL & MORGRIDGE, ARCHITECTS

2. CASEY JUNIOR HIGH SCHOOL ADDITION, BOULDER, COLO.
   HOBART D. WAGENER, ARCHITECT

Roofs

Those of most—but not all—contemporary schools are flat (3). One reason: the flatter the roof, the less roofing material generally is needed. But drainage and daylighting methods (1, 2) affect this design decision too, and so does the terrain you inhabit. One of the country's most beautiful schools (4) matches and flatters its sloping site, following it downhill and setting the classrooms on terraces, not attempting to flatten things into the "ideal" site for building. Earthmoving—particularly hillmoving—is not cheap, of course, but there are sometimes even better reasons, as shown in this photograph, for preserving a slope if it is what you start with.

3. BRIERCREST ELEMENTARY SCHOOL, SEATTLE, WASH.
   YOUNG, RICHARDSON, CARLETON & DETLIE, ARCHITECTS

4. MIRA VISTA ELEMENTARY SCHOOL, RICHMOND, CALIF.
   JOHN CARL WARNECKE, ARCHITECT

1. BOGALUSA HIGH SCHOOL, BOGALUSA, LA.
BURK, LE BRETON & LAMANTIA, ARCHITECTS

2. PHOENIX HIGH SCHOOL, PHOENIX, ARIZ.
GUIREY & JONES, ARCHITECTS

3. EDGEMONT JUNIOR-SENIOR HIGH SCHOOL, GREENBURGH, N. Y.
WARREN H. ASHLEY, ARCHITECT

Windows

They are for air and light, but sometimes they have to be *against* light, too, wearing baffles and louvers that break the glare of direct sunlight into a less jarring softness (1, 2, 4). In some climates and orientations, interior curtains, or blinds, are the simplest solution (3). And air doesn't have to enter through windows but can be pulled in through louvers in curtain wall panels (5).

5. NEAL JUNIOR HIGH SCHOOL, NORTH CHICAGO, ILL.
FISHER & BRYANT, ARCHITECTS

1. UNIVERSITY HIGH SCHOOL
MINNEAPOLIS, MINN.
MAGNEY, TUSLER & SETTER, ARCHITECTS

1. RAYMOND AVENUE SCHOOL, FULLERTON, CALIF.
SMITH, POWELL & MORGRIDGE, ARCHITECTS

Windows

Sunshading sometimes becomes almost a structural matter, as in the out-rigger (1) and exterior louvers (2) shown here. Glass framed in metal is a sun shade for an exterior corridor (3) and the old porch blinds are recalled in handsome new form (4). Another method: large adjustable vertical vanes (5) to shutter sunlight without blocking ventilation.

2. FAIRFAX ELEMENTARY SCHOOL, FAIRFAX, CALIF.
JOHN LYON REID & PARTNERS, ARCHITECTS

3. DE ANZA SCHOOL, EL SOBRANTE, CALIF.
JOHN CARL WARNECKE, ARCHITECT

5. GEORGE WASHINGTON CARVER SCHOOL, MIAMI, FLA.
ALFRED PARKER, ARCHITECT

4. TUCKER-MAXON ORAL SCHOOL
PORTLAND, ORE.
SKIDMORE, OWINGS & MERRILL
ARCHITECTS

1. CATHERINE BLAINE JUNIOR HIGH SCHOOL
SEATTLE, WASH.
J. LISTER HOLMES, ARCHITECT

2. WEST COLUMBIA ELEMENTARY SCHOOL, BRAZORIA COUNTY, TEX.
DONALD BARTHELME & ASSOCIATES, ARCHITECTS

3. MERCER ISLAND HIGH SCHOOL, MERCER ISLAND, WASH.
BASSETTI & MORSE, ARCHITECTS

Lighting

Electric lighting frequently also needs vanes or visors to block the direct brightness of its bulbs or tubes (1); and skylights almost always need this kind of control (2, 4, 5)—this last one is shown in process of being adjusted. Indoors, it is obvious that light from not just one but several sources is better for glare avoidance, even under the wide glow of a continuous ceiling of light (3).

4. SAN LORENZO VALLEY HIGH SCHOOL, FELTON, CALIF.
JOHN LYON REID & PARTNERS, ARCHITECTS

5. BRITTAN ACRES SCHOOL, SAN CARLOS, CALIF.
JOHN LYON REID & PARTNERS, ARCHITECTS

1. WHITE OAKS ELEMENTARY SCHOOL ANNEX, SAN CARLOS, CALIF.
   JOHN CARL WARNECKE, ARCHITECT

2. NORKIRK ELEMENTARY SCHOOL, KIRKLAND, WASH.
   WALDRON & DIETZ, ARCHITECTS

Lighting

Some day there may be no lighting "fixtures" as such at all, but only lighting *surfaces,* which radiate illumination from large areas, not points. To a degree the rooms on these two pages anticipate this luminosity in their use of openings, "windows," to secure natural daylight. Their designers did not think of these openings as holes to poke in a wall or roof, but as large *areas* or *ribbons* of lighting. Incidentally, there is no necessity in a single-story school for dark interior corridors (5).

3. WESTCHESTER HIGH SCHOOL, WESTCHESTER, CALIF.
HONNOLD & REX, ARCHITECTS

4. PORTOLA JUNIOR HIGH SCHOOL, EL CERRITO, CALIF.
JOHN CARL WARNECKE, ARCHITECT

5. GEORGE WASHINGTON SCHOOL, MOLINE, ILL.
MEL BECKSTROM, ARCHITECT

1. EDWARD BLEEKER JUNIOR HIGH SCHOOL, FLUSHING, N. Y.
POMERANCE & BREINES, ARCHITECTS

2. JOHN JAY HIGH SCHOOL, CROSS RIVER, N. Y.
KETCHUM, GINA & SHARP, ARCHITECTS

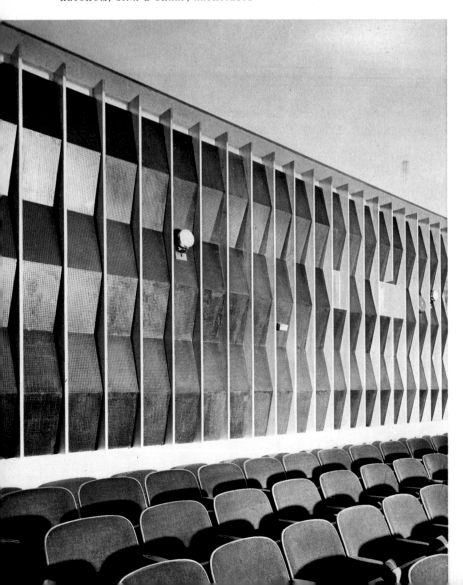

Acoustics

The patterned walls and baffles shown here (1, 2) aim at absorbing and/or dispersing the reflection of sound in order to diminish reverberation, or echoing (see chapter XI). Soft, wooly surfaces are fine for this job, but because in schools they have to stand up to especially hard daily wear, these absorptive surfaces are often covered with sheets of perforated metal. The vanes in the gymnasium (3) are intended primarily to prevent glare, but are good against blare too, deflecting sound, breaking up sound patterns, much as the vertical vanes in the band room (4) do. Another neat solution to the noise problem, but for open neighborhoods only: open the walls and let the bad air out (5).

3. BOTHELL HIGH SCHOOL, BOTHELL, WASH.
   RALPH BURKHARD, ARCHITECT

4. BOTHELL HIGH SCHOOL, BOTHELL, WASH.
   RALPH BURKHARD, ARCHITECT

5. ALAMITOS SCHOOL, ALAMITOS, CALIF.
   RICHARD J. NEUTRA & ROBERT E. ALEXANDER, ARCHITECTS

1. BELLEVUE JUNIOR HIGH SCHOOL, BELLEVUE, WASH.
    NARAMORE, BAIN, BRADY & JOHANSON, ARCHITECTS

2. LOCKMAN ELEMENTARY SCHOOL, ROYAL OAK, MICH.
    O'DELL, HEWLETT & LUCKENBACH, ARCHITECTS

3,4. BAY VIEW SCHOOL, SANTA CRUZ, CALIF.
ROBERT STANTON, ARCHITECT

Built-ins

The walls of a classroom can absorb everything from coat closets (2) to filing drawers and other small storage (5). Every year seems to bring new uses to classroom wall surfaces, plus more wall panels that reverse, or pivot—even chalkboards that come and go (1). Lunch box storage (3), teachers' files, and other closets and drawers specifically tailored to their jobs (4, 6) all help to squeeze maximum utility out of these precious teaching walls.

5. CATHERINE BLAINE JUNIOR HIGH SCHOOL, SEATTLE, WASH.
J. LISTER HOLMES, ARCHITECT

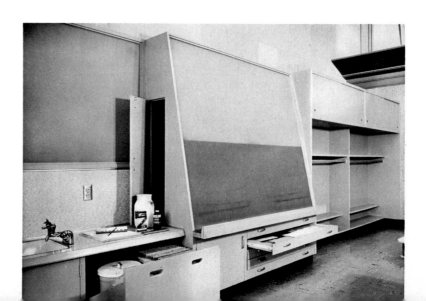

6. RAYMOND AVENUE SCHOOL, FULLERTON, CALIF.
SMITH, POWELL & MORGRIDGE, ARCHITECTS

1. NORMAN HIGH SCHOOL, NORMAN, OKLA.
CAUDILL, ROWLETT, SCOTT & ASSOCIATES AND
PERKINS & WILL, ARCHITECTS

2. WHITE OAKS ELEMENTARY SCHOOL ANNEX, SAN CARLOS, CALIF.
JOHN CARL WARNECKE, ARCHITECT

3,4. FOSTER JUNIOR-SENIOR HIGH SCHOOL, SEATTLE, WASH.
RALPH BURKHARD, ARCHITECT

5. WALKER SCHOOL, CLARENDON HILLS, ILL.
FUGARD, BURT, WILKINSON & ORTH
ARCHITECTS

6. POCANTICO CENTRAL SCHOOL, POCANTICO HILLS, N. Y.
PERKINS & WILL, ARCHITECTS

7. PALATINE ELEMENTARY SCHOOL, PALATINE, ILL.
PERKINS & WILL, ARCHITECTS

Built-ins

These sometimes include furniture too, if building it in can save on total usable classroom space. Sinks and counters (2, 6, 7) are as valued in schools as in kitchens these days, and sometimes even the teacher's desk can be absorbed neatly into a counter top (8). Devices such as folding bleachers (3, 4) are popular in today's gymnasia; or if you plan to use portable folding chairs, you should provide a convenient place to stow them (5). Outdoor built-in seating is another built-in: (1).

8. HOLMES ELEMENTARY SCHOOL, DARIEN, CONN.
KETCHUM, GINA & SHARP, ARCHITECTS

2. WHITING LANE ELEMENTARY SCHOOL, WEST HARTFORD, CONN.
MOORE & SALSBURY, ARCHITECTS

1. WESTMOOR HIGH SCHOOL, DALY CITY, CALIF.
MARIO J. CIAMPI, ARCHITECT

3. BRISTOL PRIMARY SCHOOL, WEBSTER GROVES, MO.
HELLMUTH, OBATA & KASSABAUM, INC., ARCHITECTS

4. JAMES L. MULCAHEY ELEMENTARY SCHOOL, TAUNTON, MASS.
THE ARCHITECTS COLLABORATIVE, ARCHITECTS

Art

A touch of art, in fun or serious, is a sign of civilization appropriate to schoolhouses. Sometimes the children can contribute to it themselves (they made the tiles in picture 4), but more sophisticated artists are not lost on them either. (1) Designs by architect; (2) mosaic tile mural by Henryk Mayer; (3) and (5) designs by the architect; (6) design in glazed tile by Amy Myers and John C. Harkness; (7) ground composition by Charles A. Currier and Associates; (8) ceramic mural by Anton Refregier.

6. JOHN ELIOT ELEMENTARY SCHOOL, NEEDHAM, MASS.
THE ARCHITECTS COLLABORATIVE, ARCHITECTS

5. ROXBURY SCHOOL, STAMFORD, CONN.
SHERWOOD, MILLS & SMITH, ARCHITECTS

7. WEST SPRINGFIELD SENIOR HIGH SCHOOL, WEST SPRINGFIELD, MASS.
WARREN H. ASHLEY, ARCHITECT

8. TOKENEKE ELEMENTARY SCHOOL, DARIEN, CONN.
O'CONNOR & KILHAM, ARCHITECTS

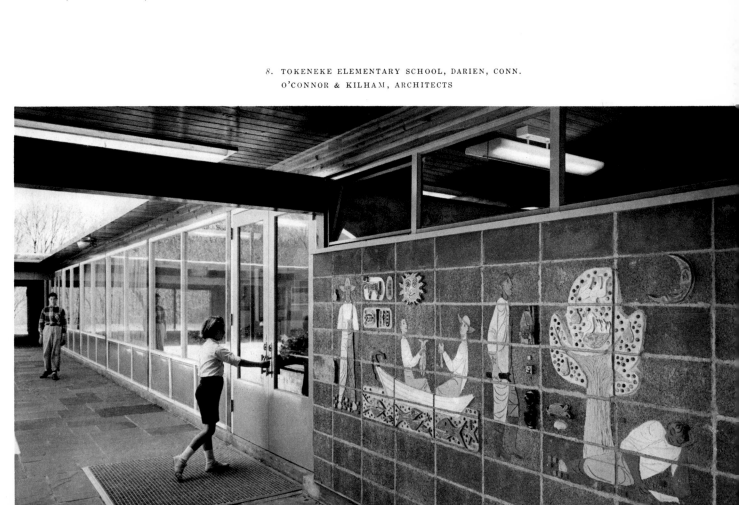

Character

Character

The personality of a building springs from the mind of its architect, and this can and should result in as many different schoolhouse personalities as there are schools and thinking architects. Since the war the number clearly has been on the increase. That old schoolhouse prototype which many adults remember—a formidable structure, varying little from one township to the next, and about as interesting as the drab bindings on old textbooks —has not disappeared. But the scene is being enlivened now all over the continent by schoolhouses of a very different character—and of different characters from each other.

It may be especially appropriate in an age worried about conformity that our new schools are as strong in their differences as in their similarities; for where else should the mark of the mind be more important? Learning itself cannot be poured out like milk; children must be interested. It is the good teacher who really interests them, of course; but a personable building, with the mark of individual aspiration on it, is appropriate to the process too. On the next few pages are a few; there are hundreds more.

HERBERT HOOVER JUNIOR HIGH SCHOOL
SAN FRANCISCO, CALIF.
ERNEST J. KUMP, ARCHITECT

1. CARMEL HIGH SCHOOL, CARMEL, CALIF.
ERNEST J. KUMP, ARCHITECT

2. MIDDLETON STATE GRADED SCHOOL, MIDDLETON, WIS.
JOHN J. FLAD & ASSOCIATES, ARCHITECTS

3. GREEN RIVER SCHOOL, GREEN RIVER, UTAH
   DEAN L. GUSTAVSON AND JOHN W. SUGDEN, ARCHITECTS

4. LINCOLN ELEMENTARY SCHOOL, LINCOLN, ME.
   ALONZO J. HARRIMAN, INC., ARCHITECTS

1. WESTWOOD HIGH SCHOOL, WESTWOOD, MASS.
   COLETTI BROTHERS, ARCHITECTS

2. CLYDE LYONS ELEMENTARY SCHOOL, GLENVIEW, ILL.
   PERKINS & WILL, ARCHITECTS

3. ABBOTT SCHOOL, SAN MATEO, CALIF.
   FALK & BOOTH, ARCHITECTS

4. MC GRATH ELEMENTARY SCHOOL, BRENTWOOD, MO.
   HELLMUTH, OBATA & KASSABAUM, INC., ARCHITECTS

1. WASHBURN ELEMENTARY SCHOOL, AUBURN, ME.
   ALONZO J. HARRIMAN, INC., ARCHITECT

2. NORTH HILLSBOROUGH SCHOOL, HILLSBOROUGH, CALIF.
   ERNEST J. KUMP, ARCHITECT

3. WHITE SCHOOL, RIO VISTA, CALIF.
   DONALD BEACH KIRBY & ASSOCIATES, ARCHITECTS

4. NORTHEAST ELEMENTARY SCHOOL, WALTHAM, MASS.
   THE ARCHITECTS COLLABORATIVE, ARCHITECTS

1. DE ANZA SCHOOL, EL SOBRANTE, CALIF.
   JOHN CARL WARNECKE, ARCHITECT

2. SAN JOSE TECHNICAL HIGH SCHOOL, SAN JOSE, CALIF.
   ERNEST J. KUMP, ARCHITECT

3. OLYMPIC VIEW JUNIOR HIGH SCHOOL, MUKILTEO, WASH.
   WALDRON & DIETZ, ARCHITECTS

4. ADDITION TO POCANTICO CENTRAL SCHOOL, POCANTICO HILLS, N. Y.
   PERKINS & WILL, ARCHITECTS

And a small final reminder

The continent was beautiful before we came to it, and much of its beauty remains today. But unfortunately, when you have a parcel of landscape to put a school on, it sometimes seems most efficient to scrape all growth from it, then replant after the building is completed. An old tree, however, is a much wiser influence around a schoolyard than a sapling, and the very newness of a good modern school frequently benefits from a touch of oldness. School Board, save that tree.

1. BRISTOL PRIMARY SCHOOL
WEBSTER GROVES, MO.
HELLMUTH, OBATA & KASSABAUM, INC.
ARCHITECTS

2. WILBERT SNOW ELEMENTARY SCHOOL
MIDDLETOWN, CONN.
WARREN H. ASHLEY, ARCHITECT

3. MEDINA ELEMENTARY SCHOOL
BELLEVUE, WASH.
NARAMORE, BAIN, BRADY & JOHANSON
ARCHITECTS

4. SAN LORENZO VALLEY HIGH SCHOOL
FELTON, CALIF.
JOHN LYON REID & PARTNERS
ARCHITECTS

Credits and bibliography

continued from page 10

Burk, Le Breton and Lamantia, New Orleans, Louisiana; Carneal and Johnston, Richmond, Virginia; Caudill, Rowlett, Scott and Associates, Bryan, Texas; Childs and Smith, Chicago, Illinois; Mario J. Ciampi, San Francisco, California; Clark, Nexsen and Owen, Lynchburg, Virginia; Colbert and Lowrey and Associates, New Orleans, Louisiana; Corlett and Spackman, San Francisco, California; Crowell, Lancaster, Higgins and Webster, Bangor, Maine; Davis, Brody, and Wisniewski, New York City; Wilmot C. Douglas, Birmingham, Alabama; Glen M. Drew, Poplar Bluff, Missouri; Falk and Booth, San Francisco, California; Finney, Dodson, Smeallie, Orrick and Associates, Baltimore, Maryland; Dean L. Gustavson Associates, Salt Lake City, Utah; L. Alex Hatton, Orlando, Florida; Hedrick and Stanley, Fort Worth, Texas; Hellmuth, Obata and Kassabaum, Inc., St. Louis, Missouri; Hewitt and Bastian, Peoria, Illinois; Holabird and Root and Burgee, Chicago, Illinois; Caleb Hornbostel and Associates, New York City; Hugill, Blatherwick, Fritzel and Kroeger, Sioux Falls, South Dakota; Jones and Bindon, Seattle, Washington; Ketchum and Sharp, New York City; Louis C. Kingscott and Associates, Inc., Kalamazoo, Michigan; Donald Beach Kirby, San Francisco, California; Kistner, Wright and Wright, Los Angeles, California; Vincent G. Kling, Philadelphia, Pennsylvania; Carl Koch and Associates, Cambridge, Massachusetts; Ernest J. Kump, Palo Alto, California; Victor A. Lundy, Sarasota, Florida; Lyles, Bissett, Carlisle and Wolff, Columbia, South Carolina; Maynard Lyndon, Los Angeles, California; MacKie and Kamrath, Houston, Texas; Maurer and Maurer, South Bend, Indiana; Mayo, Johnson and deWolf, Stockton, California; McLeod and Ferrara, Washington, D. C.; Moore and Hutchins, New York City; Richard J. Neutra and Robert E. Alexander, Los Angeles, California; O'Connor and Kilham, New York City; A. G. Odell, Jr. and Associates, Charlotte, North Carolina; Page, Southerland and Page, Austin, Texas; John B. Parkin Associates, Toronto, Canada; Perkins and Will, Chicago, Illinois; David A. Pierce, Columbus, Ohio; Uel C. Ramey and Associates, Wichita, Kansas; Vincent G. Raney, San Francisco, California; John Lyon Reid and Partners, San Francisco, California; Sargent-Webster-Crenshaw and Folley, Syracuse, New York; Howell Lewis Shay and Associates, Philadelphia, Pennsylvania; Sherwood, Mills and Smith, Stamford, Connecticut; Arthur F. Sidells, Warren, Ohio; Skidmore, Owings and Merrill, Portland, Oregon; Harold Spitznagel and Associates, Sioux Falls, South Dakota; Gordon Stafford, Sacramento, California; Eugene D. Sternberg and Associates, Denver, Colorado; Stevens and Wilkinson, Atlanta, Georgia; Jay C. Van Nuys and Associates, Somerville, New Jersey; Wilmsen and Endicott, Eugene, Oregon; Kenneth E. Wischmeyer, St. Louis, Missouri; Frank Wynkoop, Carmel, California; John G. York, Corpus Christi, Texas.

The following fabricators and subcontractors cooperated extensively with the George A. Fuller estimating department in providing technical cost data as background information:

Abbott Glass Co., Inc.; Alsynite Co. of America; Aluminum Structures Inc. of Pittsburgh; Armstrong Cork Co.; Barker Painting Co.; Benson Mfg. Co.; Builders Wood Flooring Co.; Celotex Corp.; Circle Floor Co., Inc.; Concrete Plank Co.; Corrulux Division of Libby·Owens·Ford Glass Co.; Detroit Steel Products Co.; Erie Enameling Co.; Flexicore Co.; Michael Flynn Mfg. Co.; Formigli Sales Corp.; General Bronze Corp.; E. K. Geyser Co.; Granco Steel Products Co.; H. & B. Enterprise Corp.; J. I. Hass; E. F. Hauserman Co.; Hope's Windows, Inc.; Ingram-Richardson Mfg. Co.; Inland Steel Co.; Insulrock Co.; Johns-Manville Corp.; Keystone Fireproofing Co.; Knapp Bros. Mfg. Co.; Kompolite Co., Inc.; Lally Column Co.; Macomber, Inc.; Mahon Steel Co.; Marco Co.; Marietta Concrete Corp.; Marsh Wall Products, Inc.; Masonite Corp.; A. Munder & Son, Inc.; Natco Corp.; National Acoustics; National Gypsum Co.; Neff Lathing Co.; Newell-Orr-Walsh, Inc.; New England Lift Slab Corp.; New York Roofing Co.; Owens-Corning Fiberglas Corp.; Pennmetal Co., Inc.; Pittsburgh-Corning Corp.; Pittsburgh Plate Glass Co.; Plasteel Products Corp.; Porete Mfg. Co.; Port Chester Iron Works, Inc.; H. H. Robertson Co.; Seaporcel Metals, Inc.; William Somerville, Inc.; Mr. Joseph Sparks; Steel Craft Mfg. Co.; Timber Structures, Inc.; Truscon Steel Co.; U. S. Gypsum Co.; U. S. Plywood Co.; W. F. Watson Stone Corp.

Bibliography

American Association of School Administrators. *American School Buildings, Twenty-Seventh Yearbook.* The Association, Washington, D. C., 1949

American Association of School Administrators. *Common Sense in School Lighting.* The Association, Washington, D. C., 1956

American Association of School Administrators. *Cutting Costs in Schoolhouse Construction.* The Association, Washington, D. C., 1952

American Association of School Administrators and National School Public Relations Association. *How Much Should a Good School Cost?* The Association, Washington, D. C., 1957

American Society of Heating and Air-Conditioning Engineers. *Heating, Ventilating, Air-Conditioning Guide.* The Society, New York, 1958

Birren, Faber. *New Horizons in Color.* Reinhold Publishing Corp., New York, 1955

Bormann, H. H. *Unit Costs of School Buildings.* Bureau of Publications, Teachers College, Columbia University, New York, 1941

Burke, Arvid J. *Financing Public Schools in the United States.* Rev. ed. Harper & Bros., New York, 1957

Bursch, Charles W. and Reid, John Lyon. *High Schools—Today and Tomorrow.* Reinhold Publishing Corp., New York, 1957

Caudill, William W. *Space for Teaching.* Bulletin of the Texas Engineering Experiment Station, Vol. 12 No. 9, College Station, Texas, 1941

Caudill, William W. *Toward Better School Design.* F. W. Dodge Corp., New York, 1954

Commission on School Buildings of the State of New York. *More Schools for Your Money: Finance Handbook.* The

Commission, Albany, N. Y., 1954

Committee for the White House Conference on Education. A Report to the President. Government Printing Office, Washington, D. C., April, 1956

Cyr, F. W. and Linn, H. H. *Planning Rural Community School Buildings.* Bureau of Publications, Teachers College, Columbia University, New York, 1949

Dreiman, David B. *How To Get Better Schools.* Harper & Bros., New York, 1956

Engelhardt, N. L.; Engelhardt, N. L. Jr.; and Leggett, Stanton. *Planning Elementary School Buildings.* F. W. Dodge Corp., New York, 1953

Engelhardt, N. L.; Engelhardt, N. L. Jr.; and Leggett, Stanton. *School Planning and Building Handbook.* F. W. Dodge Corp., New York, 1956

Frank, Mary and Lawrence K. *Your Adolescent at Home and in School.* The Viking Press, New York, 1956

Gans, Roma; Stendler, Celia B.; Almy, Millie. *Teaching Young Children.* World Book Co., Yonkers-on-Hudson, N. Y., 1952

Gesell, M. D., Arnold and Ilg., M. D., Frances L. *The Child from Five to Ten.* Harper & Bros., New York, 1946

Gesell, M. D., Arnold and Ilg, M. D., Frances L. *Infant and Child in the Culture of Today.* Harper & Bros., New York, 1943

Gesell, M. D. Arnold; Ilg, M. D., Frances L. and Ames, Ph.D., Louise Bates. *Youth: The Years from Ten to Sixteen.* Harper & Bros., New York, 1956

Gruenberg, Sidonie M. and the Staff of the Child Study Assn. of America. *Our Children Today.* Viking Press, New York, 1952

Harmon, Darell Boyd. *The Coordinated Classroom.* A.I.A. File No. 35-B. The American Seating Co., Grand Rapids, Mich., 1949

Herrick, John H.; McLeary, Ralph D.; Clapp, Wilfred F. and Bogner, Walter F. *From School Program to School Plant.* Henry Holt & Co., New York, 1956

Illuminating Engineering Society. *The American Standard Practice for School Lighting.* The Society, New York, 1949-50

Jersild, Arthur T. *The Psychology of Adolescence.* The Macmillan Co., New York, 1957

Jersild, Arthur T. and Tasch, R. J. *Children's Interests and What They Suggest for Education.* Bureau of Publications, Teachers College, Columbia University, New York, 1949

Landes, Jack L. and Sumption, Merle R. *Citizens' Workbook for Evaluating School Buildings.* Harper & Bros., New York, 1957

Linn, Henry H. *Reducing Costs in School Construction.* Paper delivered before AASA Convention, Atlantic City, N. J., 1954. The Association, Washington, D. C.

Linn, H. H.; Helm, Leslie C. and Grabarkiewicz, K. P. *The School Custodian's Housekeeping Handbook.* Bureau of Publications, Teachers College, Columbia University, New York, 1948

Luckiesh, Matthew. *Light, Vision and Seeing.* D. Van Nostrand Co., Princeton, N. J., 1944

MacConnell, James D. *Planning for School Buildings.* Prentice Hall, Inc., New York, 1957

McLeary, R. D. *Guide for Evaluating School Buildings.* New England School Development Council, Cambridge, Mass., 1949

National Citizens Commission for the Public Schools. *How Can We Help Our School Boards?* The Commission, New York, 1954

National Citizens Commission for the Public Schools. *How Do We Pay For Our Schools?* The Commission, New York, 1954

National Council on Schoolhouse Construction. *Guide for Planning School Plants.* The Council, George Peabody College, Nashville, Tenn., 1953

National Council on Schoolhouse Construction. *Secondary School Plant Planning.* The Council, George Peabody College, Nashville, Tenn., 1957

National Council on Schoolhouse Construction. *13 Principles of Economy in School Plant Planning and Construction.* The Council, George Peabody College, Nashville, Tenn., 1955

National Education Association, Educational Policies Commission. *Education for All American Youth: A Further Look, 1952.* Rev. ed. The Commission, Washington, D. C., 1952

Nesbitt, Marion. *A Public School for Tomorrow.* Harper & Bros., New York, 1953

New England School Development Council. *A Kindergarten Study.* The Council, Cambridge, Mass., 1953

Olgyay, A. and Olgyay, J. *Solar Control and Shading Devices.* Princeton University Press, Princeton, N. J., 1957

Olson, Willard C. and Lewellen, John. *How Children Grow and Develop.* Science Research Associates, Inc., Chicago, Ill., 1953

Perkins, Lawrence B. *Work Place for Learning.* Reinhold Publishing Corp., New York, 1957

Perkins, Lawrence B. and Cocking, Walter D. *Schools.* Reinhold Publishing Corp., New York, 1949

Pierce, David A. *School Economy Studies.* State Board of Education of Ohio, Columbus, O., 1958

School Planning. Editors, Architectural Record. F. W. Dodge Corp., New York, 1951

Schools for the New Needs. Editors, Architectural Record. F. W. Dodge Corp., New York, 1956

Sumption, Merle R. and Landes, Jack L. *Planning Functional School Buildings.* Harper & Bros., New York, 1957

The Tax Foundation, Inc. *Public School Financing, 1930-54.* The Foundation, New York, 1954

The Tax Institute, Inc. *Financing Education in the Public Schools.* The Institute, Princeton, N. J., 1956

Viles, N. E. *Local School Construction Programs.* U. S. Office of Education, Bulletin 1957 No. 20, Government Printing Office, Washington, D. C., 1957

Viles, N. E. *School Buildings: Remodeling, Rehabilitation, Modernization and Repairs.* U. S. Office of Education, Bulletin 1950 No. 17, Government Printing Office, Washington, D. C., 1950

Viles, N. E. and Hamon, R. L. *School Building Unit Costs.* U. S. Office of Education, Government Printing Office, Washington, D. C., 1954

Waechter, H. and Waechter E. *Schools for the Very Young.* F. W. Dodge Corp., New York, 1951

Wilson, Russell E. *Flexible Classrooms.* Carter Publishing Co., Detroit, Mich., 1953

Winslow, C. E. A. and Herrington, L. P. *Temperature and Human Life.* Princeton University Press., Princeton, N. J., 1949

NOTE: To those readers who wish to explore the field still further, we recommend the highly comprehensive bibliography in *American School and University, 1957-58 School Plant Reference,* published by the American School Publishing Corp., 470 Fourth Ave., New York 16, N. Y.

Periodicals

American School and University. American School Publishing Corp., 470 Fourth Avenue, New York 16, N. Y.

American School Board Journal. Bruce Publishing Co., 400 North Broadway, Milwaukee 1, Wis.

Architectural Forum. Time Inc., 9 Rockefeller Plaza, New York 20, N. Y.

Architectural Record. F. W. Dodge Corp., 119 West 40th Street, New York 18, N. Y.

Better Schools. National Citizens Council for Better Schools, 9 East 40th Street, New York 16, N. Y.

Childhood Education. Association for Childhood Education International, 1200 Fifteenth Street, N. W., Washington 5, D. C.

Child Study. Child Study Association of America, Inc., 132 East 74th Street, New York 21, N. Y.

Engineering News Record. McGraw Hill Publishing Co., Inc., 330 West 42nd Street, New York 36, N. Y.

Municipal Finance. Municipal Finance Officers Association of the United States and Canada, 1313 East 60th Street, Chicago 37, Ill.

National Municipal Review. National Municipal League, 299 Broadway, New York 7, N. Y.

National Tax Journal. National Tax Association, Box 1799, Sacramento, Calif.

The Nation's Schools. The Modern Hospital Publishing Co., Inc., F. W. Dodge Corp., 919 North Michigan Avenue, Chicago 11, Ill.

NEA Journal. National Education Association, 1201 Sixteenth Street, N. W., Washington 6, D. C.

Progressive Architecture. Reinhold Publishing Corp., 430 Park Avenue, New York 22, N. Y.

Research Bulletins of the American Institute of Architects, The Octagon, 1735 New York Avenue, N. W., Washington 6, D. C.

Research Bulletins of the Texas Engineering Experiment Station, Texas A&M College, College Station, Texas.

The School Executive. American School Publishing Corp., 470 Fourth Avenue, New York 16, N. Y.

School Life. United States Office of Education, Department of Health, Education and Welfare, Washington 25, D. C.

School Management. School Management Magazines, Inc., 22 West Putnam Avenue, Greenwich, Conn.

School Planning. School Planning, Inc., 75 East Wacker Drive, Chicago 1, Ill.

General Sources

American Association of School Administrators, 1201 Sixteenth Street, N. W., Washington 6, D. C.

American Institute of Architects, The Octagon, 1735 New York Avenue, N.W., Washington 6, D. C.

American Society of Heating and Air-Conditioning Engineers, 62 Worth Street, New York 13, N. Y.

The Association for Childhood Education International, 1200 Fifteenth Street, N. W., Washington 5, D. C.

Child Study Association of America, 132 E. 74th Street, New York 21, N. Y.

Educational Facilities Laboratories, Inc., established by the Ford Foundation, 477 Madison Avenue, New York 22, N. Y.

Illuminating Engineering Society, 1860 Broadway, New York 23, N. Y.

National Citizens Council for Better Schools, 9 East 40th Street, New York 16, N. Y.

National Council on Schoolhouse Construction, George Peabody College, Nashville 5, Tenn.

National Education Association, 1201 Sixteenth Street, N.W., Washington 6, D. C.

National Recreation Association, 8 West 8th Street, New York 11, N. Y.

New England School Development Council, Spaulding House, 20 Oxford Street, Cambridge 38, Mass.

United States Office of Education, Department of Health, Education and Welfare, Washington 25, D. C.

Other valuable sources for published and unpublished information include such continuing groups as the Texas Engineering Experiment Station, Texas A&M College, College Station, Texas, and the School Planning Laboratory of The School of Education of Stanford University, Stanford, Calif., as well as other universities and state departments of education.

Photographers

Aerial Photograph Co.; Eve Arnold; Morley Baer; Raimondo Borea; Anne Brennan; Esther Bubley; Joan Burger; Roland Chatham; Continental Air Views, Inc.; Martin J. Dain; Dearborn-Massar; Arnold Eagle; Myron Ehrenberg; Sam Falk; Harold Feinstein; Arthur Fillmore; Albert Freed; Lee Friedlander; A. John Geraci; Guy Gillette; Gottscho-Schleisner; Susan Greenburg; Suzy Harris; Hedrich-Blessing; Art Hupy; Martha Jaffe; Morris H. Jaffe; Pirkle Jones; Rudy Kahn; Simpson Kalisher; Emma Landau; Helen Levitt; Victor A. Lundy; Fred Lyon; Jay Maisel; Grete Mannheim; George McNulty; Dewey G. Mears; Ulric Meisel; Frank Lotz Miller; May Mirin; George Moffett; Joseph W. Molitor; Robert Mottar; Joe Munroe; Marc Neuhof; Don Ollis; Maynard L. Parker; Rondal Partridge; Charles R. Pearson; Louis Reens; Warren Reynolds; Romaine-Skelton; Amnon Rubinstein; Rae Russel; Gertrude Samuels; Ben Schnall; Julius Shulman; Ezra Stoller; Ted Streshinsky; Arline Strong; Roger Sturtevant; Suzanne Szasz; Ted Szymanski; Robert A. Talbot; Lew Tilley; Edward Wallowitch; Emmons Williams; Robert James Witt; William Wollin Studio; Wayne Wright; George Zimbel.

Photographic Credits

Where several unnumbered photographs appear on one page, the order of credits reads from left to right, top to bottom.

End papers: Suzanne Szasz
P. 2-3: Helen Levitt
P. 4-5: Ulric Meisel
P. 6: Rudy Kahn
P. 10: Harold Feinstein
P. 14-15: Robert M. Mottar
P. 16-17: Helen Levitt
P. 18: Lee Friedlander; Helen Levitt; George Zimbel; Fred Lyon, for *McCall's;* Sam Falk, The New York *Times;* Helen Levitt; Amnon Rubinstein; Helen Levitt; Martin J. Dain; Amnon Rubinstein
P. 22: Don Ollis; Rondal Partridge; George Moffett; Helen Levitt; George Zimbel, for *Redbook Magazine;* Albert Freed; Raimondo Borea
P. 24: Sam Falk, The New York *Times;* George Zimbel; Helen Levitt; Suzanne

Szasz; Rondal Partridge; Grete Mannheim; Robert James Witt; Morris H. Jaffe; George Zimbel

P. 25: Esther Bubley

P. 27: Sam Falk, The New York *Times*; George Zimbel; Guy Gillette; John Lewis Stage; Helen Levitt; Susan Greenburg, for *Sports Illustrated*; Susan Greenburg, for *Mademoiselle*; Rae Russel

P. 29: Rae Russel; Guy Gillette; Helen Levitt; Lew Tilley; George McNulty, *Chaminade High School*; Jay Maisel; Jay Maisel; Helen Levitt

P. 31: Helen Levitt

P. 36-37: Rae Russel

P. 38: Gertrude Samuels, The New York *Times*

P. 42: Suzanne Szasz

P. 43: Arnold Eagle, from film, "*Human Beginning*"

P. 44-45: Rae Russel

P. 46: Lew Tilley

P. 48: Jay Maisel; Robert M. Mottar; Joan Burger

P. 49: Ted Streshinsky; Emma Landau

P. 50-51: Helen Levitt

P. 54: George Zimbel

P. 56-57: Eve Arnold

P. 58-59: Helen Levitt

P. 60-61: Helen Levitt

P. 65: Edward Wallowitch

P. 66: Edward Wallowitch

P. 68: Esther Bubley

P. 69: Suzanne Szasz

P. 72: Suzanne Szasz

P. 73: Fred Lyon, for *McCall's*

P. 76: Helen Levitt

P. 77: May Mirin

P. 78-79: Susan Greenburg, for *Sports Illustrated*

P. 80: Guy Gillette

P. 83: Anne Brennan

P. 84: Robert M. Mottar

P. 85: Emmons Williams

P. 88: Simpson Kalisher, for *The Texas Co.*

P. 90-91: Albert Freed, *Blythdale Children's Hospital and Rehabilitation Center*

P. 92: Suzanne Szasz

P. 94: Raimondo Borea

P. 98: Ted Szymanski, *Chaminade High School*

P. 103: George Zimbel

P. 104-105: George Zimbel

P. 106: George Zimbel

P. 109: Fred Lyon; Esther Bubley, for *The Standard Oil Co. (N.J.)*

P. 111: A. John Geraci

P. 112-113: George Zimbel

P. 116: Helen Levitt

P. 118: Jay Maisel

P. 126-127: Raimondo Borea

P. 130: Helen Levitt

P. 132: George Zimbel

P. 133: Lew Tilley

P. 134: Suzanne Szasz

P. 136: Arline Strong; Martha Jaffe

P. 139: Susan Greenburg for *Sports Illustrated*

P. 140: Sam Falk, The New York *Times*

P. 145: Rae Russel

P. 146: Emma Landau

P. 147: Rondal Partridge

P. 150-151: Emma Landau

P. 152-153: Arnold Eagle

P. 154: Emmons Williams

P. 157: Lew Tilley

P. 159: Helen Levitt

P. 160: Suzanne Szasz

P. 165: Helen Levitt

P. 166: May Mirin

P. 169: George Zimbel, for *Parents' Magazine*

P. 174: Myron Ehrenberg

P. 176: Rondal Partridge

P. 191: Helen Levitt.

P. 196-197: Continental Air Views, Inc.

P. 198-199: Continental Air Views, Inc.

P. 200-201: Continental Air Views, Inc.

P. 202: Continental Air Views, Inc.

P. 203: Continental Air Views, Inc.

P. 204: Continental Air Views, Inc.

P. 205: Continental Air Views, Inc.

P. 206-207: Continental Air Views, Inc.

P. 208: Aerial Photograph Co.

P. 209: Robert A. Talbot, *Loring Studios*

P. 211: Julius Shulman

P. 212: *1.* Dewey G. Mears; *2.* Julius Shulman; *3.* Arthur Fillmore

P. 213: *4.* ©Ezra Stoller; *5.* Dearborn-Massar; *6.* Hedrich-Blessing

P. 214: *1.* Rondal Partridge; *2.* Roland Chatham; *3.* Victor A. Lundy

P. 215: *4.* Joseph W. Molitor; *5.* Marc Neuhof

P. 216: *1.* Helen Levitt; *2.* Arthur Fillmore; *3.* Victor A. Lundy

P. 217: *4, 5.* Roger Sturtevant

P. 218: *1, 2.* Hedrich-Blessing

P. 219: *3.* Dearborn-Massar; *4.* Julius Shulman

P. 220: *1.* Joseph W. Molitor; *2.* Hedrich-Blessing

P. 221: *3.* Marc Neuhof; *4.* Gottscho-Schleisner

P. 222: *1.* Arthur Fillmore; *2.* Ulric Meisel

P. 223: *3.* Morley Baer; *4.* Arthur Fillmore; *5.* Julius Shulman

P. 224: *1.* Roger Sturtevant; *2.* Julius Shulman; *3.* Art Hupy

P. 225: *4.* Wayne Wright; *5.* Arthur Fillmore; *6.* ©Ezra Stoller

P. 226: *1.* ©Ezra Stoller; *2.* Joseph W. Molitor

P. 227: *3.* Joseph W. Molitor; *4.* Art Hupy

P. 228: *1.* Charles R. Pearson; *2.* ©Ezra Stoller

P. 229: *3.* Charles R. Pearson; *4.* Ulric Meisel; *5.* Dearborn-Massar; *6.* Gottscho-Schleisner

P. 230: *1.* Julius Shulman; *2.* George Zimbel; *3.* Roger Sturtevant

P. 231: *4.* Joseph W. Molitor; *5.* Dearborn-Massar

P. 232-233: Rondal Partridge

P. 234: *1.* Charles R. Pearson; *2.* Hedrich-Blessing; *3.* Victor A. Lundy; *4.* Frank Lotz Miller

P. 235: *5.* ©Ezra Stoller; *6.* Warren Reynolds, *Infinity Inc.*; *7.* Joseph W. Molitor

P. 236: *1.* Julius Shulman; *2.* Wayne Wright

P. 237: *3.* Charles R. Pearson; *4.* Rondal Partridge

P. 238: *1.* Frank Lotz Miller

P. 239: *2.* Julius Shulman; *3.* Joseph W. Molitor; *4.* Warren Reynolds, *Infinity Inc.*; *5.* Hedrich-Blessing

P. 240: *1.* Julius Shulman; *2.* Roger Sturtevant

P. 241: *3.* Morley Baer; *4.* Dearborn-Massar; *5.* ©Ezra Stoller

P. 242: *1.* Charles R. Pearson; *2.* Ulric Meisel; *3.* Art Hupy

P. 243: *4, 5.* Roger Sturtevant

P. 244: *1.* Rondal Partridge; *2.* Dearborn-Massar

P.245: *3,4.* Julius Shulman; *5.* Hedrich-Blessing

P.246. *1.* Ben Schnall; *2.* Joseph W. Molitor

P.247: *3,4.* Charles R. Pearson; *5.* Julius Shulman

P.248: *1.* Charles R. Pearson; *2.* Joe Munroe

P.249: *3,4.* Maynard L. Parker; *5.* Charles R. Pearson; *6.* Julius Shulman

P.250: *1.* Hedrich-Blessing; *2.* Rondal Partridge; *3,4.* Charles R. Pearson *5,6.* Hedrich-Blessing

P.251: *7.* Hedrich-Bessing; *8.* ©Ezra Stoller

P.252: *1.* Rondal Partridge; *2.* Joseph W. Molitor; *3.* ©Ezra Stoller; *4.* Ben Schnall

P.253: *5.* Joseph W. Molitor; *6.* Louis Reens; *7,8.* Joseph W. Molitor

P.255: Roger Sturtevant

P.256: *1.* Roger Sturtevant; *2.* William Wollin Studio

P.257: *3.* Romaine-Skelton; *4.* Joseph W. Molitor

P.258: *1.* Joseph W. Molitor; *2.* Hedrich-Blessing

P.259: *3.* Roger Sturtevant; *4.* Arthur Fillmore

P.260: *1.* Joseph W. Molitor; *2.* Roger Sturtevant

P.261: *3.* Pirkle Jones; *4.* ©Ezra Stoller

P.262: *1.* Morley Baer; *2.* Roger Sturtevant

P.263. *3.* Art Hupy; *4.* Hedrich-Blessing

P.264: *1.* ©Ezra Stoller; *2.* Joseph W. Molitor; *3.* Charles R. Pearson; *4.* Julius Shulman

P.271: Helen Levitt

Architectural credits, opening pages

P.2-3. Hollow Tree Elementary School, Darien, Conn.: Ketchum, Gina and Sharp, Architects

P.4-5. San Jacinto Elementary School, Liberty, Tex.: Caudill, Rowlett, Scott and Associates, Architects

P.6. White Oaks Elementary School Annex, San Carlos, Calif.: John Carl Warnecke, Architect

PRODUCTION DATA

Sheet-fed gravure and offset reproduction: Photogravure & Color Company and The John B. Watkins Company
Binding: Russell-Rutter Company, Inc.
Paper: Mohawk Super-fine Special
Type: Linotype Century Expanded, and ATF Craw Clarendon Book